Meet M
Jim & Andy's

Meet Me at Jim & Andy's

JAZZ MUSICIANS AND THEIR WORLD

Gene Lees

New York   Oxford
OXFORD UNIVERSITY PRESS
1988

Oxford University Press

Oxford   New York   Toronto
Delhi   Bombay   Calcutta   Madras   Karachi
Petaling Jaya   Singapore   Hong Kong   Tokyo
Nairobi   Dar es Salaam   Cape Town
Melbourne   Auckland

and associated companies in
Berlin   Ibadan

Copyright © 1988 by Gene Lees

Published by Oxford University Press, Inc.,
200 Madison Avenue, New York, New York 10016

Oxford is a registered trademark of Oxford University Press

Library of Congress Cataloging-in-Publication Data
Lees, Gene.
    Meet me at Jim & Andy's: jazz musicians and their world
Gene Lees.
        p.   cm.
    ISBN 0-19-504611-0
        1. Jazz musicians—United States—Biography.   2. Jazz music—
United States—History and criticism.   I. Title.
ML394.LA 1988
785.42′092′2—dc19   88-4865   CIP
    [B]   MN

2 4 6 8 9 7 5 3 1

Printed in the United States of America
on acid-free paper

CONTENTS

INTRODUCTION:
DON DeMICHEAL

SIBELIUS, reputedly, was author of the observation that "no one ever erected a monument to a critic." Whoever said it first, musicians have repeated it with relish ever since, overlooking that society has not been conspicuously generous with monuments to musicians either.

One can understand an artist's resentment of the critic. His career, his very livelihood, can hang on the opinion of someone who may or may not know what he is talking about and, even if he does, whose aesthetic philosophy may or may not accord with one's own. But criticism, as Virgil Thomson put it, is "the only antidote we have to paid publicity." And musicians and other artists incline to slighting the serious work done on their behalf by men they rarely bother to acknowledge. The writings over the years of Otis Ferguson, Leonard Feather, John S. Wilson, Whitney Balliett, Nat Shapiro, Grover Sales, Max Jones, Stanley Dance, James Lincoln Collier, and more have given jazz the chronicle the musicians themselves never bothered to set down.

One of the most valuable of these men was Don DeMicheal, whose archives of material he had been gathering since his boyhood now rest at the University of Chicago.

I met Don in Louisville, Kentucky, in 1955, shortly after I joined the staff of the Louisville *Times* as its classical music critic. I settled into my job and eventually became drama and movie critic, and entertainment editor as well. My main assignment was covering the Louisville Orchestra's program of commissioning and recording new music by contemporary classical composers. For three years I assiduously attended not only the concerts but the rehearsals as well. I would hang out with the musicians from the orchestra and discuss the new pieces in detail. Many of them did not like most of the music very much, but a gig is a gig, and they played it and played it well.

Not by design but by my natural inclination, I became friends with all the jazz musicians in town, one of whom was Don DeMicheal, who played vibraharp and drums.

Don had a quartet that played for dancers in some little road-house on the edge of town. The group sounded not unlike the Modern Jazz Quartet, given its instrumentation and DeMicheal's deep admiration for that group and for the work of vibraphonist Milt Jackson in particular. Don was a very good player on both his instruments. His drumming had a loose, comfortable Cliff Leeman kind of feeling. Don had a peculiar habit. He always played drums in his stocking feet. He said it let him feel the pedals better. He used to drive his car that way too.

There was something interesting about him, something hidden, and I got to know him better. It required a little pulling. Perhaps this had to do with the fact that he was Italian by ancestry in an area in which there were not many Italians. And he was by birth that very rare bird, an Italian Protestant. He seemed in those days something of an outsider, no doubt because he had not yet found his true calling, or, for that matter, his own perception of himself.

Don had a wonderful collection of old 78 rpm recordings, some of them very rare. He had acquired parts of it, he said, when he was a little boy, knocking on doors in the black neighborhood and asking people if they had any old records they didn't want. In attics and basements he uncovered forgotten treasures and bought them for five or ten cents each. One must wonder what some of those people thought of the little dark-haired white boy who was interested in such old music.

Louisville society was making much of its orchestra's commissions, but the extended exposure to all of this new "classical" music served increasingly to convince me that jazz was all that my intuition told me it was: the most valuable music America had produced. Or even, if you like, what Billy Taylor calls it: America's classical music. Henry Pleasants' book *The Agony of Modern Music* came out about this time, and it emboldened me to observe that much of what the Louisville Orchestra was playing was claptrap— or rum-tum, to use George Bernard Shaw's vivid term. I was constrained from saying so as forcefully as I might have wished by the fact that the paper's managing editor was also president of the orchestra. On at least one occasion one of my reviews was altered overnight and behind my back: a review of Rolf Lieberman's pretentious and sterile opera *The School for Wives*. The qualifying adjectives I had used were removed, and the damnation by faint praise that I had attempted, knowing that it was all I could hope to get away with, had been turned into warm praise. I was delighted when a while later the New York critics accorded that work the public execution it deserved.

It was not to be my last brush with the politics of publishing.

I spent 1958 in Europe on a Reid Fellowship. When I returned to Louisville in the spring of 1959, DeMicheal was still playing at the roadhouse, and still working what musicians normally call a day gig—except that his was a deep-of-the-night gig. Don's family owned a small bakery, and after his roadhouse job he would go there and work till daylight, baking buns that were sold on contract to the White Castle hamburger chain. While I had been away, Don had been taking an extension course in sociology at a branch of Indiana University in Jeffersonville, which lies across the Ohio River from Louisville. Thereupon began a joking argument between us that never ended. "Sociology," I used to kid him, "is the elaborate compilation of statistics to explain the perfectly obvious."

Don had written a term paper which he asked me with a certain diffidence to read, to give him a judgment on it as a piece of writing. He had never written anything before. The paper was an examination of a jazz group from a viewpoint of sociology, and in it he hypothesized a phenomenon he called "rotary leadership." In the course of an evening of playing, he said, the leadership of a group keeps passing from one player to another, and the leader at any given moment is not the group's acknowledged leader or even necessarily the soloist. It was a good and interesting essay.

That spring Don Gold resigned from his position as editor of *Down Beat*. A friend, a publicist for the Walt Disney studio who happened to be visiting Louisville that week, urged me to apply for the job. I was hesitant. He picked up the phone saying, "It's Disney's dime," and called *Down Beat*'s publisher, Charles Suber, in Chicago. He thrust the phone at me, and I found myself talking. Suber asked me to fly up to Chicago for an interview. I made the trip that weekend, and on Monday handed in my resignation at the Louisville *Times*.

The *Times* and the *Courier-Journal* were owned by the same man, Barry Bingham, and the editorial staffs of the two papers occupied opposite ends of a large office. I had a friend over on the *Courier-Journal* side named Tom Carsell. On my last night I went into the office to clean out my desk. Tom came by and sat on it as I stripped its drawers.

"So you're going up to Chicago to edit a jazz magazine," he said.

"Yep."

"Do you read our sports pages?"

"Never," I said.

"Why?"

"Because I don't know what they're talking about. They're written in jargon, and they assume prior knowledge."

"Exactly," Tom said. "Well I don't know a thing about jazz, so when you get to *Down Beat,* keep me in mind. Edit it so that I can understand it. Edit that magazine for me."

And I always did.

The first issue bearing my name on the masthead is that of April 16, 1959, the lead story of which is the death of Lester Young.

Down Beat's special annual volume was about to be put together, and needed material. I remembered DeMicheal's essay on "rotary leadership" and phoned him to ask if he would be interested in rewriting it into an article. He was, of course, thrilled to do so. It was the first piece of Don's writing to be published.

I then asked him to be Louisville correspondent for the magazine, and he began to send me tidbits of information about jazz activities there. One time he included an item about the legendary blues singer Blind Orange Adams.

Because I so respected and therefore trusted Don's knowledge of the earlier forms of jazz and the blues, I didn't question the item. When the next issue came out, Don phoned in panic. "That was a joke," he said. "I thought you'd get a laugh and take it out of my copy. It's a pun on Blind Lemon Jefferson! Jefferson, Adams—get it?"

"Too late now," I said, and started to laugh.

Later I told Jack Tynan, the magazine's west coast editor, about it on the phone. And of course I told Chuck Suber, who found it as funny as Tynan did. We began dropping references to Blind Orange into the Chicago and Los Angeles copy, and among us we had the non-existent Mr. Adams appearing at rent parties and other functions all over America.

When I first joined the magazine, I was the Chicago editorial staff. I was it, all of it. I worked eighteen hours a day in those first months. Finally, with Chuck Suber's support, I managed to get the owner to give me a budget to hire an assistant editor and, later on, an art director as well. I gave considerable thought to the choice I had to make. At last, and under the weight of knowing I would be changing a man's life entirely, I picked up the phone and called DeMicheal in Louisville. I asked if he would be interested in tossing up his job in the bun business, packing up his drums and vibes and wife and son, and moving to Chicago to work for and with me. I think he was stunned. He said, "Yes."

My instincts about him proved to be accurate. He was a worker, and he was a learner. Fearful at first of having to assimilate a new profession, the exacting one of journalism, under pressure and on the job, he did it with remarkable speed. As I edited his writing, I would explain exactly what I was doing and why. Long afterwards he said in an interview that I was the toughest son of a bitch he had ever worked for, and he had learned everything he knew about writing from me. Since he had become by then an assured and excellent writer, I treasured the compliment, and still do. But

I learned from him as well. Don's knowledge of early jazz history was extraordinary, and in that aspect of our work together, I was the student.

The career of Blind Orange Adams blossomed during those years. Soon there was mail about him, and DeMicheal went so far as to rent a postal box and found the Blind Orange Adams Appreciation Society. Don blossomed too. He was tall, with a slight stoop. He had a long face, sharp features, straight dark hair, and a deep-toned Italian skin. And he had a sense of humor beyond anything he had ever revealed in Louisville.

We used to hang out with all the Chicago musicians—Johnny Pate, Eddie Harris, Art Hodes, who was a particularly close friend of Don's, George Brunis, Dick Marx, John Frigo, Ahmad Jamal, Eddie Higgins, Larry Novack, Ira Sullivan, Cy Touff, Joe Farrell, Johnny Griffin, and so many more. I tended to hang with the beboppers, Don with the older players, but the division was hardly a strict one, and we were both friends with John Coltrane, who came to Chicago often.

One night Don was with John at the Sutherland Lounge. Coltrane played a quirky melodic figure that piqued DeMicheal's curiosity. After the set, he sang it back to John and asked him the reason for it. "Oh *that*," John said. "I was just trying to get the rhythm section to tighten up."

Don had lunch with Paul Desmond, Dave Brubeck, and Dizzy Gillespie. Dizzy's quintet and the Brubeck group were about to go to Europe. Dizzy suggested that they do a concert together in Berlin, then tour France, Scandinavia, the Far East. "Ah yes," Desmond said, "today Germany, tomorrow the world." DeMicheal chuckled over that for days.

At that time *Down Beat*'s office was on the fourth or fifth floor of an old building at 203 West Monroe Street, immediately west of the Loop. A wrecking crew set to work tearing down a similarly venerable building across the street from us. Some of those buildings were exceptionally well made, and day after day the big crane would swing its great steel wrecking ball and smash in some more of the wall, pulverize more of the reinforced concrete. Every day at noon, on our way to lunch, Don and I would stop for ten minutes or so among all the other sidewalk superintendents to contemplate the slow progress of this destruction.

Finally the process was nearly completed. The ruins were now down almost to ground level, a last island of rubble in a plane of broken brick. And suddenly Don pulled a folded paper from the inside pocket of his suitcoat, waved it in mock alarm, and ran toward the ruins yelling at the top of his voice, "Wait a minute, we've got the wrong building!"

He played one of his practical jokes on me, and to great effect.

I wrote something or other in the magazine that Charles Mingus didn't like. Mingus was prone to threaten with dire consequences anyone who aroused his ire, and his ire was easily aroused. He once threatened Oscar Pettiford, who instantly knocked him flat. One young saxophonist in his group was so afraid of Mingus that he carried a holstered .32 automatic on the bandstand. In truth I liked Mingus, and some of his most aberrant actions struck me as the funniest possible responses to a mad world. But he did have that violent streak.

I got a call from him from New York. He was calm at first as he complained about the article. But his rage rose and finally he screamed, "You're a dirty white motherfucker!" and he hung up.

Ten or fifteen minutes later, he called back. "This's Mingus. I shouldn't have spoken to you that way. We should be able to discuss this like gentlemen." And then his anger took possession of him again and he began to crescendo and finally with another scream of "You're a dirty white motherfucker," he hung up again.

This happened several more times in the course of the morning. Finally he introduced a variant: "I feel like getting on a plane and flying out to Chicago and coming up to your office, and I'll pick you up and throw you over all the desks and then run down and catch you, so I don't break your puny back." So colorful a threat is not readily forgotten. Then, after calling me a dirty white motherfucker one more time, he hung up and I heard no more from him.

Don of course was watching all of this with amusement. Ted Williams, a great photographer who did a lot of work for us, came by to deliver some pictures. I told Ted what was going on. Ted suggested that we all go to hear Oscar Peterson that evening at the London House.

In mid-afternoon our switchboard operator said to me, "There was a call from the airport from a man called Mingus. He said he's on his way here to see you." This was conceivable: the flight from New York was only about an hour. All I could do was confront him. I waited. Five o'clock came, and still I waited. No Mingus.

We went to hear Peterson that night. I told Oscar, who had himself had a brush with Mingus, what was going on. And Ted Williams said, "I don't know why you're so upset about this. I don't think anybody takes it seriously except you and Mingus."

Oscar Peterson and Don DeMicheal nearly strangled with laughter.

The next day I found out that DeMicheal had put our switchboard operator up to that message.

Don was playing gigs around Chicago, and Blind Orange Adams was becoming the legend we said he was.

One day I got a letter from a New York record label that specialized in folk music. They wanted to find and record Blind Orange Adams! I tried a desperate ploy. I wrote to the company saying that Blind Orange didn't trust people, and the only one he would deal with was DeMicheal. He would agree to do an album only if DeMicheal and I produced it.

One of my frequent companions of that period was the tenor saxophonist Eddie Harris, who used to sing incredibly funny satires on the blues. If I could seduce the label into going for it, I planned to record Eddie as Blind Orange and make the put-on complete.

But the company was immediately suspicious, and insisted on meeting Blind Orange face to face. I can no longer say with certainty what we did to resolve the situation, but I seem to recall that Don wrote a story killing Blind Orange off in a car crash.

The situation at *Down Beat* was growing untenable for me. Someone once suggested to Jack Tracy, who was its editor before

Don Gold, that he should organize a reunion of all the former *Down Beat* staffers. "What would we do," Jack said, "sit around and bitch about John Maher?"

John Maher, the magazine's owner, was an Irish Catholic Republican. He was a very handsome man, avuncular and charming, and always beautifully dressed. He knew nothing about music. He was a printer by profession who had acquired the magazine by default when its previous owners were unable to pay their bill. He was notoriously parsimonious, and though he loved to take staff members to lavish lunches at which he could affect *largesse,* he paid poorly, and the magazine's operating budgets were thin. He disliked paying for photographs, which he felt should be provided to us free by record companies.

He repeatedly told me I was putting pictures of too many black musicians—or Negro musicians, as polite language at that time had it—on the cover. I pointed out that thirty-four of the thirty-seven winners of the magazine's own popularity poll were black. To bar them from the cover, quite aside from any consideration of ethics or civil rights or history and the fact that black Americans had invented this music, was to exclude the people our own readers most wanted to read about. However one felt about it morally, and I felt hotly about it, it was, to paraphrase an old joke, a hell of a way to run a magazine.

But Maher insisted that black faces on the cover hurt magazine sales in the South. And I said, somewhat hyperbolically, "Southerners don't listen to jazz anyway, they listen to hillbilly music."

As Don put it, in his laconic Kentucky way, "We don't have but two readers in Atlanta."

One day Lou Didier, who held the post of president of the magazine, came into my office and said, "Mr. Maher says to tell you: absolutely no more Negroes on the cover."

"Then you go back to Mr. Maher," I said, "and give him a message for me: I quit."

Didier, alarmed, went into Chuck Suber's office. Chuck and I had by then become good friends. Lou urged him to speak to me because I was going to resign. Chuck asked him why. Didier told him.

"Then you can tell Mr. Maher something for me too," Chuck said. "I quit too."

I never forgot that. The proscription of blacks on the cover was rescinded. Chuck Suber was one of the most significant figures in launching the jazz education movement in the high schools and colleges of the United States. He is now on the staff of Columbia College in Chicago.

I went on for a while longer, and then Maher, on one of his cut-the-budget sprees, ordered me to fire our brilliant young art director Bob Billings. I resigned instead, and Don DeMicheal succeeded me as editor.

A few months later, on February 1, 1962, I left on a six-month tour of South America with the Paul Winter Sextet. I learned Spanish before we left. I managed the tour, and I lectured at various universities along the way. In Rio de Janeiro I met the composer Antonio Carlos Jobim and translated some of his songs into English, songs that would soon become well known.

We returned to the United States in July of that year, and I stayed in New York. Except three times, for brief visits, I never went back to Chicago. Thenceforth I saw DeMicheal only when he came to New York, where he would meet me for lunch, usually at Jim and Andy's. He said that the Blind Orange Adams Appreciation Society was still getting mail. He cherished a curious illusion that John Maher would leave the magazine to him in his will. I told him he was crazy and should re-read Machiavelli, if that was the lure that was being held up in front of him like the stuffed rabbit at a dog track.

One evening he called me from Chicago. He said, "The Old Man's dead."

"So?" I said.

"Is that all the reaction you have?"

"Yeah. Everybody dies."

John Maher had not left him the magazine, and in due course Don too resigned from *Down Beat*. For some years he worked for an engineering mazagine.

On arriving at *Down Beat,* with Tom Carsell in mind, I circulated a memo to its regular contributors. I told them that the first purpose of a magazine is to be a good magazine, whether it is about music, sports, or collecting butterflies. If it isn't a good magazine—readable, reliable, and entertaining—it can't serve the needs of its subject. Its first duty then is to itself. Don learned that, and he was an extremely good editor of an engineering magazine, and later of a magazine devoted to the collection of *objets d'art*. This was not as far-fetched as it might seem—not for a little boy who went through Louisville asking for dusty old records that nobody much valued but he.

During those three years in Chicago and the seven subsequent years in New York I formed most of the personal relationships that would last through the years ahead. Musicians I first met in Chicago became close friends in New York. At first gradually and then more rapidly, it became clear to me that the archetypical jazz musician did not exist, that these were people of great and indeed exaggerated individuality, and I grew tired of reading that jazz musicians are inarticulate men. They are anything but that. What is more, I became uneasy with the history of jazz as it was up until then described in the books. In conversations with Coleman Hawkins, Jo Jones, Dizzy Gillespie, George Brunis, and others, I began to sense that there was something a little off about the accepted chronicle of this music's genesis.

This book is about some of those musicians and those years and what I learned about them and from them and about the music. If a lot of the people described in this book are gone now, I'm sorry about that, in more ways than one. They were—or are—remarkable human beings who deserve to be remembered. Though it deals with a number of lives that are ended, this book is not about death. It is about life, and if it has been my sad lot and yours to share several decades with some of history's most appalling people, it is also a privilege to have lived in the time of the people in this book.

All the material in this book, with an exception I'll note in a moment, appeared originally in the *Jazzletter,* a publication I founded in 1981, which was from its first day financed and supported primarily by a subscription list of America's (and some of Europe's) most distinguished musicians—far too long to include here. I have always considered the publication to be theirs as much as mine, and they set its tone and thus that of these essays. It is probably helpful to note that not only did I know, and in most cases know well, the people I have written about in this book; most of the people reading the essays knew them too. These are personal and subjective pieces; they were meant to be. They were written about friends for friends.

The exception I mentioned is the portrait of Bill Evans. Part of the material originally appeared in an annotation for the reissue of his Fantasy albums, and is used here with the permission of Fantasy Records Inc.

I never lost contact with DeMicheal who, while continuing to work as an editor in Chicago, pursued an active career as a musician, playing with such people as Kenny Davern, Dick Wellstood, and Art Hodes. He became an integral and important part of the musical life of Chicago, amassing a collection of friends who loved him. In 1981 he appeared at the North Carolina Jazz Festival. I hadn't spoken to him in several months and was planning to call him, to ask him to write some pieces for the *Jazzletter*, when I learned it was too late.

Don died February 4, 1982, of liver cancer. He was fifty-three.

Mark Twain said every man is a genius if you can only place him. Once I thought I saw a talent in a friend and I gave him a chance to develop it. There are things you do in your life that you're proud of, others that you're not. I'm proud of Don DeMicheal, who didn't die baking a bun in Louisville.

True, they don't build monuments to critics. But I can at least dedicate a book to one.

So this book is for Don.

And for Jimmy Koulouvaris.

Ojai, California   G. L.
June 1988

Meet Me at Jim & Andy's

1

MEET ME AT
JIM AND ANDY'S

WHEN AND IF, in some far future, a definitive history of jazz is ever written, there will undoubtedly be justified mentions of the record producers and critics who were its champions. It is unlikely that any historian will give an appreciative nod to one James Koulouvaris. Jimmy did nothing but run a bar. But many a great jazz musician remembers that establishment, known as Jim and Andy's, with an almost mystical affection.

Jim and Andy's was one of those New York bars that become centers of an art or an industry. Over on Eighth Avenue, the actors had Downey's. On Sixth Avenue, surrounded by Rockefeller Center, there was the odd little enclave called Herlihy's, an Irish bar where the television people hung out. Jazz musicians had Jim and Andy's, located about sixty paces west of Sixth Avenue on 48th Street.

Its entrance was obscured by a flight of steps rising to an adjacent building. It was easy to pass by, particularly at night, for the small pink electric sign in its window, *Jim & Andy*, was muted by the more assertive neon voices around it. You descended into Jim and Andy's on a slight ramp with a fall of about a foot. The place had a curious cave-like sense of safety about it which, to men in an insecure profession, was undoubtedly part of its appeal. The bar was on the right as you entered. A line of booths ran along the left wall and another line of smaller booths split the place down the middle.

I was introduced to it by Art Farmer. I returned from a State Department tour with Paul Winter of South America in July of 1962 and called Art the minute I hit New York. Art said, "Meet me at Jim and Andy's."

"Where's that?" I said. Art told me.

Through the remainder of the '60s, Jim and Andy's was for me, as it was for almost every musician I knew, a home-away-from-home, restaurant, watering hole, telephone answering service, informal savings (and loan) bank, and storage place for musical instruments.

It was not uncommon to walk into Jim and Andy's in the late afternoon and encounter Gerry Mulligan, Lalo Schifrin, Alec Wilder, Eddie Safranski, Marion Evans, Mundell Lowe, George Barnes, Carl Kress, Clark Terry, Pat Williams (this was before a record company presented him with roses on the assumption that he was a girl singer, causing him to change it to Patrick), Al Klink, Nick Travis, Willie Dennis, Jo Jones, Coleman Hawkins, Grady Tate, Ben Webster, Richard Davis, George Duvivier. If you sat there for a while, you'd see Bob Brookmeyer, Doc Severinsen (then only known for being one of the best lead trumpet players in New York), Hank d'Amico, Will Bradley, Budd Johnson, Eddie (Lockjaw) Davis, Phil Woods, Al Cohn, Bill Crow, Milt Hinton, Claus Ogerman, Willie Rodriguez, Zoot Sims, and Richie Kamuca. Occasionally Harry Belafonte, Lena Horne, Sarah Vaughan, or Tony Bennett would drift in. Once a certain famous jazz producer, noted for his light-fingered way with royalties, came in. Clark Terry muttered, "What's he doing in here? Looking for a friend?"

A postcard-covered bulletin board near the front door kept everyone up to date on friends who were out on the road. The coat closet was so jammed with instrument cases that nobody was ever able to hang a coat there. The jukebox had probably the best selection of any in the country but it was rarely played.

Willis Conover, the Voice of America's renowned jazz broadcaster, said once, "What the Mermaid Tavern was to literature in Elizabethan England, Jim and Andy's is to jazz in America today."

He was not far from the mark. Jim and Andy's—known to its bibulous patrons as J. and A.'s, Jim's, and then the Gym, and finally, by a logical progression, the Gymnasium—had all the attributes of a private club, though it had no membership list, no dues, and no rules beyond the requirement that its clients behave themselves, which they did. Indeed, no bar in America could boast a more circumspect clientele.

The proprietor of this curious musical center was the aforementioned Mr. Koulouvaris, an ex-Seabee of Greek extraction, a veteran of the war in the South Pacific. He had a thick head of black hair and smooth, dark, Mediterranean skin. He was stocky, with solid shoulders and powerful cord-muscled arms. He always wore black shoes, shiny old black pants, and a white short-sleeved shirt open at the neck. He was a genuinely tough man, in the most admirable sense of the term.

Jim Koulouvaris operated the Gymnasium at that location from 1956 until, in the late 1960s, the encroaching steel-and-glass towers caused the demolition of that whole colorful block, between Sixth and Seventh Avenues, of excellent dusty bookshops, music stores, and small restaurants. Jim had a big heart, a gruff manner, an uncanny instinct about people, a genuine affection for musicians, and a ribald sense of humor. "Jimmy gives something that has almost disappeared from society," Willis Conover said. "Service."

While other taverns were decorated with signs saying, "No Checks No Credit," Jimmy accepted checks and extended credit to all his regular customers. He would send each of them a bill at the end of the month. If a musician happened to be going through a time of hardship, the bills mysteriously stopped coming. They resumed when Jimmy knew his man had passed through the doldrums.

In fact, Koulouvaris not only permitted credit to continue when a regular was broke—the plain but excellent food from his small kitchen kept more than one later-famous musician alive during a lean time. He would, as often as not, reach into his own pocket to find the man a little walking-around money. Jim Hall said once, "We can't stop coming here. We all owe Jimmy too much money."

The most astounding example of Jimmy's generosity—and his faith, if not in the whole human race, at least in his specialized clientele—was recalled by one of the regulars who preferred to remain anonymous:

It was on a Monday or Tuesday. The man went in, long in the face. Jim asked, "What's the matter, H-----?"

He replied, "My wife's divorce lawyer says if I don't come up with four thousand dollars by Thursday, he'll ruin me completely." Four thousand dollars then equaled twenty or twenty-five today.

"How do you want it?" Jim asked. "In cash, or a check?"

"Jim," the man said, "don't make jokes."

"I'm not joking. Cash? Or a check?"

"Really, Jim," the man said, "I didn't come here to borrow money."

"Look, H-----, I'm busy! For Christ's sake, do you want cash or a check? I gotta get back to work, and you're holding me up."

"It'll take me a long time to pay you back."

"Why should we both worry?" Jim said.

"Well, okay. Check, I guess. Jesus, Jim, thank you."

"Come in Thursday morning at ten," Jim said as he walked back to the bar.

Jimmy claimed that in all the years he ran the place, he was clipped only three times. "The funny thing is that it's been for small amounts each time, twenty or thirty bucks.

"The guys are always good for the money," he said. "They may hold you up for a while, but they always pay in the end. Oh, I've lost out two or three times when guys died. No, I never tried to collect from the estate. Maybe the guy's wife needed the money.

"Musicians are good people. They always pay their debts."

Because of Jimmy's attitude, his patrons felt that their obligations were debts of honor. When a young trumpeter went into the Navy, he sent a postcard from Gibraltar saying, "Sorry, I didn't get a chance to see you before I left. I'm sending you the money I owe next payday. Regards to everybody."

Every so often someone would wander into Jim and Andy's and ask for Andy. This elicited laughter from the regulars. There was no Andy. In fact Jim Koulouvaris was not even the Jim of the bar's name. The original Jim and Andy opened the place in 1945. Ten years later they decided to get out of the tavern business and Koulouvaris bought it. Thus, when someone asked for Andy, he marked himself as an outsider, probably a salesman.

For a while Jim told everybody that Andy was the cat. "Oh yeah," he said, "we had a cat named Andy. Only one day one of the customers came in and said, 'Hey, Jim, Andy's a lady.' So I said, 'Are you sure?' He just grinned and said, 'That was no cat-fight I saw in the parking lot.'

"A while after that she had kittens, but we still called her Andy."

It was part of the tradition at Jim and Andy's that the customers answered the telephones. There were two telephones in booths at the rear of the place, and they never stopped ringing. Someone would answer, then lean out and yell, "Has anyone seen Jim Hall?" Or they would hang up and say to Jimmy, "If Stan Getz comes in, tell him to call Betsy at Verve Records." Jimmy never wrote any of these messages down, yet he never failed to deliver them.

Jim and Andy's served not only as a social club for its "members" but as a clearing house for employment. At recording studios all over New York it was known that the place was always filled with musicians and that they were among the best in the world. Outside of Los Angeles, there was not then and is not now a city in the world with as large a pool of great musicians, and the cream of New York's musicians hung out at Jim and Andy's. Often, when a producer or arranger needed a bass player or a trumpeter on short notice, he would bypass the standard hiring procedures and simply call the Gymnasium. Whoever answered the call would bawl out, "Are there any bass players looking for a gig?"

The building next to Jim and Andy's housed A&R, one of the best and busiest recording studios in the city. Its engineers ran a line down into Jim and Andy's and connected it to a small loud-speaker on the rear wall. Every so often it would crackle into life and the disembodied voice of engineer Phil Ramone would resound, "Hey, we need a trombone player up here. Is there any-body around?" He might get J. J. Johnson or Willie Dennis or Frank Rehak or Wayne Andre or, if bass trombone should be needed, Tony Studd.

What all the Gymnasium regulars did not realize was that this sound system worked two ways. The speaker was over the rearmost booth of the place, the one to which a romantically inclined musi-cian would retreat with a lady, not necessarily his wife. With a flick of the switch, Ramone and the other recording engineers could hear the conversations in that booth. "Sometimes we hear some pretty funny ones," Ramone said.

Funny stories abounded in Jim and Andy's. Some of them sprang from the late Zoot Sims. Zoot, a man of phenomenal stam-ina and a heroic capacity for alcohol, usually came in wearing a sweater and looking most casual. One noon he turned up in a dark suit, white shirt, and a tie. "Hey, Zoot," someone said, "you're looking mighty dapper today. What happened?"

Zoot looked down the length of his own splendor and said, as if puzzled, "I don't know. I woke up this way."

On another occasion, Zoot turned up during the morning after having worked until four or five a.m. He'd had no sleep and faced a heavy day of recording. Lamenting his condition, he asked if any-one might have a pill to help him through the day. The fiancée of a fellow musician offered him one.

Zoot looked at it lying on his palm. "I've never used this kind before," he said. "Is it strong?"

"Sort of," the girl said. "You can take half of it and throw the rest away."

"*What*," Zoot said in mock indignation. "Throw that good stuff away? Do you realize there are people in Europe *sleeping*?"

On one wall of Jim and Andy's there was a cartoon showing Jimmy answering the telephone and saying, "Zoot who?" On each of the four walls was a sign. One said Jim and Andy's East, the others Jim and Andy's West, North, and South. All were on the wrong walls. In the doorway to the small kitchen at the back was a centerfold from *Playboy*. Across the girl's bosom the arranger and composer Gary McFarland had written:

To Gary, dearest:

As you strive to make your way to fame and fortune in Gotham, I hope you won't forget this homely bit of backwoods philosophy: It doesn't matter how you play the game—it's who wins, baby!!!

Love from . . .
Your Mom

A few non-musicians hung around Jim and Andy's. One of them was a loan shark, who never plied his trade there. There were one or two hookers as well, nor did they ply their profession: they came in there *not* to be bothered, and the musicians accepted them with that tolerance that seems to go with playing jazz. One of them was named Marge. Everyone liked her. She died at thirty-six of alcoholism.

Still another regular I'll call Buddy Butler. He was getting on in years, had one eye that was rheumy and another that was whitened by a cataract. He was heavy-set and had a pocked face. Everybody knew Buddy's history. He was a semi-retired thief. His specialty had been shoplifting, or boosting, as he called it. He once showed me the big pockets of a raincoat that facilitated his activities in department stores. "But I can't do it any more," he growled in an accent out of Damon Runyon. "Legs are shot." After that he startled me with "I'm trainin' my daughter in the business."

The staff of Jim and Andy's consisted of Jimmy, Pete Salvato, the pint-sized cook, and Rocky Mareno, a Brooklyn-born bartender whose stub of cigar looked as if it had been welded into his face. Rocky would curse the customers, and they would curse him back. He had especially insulting names for some of them—his favorites, one suspected. His pet form of address was, "Hey, stiff, what're you drinking?" The first time Rocky would yell to a customer, "Why don't you answer the goddamn phone?" the man knew he had become one of the regulars.

When the place got more than usually busy, Buddy the Booster would be impressed into duty as assistant bartender. Jimmy trusted him with his cash register, and the musicians, sometimes with large sums of cash they didn't want to carry in the streets, trusted him with their money. Buddy never stole anything from any of *us*. It would have been unthinkable to him.

Once he acquired a quantity of blue-black gabardine raincoats, which he sold to the regulars for twelve dollars each—so many in fact that they had to write their names inside them. At closing time it looked as if the Navy were leaving. Another time he unloaded some hot radios. A musician who bought one set it on a table in one of the booths and walked away to talk to a friend. Buddy said to him, "Hey, somebody's gonna steal that!" The musician gave him a quizzical look that prompted Buddy to shrug and deliver himself of an outstanding piece of folk philosophy: "De second t'ief is de smart t'ief."

For the most part, the musicians were family men, and many of the bachelors were on their way to that condition. As often as not, their courtships were conducted in Jim and Andy's, with, no doubt, many of their tenderest sentiments overheard by Phil Ramone from that back booth. On Christmas Eve, the musicians would sing carols. Christmas Eve one year found Judy Holliday singing a high, sweet, and sensitive soprano lead and Willis Conover singing basso, with various jazz musicians working on the inner lines. Gerry Mulligan was the conductor.

Jim and Andy's began to be a musicians' bar in 1949, more or less by accident. Phil Sapienza, a widely respected repairman of reed instruments, came in one day, bringing with him Paul Ricci, a clarinetist on the staff of NBC, which was just around the corner on Sixth Avenue in Rockefeller Center, and Irving Horowitz, an English horn player at ABC. They continued to come and brought other musicians. In the middle 1950s, as more and more jazzmen turned to studio jobs, they too discovered the place. By the 1960s, they had begun to feel that they owned it. When Koulouvaris tried to redecorate it, the regulars complained. "What are you trying to do?" one of them demanded. "Make the place ritzy?" The pink leatherette seats in the booths were torn and patched, having taken severe and prolonged beating from the instrument cases that musicians would casually sling into them when they arrived. They liked the place as it was.

Jimmy used to close up in July, which disoriented everyone. As one patron put it, "My God, I ended up meeting a buddy of mine in a tea room. It was awful."

For countless musicians the historical events of the 1960s are linked in memory with Jim and Andy's and, faintly, to the flavors of a sautéed dish known as shrimps Romeo and a crisp Greek salad made with feta cheese. During the week of the Cuban missile crisis, when people walked through supermarkets almost on tiptoe and everyone in New York knew we were at Ground Zero of Target Number One, I spent every afternoon in J. and A.'s with Bob Brookmeyer, drinking—with gallows humor—Moscow mules.

On that ghastly afternoon when John F. Kennedy died, Gary McFarland and I went listlessly up the stairs to A&R Studios, where Woody Herman was recording an album for Phillips. The band was playing Bobby Scott's *A Taste of Honey*. Everyone had heard the news and there was in that performance a mournfulness that is not in the arrangement, not in the notes themselves, but in the attitude of the band, whose personnel at that period included Nat Pierce, Sal Nistico, Phil Wilson, and Bill Chase. You can hear it in the record. It is a striking track, deeply sad, and it shows how jazz can reflect public events and the consequent moods more immediately than any other art. Woody finished the take and canceled the rest of the date. Everyone went down to Jim and Andy's for a drink before going home to continue the numbing vigil in front of the television set.

But most of the memories of J. and A.'s are happier stuff. Late one afternoon I was having an early dinner with the great arranger Marion Evans, disciple of Robert Farnon and teacher of many other arrangers and composers, including J.J. Johnson, Pat Williams, and Torrie Zito. A strange looking woman, who resembled Yvonne DeCarlo in *The Munsters*, except that she wore a wide floppy hat and a loose flower-print blouse, was looking intently at a sheet of paper in an adjacent booth. "Are you fellows musicians?" she said.

"I guess you could say that," Marion replied in a soft Georgia voice.

She approached and stood by our table and showed us a piece of sheet music, pointing to a whole note, second space up on the bass clef. "What's this note?" she asked.

"Well just think about it," Marion said. "All Cows Eat Grass."

"I *know* that," she said, "but what's this *note*?"

"It's a cow," I said. I thought Marion would choke.

When he had recovered his composure, he told her the note was C. She left, satisfied, and Marion crossed his arms at the wrists, fluttered his hands like an ascending bird, and whistled a rising tremolo.

Another time, as we sat at the bar, Marion was telling me about his troubles with the recording engineers at Columbia Records. He had written the charts for an album by Steve Lawrence and Edie Gorme. Hearing the mix at home, he went into a slow steam. He took the tape to the chief engineer at Columbia (he always argued that Columbia promoted janitors to engineers) and demanded that the man play it. He asked the engineer how many musicians he could hear.

"You could see the wheels turnin' in his head," Marion said. "He knew it was more'n ten an' less'n a hundred. Finally he said, 'About twenty.'"

"That's what I hear too," Marion told him. "An' I used thirty-five men on that date. Now I have a certain interest in finance an' I have worked it out that Columbia Records is wastin' about three million dollars a year on recordin' musicians who never get heard."

Marion did indeed have an interest in finance. Disgusted with writing, as he put it, "music by the pound," he quit the business to devote himself to the stock market, growing wealthy in the process.

Everyone who went to Jim and Andy's remembers something—or someone—funny. Bassist Buddy Clark recalls a trombone player, a man of dapper manner and attire, who used to come in after gigs, take off his coat and hang it up, take off his hat and hang it up, then take off his toupee and hang it up.

Around four a.m., Jimmy would start clapping his hands and calling out, "All right, you guys, everybody out!" And we would find ourselves on the sidewalk in little groups, bidding our goodnights.

Jim and Andy's was a Mecca not only for all the musicians of New York but for those of the West Coast as well. When any of the Los Angeles crowd would get into town—Shelly Manne, Johnny Mandel, Jack Sheldon, Frank Rosolino—they would usually turn up at Jim and Andy's shortly thereafter. There was a joke about a shy West Coast jazz musician who arrives at then-Idlewild Airport and tells the cab driver to take him to Jim and Andy's on West 48th Street. The cab driver turns out to be one of New York City's licensed psychopaths, weaving in and out of traffic at high speed and pounding over the potholes. Finally, the L.A. musician, squirming in the back seat, says, "Oh, man, just play melody."

Bob Brookmeyer was once asked the question that became anathema to jazz musicians: "Where is jazz going?"

"Down 48th Street to Jim and Andy's," Bob said.

Brookmeyer was the author of another much-quoted line. A rumor swept Jim and Andy's that a certain musician, politely detested by his fellows, had undergone open-heart surgery. "What'd they do, take one out or put one in?" Brookmeyer asked.

Many of the Jim and Andy's patrons of those days are gone now. Willie Dennis died in a car crash in, of all places, Central Park. A lot of impromptu wakes were held in Jim and Andy's, all of them quiet and sad. Nick Travis, one of the great lead trumpet players in New York, died of a heart attack. A week or so later, on the West Coast, Conrad Gozzo, another great lead trumpeter, died. A sad little joke went around Jim and Andy's. Nick dies and goes to heaven. Gabriel greets him at the gate, his own horn in hand, and says, "Hello, Nick, we've been waiting for you. We're putting together a new band and we want you to play lead." Gabriel takes

Nick to a rehearsal. Nick plays through the charts and says, "Hey, Gabe, this is a tough book. I think we'll have to have a split lead." "Who do you want?" Gabriel says. "Gozzo," Nick says. "You got him," Gabriel says.

Jim used to close the place for certain of the holidays. On one of those days, Gary McFarland met a friend at some other bar, a civilian bar, as it were. Someone slipped liquid methadone into their drinks. Gary died right there, his friend a day or two later. Jim was haunted by this, wondering if Gary would still be alive had J. and A.'s been open that day.

When Jimmy received notice that the building was to be torn down to make way for the continuing dehumanization of New York, he found a location on West 55th Street. He tried to make it as much like the old place as possible. The seats in the booth were the same pink as the old ones. A brick from the old building was on display in a small glass box, and the old neon sign hung in the window. But somehow it wasn't the same. The new J. and A.'s was too far west and too far north. It was also close to Eighth Avenue, which had long since gone to seed, and the neighborhood didn't feel as safe as the old one.

And finally Jim Koulouvaris, who used to come to work at noon and stay until four a.m., when he threw the last customers out, died of a heart attack. At home, and behind their backs, he used to refer to his customers as "my boys." For their sake, his widow, Catherine, tried to keep the place going with the help of Rocky Mareno, but it couldn't work without Jimmy, and she closed it forever. Long into the 1980s, Jimmy's boys stayed in touch with her, hovering over her a little.

Jim and Andy's was hardly Camelot, but for a time there it was indeed a most congenial spot and an extraordinarily important part of musical Americana. Perhaps its ultimate tribute came from Phil Woods who, excoriating a certain critic noted for obscure theorizing and impenetrable prose, said, "What the hell would he know about jazz? He never comes into Jim and Andy's."

2
THE MASK:
SHORTY PEDERSTEIN

JAZZ MUSICIANS who are, as the French say, of an age, and serious listeners as well, remember the Shorty Pederstein interview. This was a comedy record on the Fantasy label in which an earnest interviewer tries to get a mumbling, inarticulate, and fogbound bebop musician to say anything intelligible about the music. The interviewer is bemusedly serious; Shorty Pederstein's reluctant replies are an opaque wall of bebop slang and attitude.

Musicians loved the record. Shorty Pederstein immediately became the archetype of the jazz player.

Steve Allen contributed to the myth with a record called *Bop Fables*, which he wrote and which the disk jockey Al (Jazzbo) Collins narrated in the role of a musician telling in his own esoteric style such fairy tales as *Little Red Riding Hood* and *The Three Little Pigs*.

The late Lenny Bruce built the style of his comedic delivery on the argot of jazz musicians. So did Mort Sahl.

The musicians gleefully abetted the Shorty Pederstein image of themselves with a series of what were called bop jokes. Sample:

Road musician comes back to his hotel room after a matinee movie. The room reeks of marijuana fumes. His room-mate is kneeling, ear to the floor. "What're you doin', man?" the first says. "C'mere an' listen to this," the second says in a stoned voice. The

15

first musician kneels, listens, and says, "I don't hear a thing." "I know, man," says the second, "it's been like that *all day*."

Another: Bebop musician is leaning against a building on 72nd Street in New York. Little old lady approaches him and says, "Crosstown buses run all night?" "Doo-dah," the musician answers airily.

A third: Little old lady approaches musician in New York and says, "How do you get to Carnegie Hall?" "Practice," he replies. This was probably the most widely circulated of the bop jokes. There is a footnote to it. Legend has it that the late Bobby Hackett and Dizzy Gillespie were walking down Seventh Avenue when a woman said to them, "Pardon me, gentlemen, can you tell me how to get to Carnegie Hall?" One can well imagine the impish look on Dizzy's face, the glance from side to side, the perfect pause, then, "Practice," he said. And Bobby Hackett had to hold himself up with the help of a nearby pole.

One year there circulated within the jazz community a Christmas card on the front of which was an elegant little cartoon, a line drawing of two musicians standing under a Dickensian lamp-post in the falling snow. One carries under his arm a trumpet in a soft leather covering—known in the profession as a bop bag—and the other holds a saxophone case. In the caption below it, one is saying to the other, "Like, have a Merry." Whoever did that cartoon knew musicians. Everything about it was perfect, the clothes and the lazy S-curve stance of the figures. It was not only a funny cartoon, it was a touching one. In a moment of emotion, the musician is able to say no more than that.

How true to life were those jokes and fables? How accurate was the Shorty Pederstein characterization?

The Shorty Pederstein manner was always to some extent a protective camouflage. Yet one constantly reads in newspaper articles and liner notes, "Jazz musicians are a shy and inarticulate group," or variations thereon. No one who hung out at Jim and Andy's would believe that. You could drown in the incessant conversation of that place. One wonders from whom these journalists drew this image. Bill Evans? Lockjaw Davis? Duke Ellington, who spoke a lofty patrician kind of prose? Dizzy Gillespie? Paul Desmond, whose wit was legend and who had originally intended to be a writer? Pianist Chuck Folds, who used to be an editor at *American Heritage* magazine? Cornetist Richard Sudhalter, who was for twelve years a correspondent in Europe for United Press International, covering such things as the Soviet invasion of Czechoslovakia, and is co-author of the classic biography *Bix: Man and Legend*? Richard Hadlock, the clarinetist and jazz historian? Pianist and singer Ben Sidran, whose degree is in sociology and who wrote the excellent study of jazz titled *Black Talk*? Trombonist, historian, and novelist James Lincoln Collier? Charles Mingus, whose book *Beneath the Underdog* is a volcano of rich prose? Joe Williams? Bobby Scott is an excellent writer. Art Hodes and Dave Tough both wrote columns for *Down Beat*. Kenny Dorham wrote record reviews for the same magazine. Bix Beiderbecke was always quoting Wodehouse. Artie Shaw, who gave up playing to pursue successfully his original ambition of being a writer, speaks Spanish. Art Farmer speaks German, Clare Fischer speaks Spanish and Portuguese, Oscar Peterson, who is powerfully articulate, speaks French, Sahib Shihab speaks Danish, Dick Wellstood, who had a law degree, spoke Chinese. Michael Zwerin, who has pursued parallel careers as a trombonist and journalist, speaks French. Drummer Al Levitt, like Zwerin, lives in Europe and writes for many magazines. Composer and pianist Denny Zeitlin is also a psychiatrist—and any number of doctors are musicians of professional stature, including the Toronto pianist Barry Little, who is also a neurologist. Actor Michael Moriarity is a pianist. Trombonist Conrad Janis is an actor. Dudley Moore was a jazz pianist before he was an actor and has an Oxford degree in composition. Bassist John Heard is an admired portrait painter and sculptor. George Wetling was an artist. Bill Perkins has a prodigious background in electronics. Pat Williams has a degree in history. Jack Teagarden held patents for a number of his inventions. And saxophonist Frank Trumbauer finally surrendered to his second passion, giving up music to become a test pilot.

A psychologist with many friends among jazz musicians said, "I find jazz musicians to be very broad, well-read, intelligent and articulate—a great deal more so than doctors. I think the reason is not hard to find. When they are on the road, all they do is read.

"Another thing. I am fascinated by the way they play chess and do things like building paper airplanes. When they get involved in that, you'll find they've read just about everything on the aerodynamics of the subject. They have used their road time well, the dead time spent on airplanes and buses and in hotel rooms. After they've drunk and smoked everything, they say, 'Now what can I do that's interesting and creative?'"

Once, in the mid-1960s, I was driving back to New York from a concert at the University of Pennsylvania with Coleman Hawkins and some other musicians. The concert had been booked by Abe Turchen, Woody Herman's manager, and I was driving Abe's Cadillac. I did not know Coleman Hawkins well at that time, did not know that he was an art lover and an intellect of substance. The Pennsylvania Turnpike on the down trip had been dangerously foggy, and now, late at night, I decided to go home by a freeway that was rather new. Hawkins told me I was making a mistake, that this route would take us through every tiny town along the way, and we would not get back to New York until dawn. I told him I had come upon this road a year or so earlier, driving in from Chicago, and that it would take us straight home.

I was right. He sat beside me in the front seat, quietly watching all the exit signs to various communities as we made swift smooth time. "Damn," Bean said after a while. "We used to have to go through all these little towns. Now you just read about 'em."

You may call that laconic but hardly inarticulate.

Yet anyone who has been around the jazz world to any extent has met what seems to be, if not Shorty Pederstein's brother, at least his cousin. At one time or another, we have seen many of these people take on a little touch of Shorty in the night. Why?

"I think they were slightly embarrassed by the conditions under which they had to live and work," Mundell Lowe said. "That was one of the things that killed Davey Tough, a brilliant and very literate guy. I remember doing that number myself on occasion, when I'd be working at Birdland with Mingus or some other group. You didn't want anyone to realize that you knew anything more than the job seemed to require."

That remark illuminates a remark made by Dizzy Gillespie: "I know more than they think I know."

Since black musicians invented jazz and were its first heroes, they set the style and even social behavior of the young white musicians who idolized them.

Out of the black experience in the United States grew a calculated dissembling whose purpose was defense. Blacks deliberately created an impression that they were dull-witted, slow, so brainless that they could not do anything that required precision. The white slave-owner, or later, boss, would be more forgiving of someone he considered merely stupid. The black photographer Ted Williams said, "And appearing stupid had the additional advantage of letting the boss think you were no threat to him."

The air of vagueness and the slang developed by blacks— actually a clever code—was in accord with military wisdom: try to make the enemy underestimate you. The very word *ofay*, applied by blacks to whites and widely used in Louis Armstrong's youth but now apparently vanished from ghetto vocabulary, was pig Latin for *foe*.

It is part of the mythology of jazz that the music has been despised by the Establishment since its development. The fact is that it was widely acclaimed by such musicians in other fields as Maurice Ravel, Ernest Ansermet, and John Philip Sousa, and even by many classical-music critics. It was condemned by puritanical social leaders who saw it, as their predecessors saw the waltzes of Strauss, as a corrupting influence on the morals of youth. Young white musicians and even many blacks—Fats Waller, for one— who took up jazz were often castigated by their families, but no more so than Haydn, when he told his family he was going to be a musician, and no more so than they might have been had they announced they intended to be actors. There was once a law on the books forbidding any actor from living within a mile of Buckingham Palace. The artist, in whatever field, has always been seen as a Gypsy, and the life of Bix Beiderbecke was not unlike that of Van Gogh, Gauguin, or Arthur Rimbaud.

Respectable black families saw jazz as devil's music, though there can be little doubt that the problem was worse for Beiderbecke, coming from a solidly prosperous Middle-West and middle-class family, than it was for Louis Armstrong, who came from direst poverty. For Armstrong, a life in music was a step up; for Bix, in his family's eyes, it was a descent into the abyss.

The conditions in which the first jazz musicians played undoubtedly reinforced the slave's shrewd affectation of a brainless invisibility. They worked in Chicago and New York nightclubs invariably owned by mobsters such as Owny Madden and Al Capone, people who could simply have you removed if they didn't like the cut of your smile. Bix's friend, the clarinetist Don Murray, was casually beaten to death by Chicago gangsters, apparently for paying too close attention to the girlfriend of one of them.

The black musicians who inspired the young whites to take up the music no doubt taught them as well how to get away with it: how to hide your intelligence, how to make yourself seem a harmless eccentric. They had devices of behavior and even a private language developed during generations of experience at handling a dangerous world. It wasn't only that the young white musicians began using the the slang because it was the speech of their heroes, although that was undoubtedly a factor. In the conditions in which they were forced to work, the coded speech, the vagueness, the abstracted attitude, were more than colorful: they were *useful*.

The image of jazz musicians as a subculture was most vivid in the early bebop days, toward the end of and right after World War II. By then they were going out of their way to seem alienated, separate. Though the idea that jazz was a music condemned by the musical Establishment is essentially false—the work of journalists of the political left—the beboppers faced ferocious hostility from within the jazz community itself. The music was hated by some of the musicians of the older school, disparaged by the very man whose work defined forever how jazz would be played: Louis Armstrong.

The boppers behaved according to a classic psychological pattern: before you have the chance to reject me, I will reject you. They rejected the social conventions, cultivating eccentricity in speech and manner for their own sake, and for the humor of it. *Life* magazine ran an article about bebop and Dizzy Gillespie, paying more attention to his beret and thick-rimmed glasses than to the significant developments in the music itself. Dizzy, who has an extraordinary gift for comedy and has developed the put-on almost into an art form, undoubtedly enjoyed the situation thoroughly. And he set the style for a lot of musicians, not to mention their fans. Bop glasses and berets became for a while almost a uniform. That was the period when everybody was supposedly going around making the sign of the flatted fifth, a gesture I for one never saw in real life. But the slang was real.

Nobody drove a car. One drove a short. One did not have an apartment, one had a pad. The term *short* has passed from use, though *pad* and *dig* have been absorbed into general American speech. One encounters people who have never heard jazz in their lives using argot that was once the arcane vocabulary of the jazz musician. *Latch onto* seemed fresh, funny, and descriptive; years later I saw it in a *New York Times* editorial. *Too much* has similarly become commonplace, along with a grammatical aberration I came to think of as the dangling superlative: the adjective used without the logically following noun, as in *the lowest, the greatest, the worst*. *Like* was dropped into the bopper's conversation about every third word, as if he were reluctant to commit himself to anything. It became a sort of audible comma, which one still encounters now and then, though it has been largely replaced by the ubiquitous *y'know*. Used in combination, they achieved some sort of ultimate of the inexpressive, as in *Well, like, y'know, man . . .*

What pleased you *knocked you out*. If it amused you, you *fell out*. What was good was at first *groovy* and, later, *gone* or *crazy*. Several members of the Les Brown band were in a restaurant sometime around 1948. One of them asked the waitress for the cherry pie on the menu. She said, "I'm sorry, it's gone." "Crazy," he said, "bring me two pieces." Needless to say, the others fell out.

Bix Beiderbecke is credited with inventing the term *corny*, from *corn-fed*, meaning countrified and backward as opposed to urban and hip. By now it had been replaced by *square*. Today *square* is used even by squares, along with groovy. *Gone* is gone. But *man*, which once seemed characteristic of the jazz musician and later of his followers—as in Dave Frishberg's lyric, "I even call my girlfriend 'man,' I'm so hip"—is now used by little boys in schoolyards.

But in the late 1940s, jazz was still a young music, played by young men. Dizzy Gillespie was in his early twenties when bebop developed. Gerry Mulligan was eighteen when he wrote *Disk Jockey Jump* for Gene Krupa. Miles Davis was twenty when he hit New York. The fans were younger still. The young do not need the hostility of society to wish to feel separate, living in a world of their own. The slang, the self-indulgent eccentricities, created unity in a group that felt and, perversely, wanted to feel, misunderstood. What could not be understood by the masses was clearly superior. The slang helped to keep the bebop subculture a sort of secret. Its very intent was to keep anyone from the "square" world from knowing what you really thought or felt.

That is in part what makes Shorty Pederstein so funny even now: we're never quite sure whether Shorty is as dumb as he seems or is merely putting the interviewer on. (*Putting him on* was originally a jazz expression.) There is a flash of self-recognition in Shorty's low-keyed, "Go, man."

There was a darker side of it all, to be sure, quite aside from the echoes of slavery. Some of the vocabulary was drawn from that of the drug addict. Heroin use was in sinister flower in the jazz world, killing some of bebop's most important figures, pre-eminently Charlie Parker. That slow and indifferent diction echoed the cheek-scratching speech of the nodding-out junky.

There was, I think, another reason why jazz musicians created a barrier of behavior and colorful slang. They are, in my experience, extremely sensitive people. All art is created with and out of sensitivity, the ability to make the calculating and imaginative sides of the brain work in balance. That balance is usually uneasy and short-lived, which is why there are days when you have it and days when you don't. Aldous Huxley said that art is created in a state of relaxed tension. You must be relaxed enough to let the dreams flow, alert enough to know what to do with them, grab them out of the incorporeal air as they rush by and turn them into something that others can perceive and be moved by.

Being, then, usually very sensitive—romantic, imaginative, and desperately in love with music, so much so that they want to create it spontaneously, instantaneously, and go on to the next thing, always relishing the flashing joy of creation—jazz musicians were guarded among those they had not learned to trust. Some of the still are. Making jazz is a very naked thing to do.

That anyone can do anything at all but stand there in paralyzed amazement when the chord changes are going by, that musicians can function with minimal premeditation and great creativity within the materials of a song's structure, is more remarkable than even the most expert practitioners themselves seem to appreciate. It requires both tremendous knowledge, whether intuitive or acquired, and the physical reflexes of an athlete. Jazz is not only one of the most remarkable achievements in the history of music, it is one of the most striking achievements in the history of human thought.

In recent years, jazz musicians seem to have become more thoughtful, more articulate. Not so. They always were, among those they trusted. With maturity, and in an atmosphere of respect for the music, which is now taught in colleges and universities everywhere, they simply abandoned the pose. They still will be heard using the old slang, but that has become common vocabulary, and they have invented nothing new to replace it. The slang that comes into general use still originates largely in the ghetto but it passes into use through rhythm-and-blues and rock-and-roll, not jazz.

There was one musician who sort of did fit the Shorty Pederstein image. No one acted out the bebop archetype better than Frank Rosolino. And Frank did it only too well, right down to the terrible end. Apparently incapable of expressing his true inner feelings, his anxiety and pain and fear, he seemed to have stepped directly out of that bebop Christmas card.

For the most part, though, jazz musicians, caught in their element, in their homes or in Jim and Andy's and other favored hangouts, were a far cry from their general image, a remarkably variegated and intelligent group of people. In participating in the perpetuation of that image, which a lot of them did, just for the hell of it, just for the inside joke of it, they unthinkingly did themselves a disservice.

3

THE MYTH

IN A 1983 liner note, Nat Hentoff wrote that "Coleman Hawkins and Lester Young were never admitted to 'official' American culture. No Pulitzers, no invitations to join National Academies of Arts and Letters, no artist-in-residence appointments at any universities (white or black)."

Hentoff has been writing things of this kind throughout his career, contributing substantially to the biggest of all the many myths about jazz: namely, that poor uneducated black folks invented it out of inspiration and thin air, thereby creating America's Only Original Art Form, which a malign WASP establishment has ever since kept on the outside looking in, as the classical music world frowns down on it with disdain.

It is mystifying that Hentoff keeps it up when there are an estimated 30,000 jazz bands of one sort or another in the high schools, colleges, and universities of the United States. If Coleman Hawkins was never appointed to a university staff, Dave Baker has been head of the department of jazz studies at Indiana University since 1966. If Lester Young was never artist-in-residence at a university, Mary Lou Williams was. She held that position at Duke University, where she taught full time in the last years of her life. Benny Carter was artist-in-residence at Baldwin-Wallace College in 1970, and later gave seminars at various universities and colleges. In 1973 he was visiting lecturer at Princeton, which made him an

Honorary Doctor of Humanities the following year. Dr. Billy Taylor is artist-in-residence at Long Island University, Brooklyn Campus, and has taught at the Manhattan School of Music, Columbia University, and Howard University. He has a combined master's degree and doctorate from the University of Massachusetts. He has been a Yale Fellow at Calhoun College for some years and has been appointed a Duke Ellington Fellow by Yale. And he broadcasts regularly about jazz for CBS-TV's *Sunday Morning* program. Willie Ruff, educated at Philadelphia Musical Academy, is on the faculty at Yale. Teddy Wilson was teaching at Juilliard more than thirty years ago. Kenny Barron is on the faculty at Rutgers University.

Any number of jazz musicians have honorary doctorates from universities. Oscar Peterson has at least six, including three LL.Ds. In 1973, he was made an officer in the Order of Canada, the Canadian equivalent of a British OBE. And if Lester Young and Coleman Hawkins did not have Pulitzers, jazz works *have* been nominated for it. Ornette Coleman was awarded a Guggenheim. So was Johnny Carisi.

The performance of this music is taught at thousands of colleges and universities, and jazz appreciation courses are offered at as many more. Clark Terry is one of the most respected clinicians in America, and Dizzy Gillespie turns up in Denton, Texas, to play with the North Texas State University Lab Band. And there are five such bands on that campus alone.

Indeed, the gravest danger facing jazz may lie in this comfortable acclimation to the academic world. The easy way to teach anything is to standardize it—to say that this and this only is the correct way to learn the trumpet, not blowing into a garden hose, the way Clark Terry did as a boy. It will leach the individuality out of the art, and you will get players as precise, mechanical, and cold as Wynton Marsalis. It faces another danger, too, over which Clark Terry has expressed concern: Ghetto children aren't learning jazz; they're learning whatever offers a hope of making much money quickly, which is rock and roll or rhythm and blues, not jazz. If present trends continue, jazz is in danger of being largely abandoned by the ethnic group that invented it. Johnny Griffin has said, "The American jazz audience today is predominantly white. Let's hope that those faithful white connoisseurs of jazz will hang in there long enough for the people back in the hood to get the message."

The idea that the music was intuitively created by uneducated people is subtly racist in its implicit acquiescence to the myth of those happy singin' an' dancin' folks with their natural rhythm. And it demeans many seminal figures in the music's history, who achieved what they did, not because they were black and had "natchal" rhythm but because they were superior musicians who mastered their craft the only way it can be done, by education, formal or otherwise, and hard work.

Benny Carter mentions studying the Forsythe orchestration treatise probably toward the end of the 1920s. Claude Hopkins studied at the Washington Conservatory and had a bachelor's degree from Howard. The Canadian-born pianist Lou Hooper— for a short time one of Oscar Peterson's teachers—who was a figure in Harlem jazz of the 1920s, graduated from the Detroit Conservatory in 1916, and ended his career on the faculty of the University of Prince Edward Island. Paul Whiteman's father, a Denver music educator, numbered among his students Jimmie Lunceford, who went on to get a bachelor's degree from Fisk. Lil Hardin Armstrong had studied at Fisk. Don Redman was the son of a prominent music teacher. By the age of twelve, Redman played all the reeds, including double reeds. He studied at both the Chicago and Boston conservatories.

Even Buddy Bolden was a high school graduate and a reading musician. And if you take a close look at the one surviving photo of the Bolden band, taken about 1905, you will note that Jimmy Johnson's left hand on the neck of his bass is in the correct position used by symphony bassists, with the two middle fingers close together to accommodate the half step between the third and fourth degrees of the major scale. Show that photo to any bass player, and he will tell you instantly that Johnson was a well-trained bassist.

In music, private teaching has always meant more than class instruction, and a great many of the early black musicians had solid training behind them, whether they had degrees or not.

Given the background of men like Carter, Redman, Hooper, Hopkins, and Lunceford, it is inconceivable that they were unaware of the revolutionary turn-of-the century developments in European music. By 1927, William Grant Still—who had a degree in music—was studying with the avant-gardist Edgard Varèse, and had previously studied with George W. Chadwick while Chadwick was director of the New England Conservatory of Music. Another of Still's influences was Will Vodery. Educated as a scholarship student at the University of Pennsylvania, Vodery became one of the outstanding arrangers of the 1920s and '30s. He wrote scores for at least twelve theatre musicals, and from 1913 into the 1920s he arranged music for the *Ziegfeld Follies*. He was in heavy demand through the 1920s and worked as an arranger on the Kern-Hammerstein *Show Boat* before moving to Hollywood to be an arranger and musical director at Fox Films. He was the first black musician to penetrate that world.

James Reese Europe, who was musical director for Vernon and Irene Castle in 1913-14, had been trained on violin and piano in Washington, D.C. He was the first black bandleader to make records, and was the first man to play something akin to jazz in Carnegie Hall, somewhere between 1911 and 1914—the date is uncertain. This was a quarter century before the famous *From Spirituals to Swing* concert in Carnegie. When Europe formed his own band, he hired skilled and schooled musicians. Eubie Blake, who played piano in it, said, "That Europe gang were absolute reading sharks. They could read a moving snake and if a fly lit on that paper, he got played." Blake noted the irony that the band's members were not allowed to enter through the front door of many of the places where they played.

The great stride pianist James P. Johnson had solid "classical" piano training. Scott Joplin studied composition and theory at George Smith College for Negroes.

To insist on some sort of intuitive invention of jazz by an uneducated "folk" is an appalling slight to the achievement of black musicians who were able, more than half a century ago—and some nearly a century ago—to get into and graduate from universities and major conservatories. To describe it as a folk music is to demean both the music and the men who developed it. "Jazz is no folk music," the great trumpeter Harry "Sweets" Edison asserted. "It's too hard to play."

There is no single element in jazz that was or is original, not the harmonic-melodic system, which is European, not the rhythmic character, which is African, not even the idea of improvisation, since improvisation has always been a part of the European tradition. Bach, Mozart, Beethoven, Chopin, Liszt were all master improvisers. Church organists have always been trained in keyboard improvisation, with the best of them able to create spontaneously large and complicated structures that go beyond anything yet attempted by jazz musicians.

The originality arises in the combination of elements. Art Blakey insists: "This is American music. There's nothing like it anywhere on the planet. People are always trying to connect it to something else, to African music, to Latin music. It's not. It's American music. And no one else can play it. Now they say, 'Art Blakey, he's black. That makes him an African.' I'm not. I'm an American and this is American music." He narrows the case a little: there are now innumerable excellent jazz musicians of nationalities other than American. But he could rightly say that they succeed in this music only insofar as they Americanize their aesthetics. And certainly he is quite correct in asserting that it is American music in that the particular cultural cross-pollination that produced it occurred in the United States. But to suggest that the early jazz musicians did not look to "educated" music to pick up a few tricks is to imply that they were stupid or deaf when they were obviously neither.

Nor is it true that the classical establishment universally has disdained jazz. Virgil Thomson long ago affirmed, "Jazz is the most astounding spontaneous musical event to take place anywhere since the Reformation." In 1947, Leonard Bernstein said, "Serious music in America would today have a different complexion and direction were it not for the profound influence of jazz." In 1944, the Chevron School Broadcast published an appreciation of authentic jazz for use in public schools. The extensive notes in praise of the music were by the well-known classical music critic Alfred Frankenstein. In 1941, Louis Harap wrote in *The Musical Quarterly*, "The most valid and vital music created in America in this century has been hot jazz, while classical composition here during the same period has been something less than vital." In the early 1930s, the British composer and essayist Constant Lambert deplored the sterility of contemporary classical music in comparison with the vitality of jazz, particularly the work of Duke Ellington, which he admired enormously. And continuing in his path, Henry Pleasants, who had been the Philadelphia *Evening Bulletin*'s classical music critic from 1930 to 1942, published a series of books, starting with *The Agony of Modern Music* in 1955, excoriating contemporary classical music and praising jazz as the most important music of our time. The Austrian pianist Friedrich Gulda, noted as a Mozart and Beethoven specialist, has taken a similar position.

In August 1924, *The Etude*, the most pervasive journal for music teachers, published an issue devoted to what it called *The Jazz Problem*. It surveyed a number of then-famous people (some of them now largely forgotten) on the subject. It got a result it apparently did not anticipate: extensive praise of the music, along with a few derogations. These statements are a little startling to read today.

The magazine's own editorial on the subject seems confused, as if approval of the music by men such as Leopold Stokowski left it uneasy about its bias. That editorial is worth quoting in full.

> *The Etude* has no illusions on Jazz. We hold a very definite and distinct opinion of the origin, the position, and the future of jazz.
>
> *The Etude* reflects action in the music world. It is a mirror of contemporary musical educational effort. We, therefore, do most emphatically not endorse Jazz, merely by discussing it.
>
> Jazz, like much of the thematic material glorified by the great masters of the past, has come largely from the humblest origin.

In its original form it has no place in musical education and deserves none. It will have to be transmogrified many times before it can present its credentials for the Walhalla of music.

In musical education Jazz has been an accursed annoyance to teachers for years. Possibly the teachers are, themselves, somewhat to blame for this. Young people demand interesting, inspiriting music. Many of the Jazz pieces they have played are infinitely more difficult to execute than the sober music their teachers have given them. If the teacher had recognized the wholesome appetite of youth for fun and had given interesting, sprightly music instead of preaching the evils of Jazz, the nuisance might have been averted.

As it is, the young pupil who attempts to play much of the "raw" Jazz of the day wastes time with common, cheap, trite tunes badly arranged. The pupil plays carelessly and "sloppily." These traits, once rooted, are very difficult to pull out. This is the chief evil of Jazz in musical education.

On the other hand, the melodic and rhythmic inventive skill of many of the composers of Jazz, such men as Berlin, Confrey, Gershwin, and Cohan, is extraordinary. Passing through the skilled hands of such orchestral leaders of high-class Jazz orchestras conducted by Paul Whiteman, Isham Jones, Waring and others, the effects have been such that serious musicians such as John Alden Carpenter, Percy Grainger and Leopold Stokowski, have predicted that Jazz will have an immense influence upon musical composition, not only of America, but also of the world.

Because *The Etude* knows that its very large audience of wideawake readers desires to keep informed upon all sides of the leading musical questions, it presents in this midsummer issue the most important opinions upon the subject yet published. We have thus taken up the "Jazzmania" and dismiss it with this issue. But who knows, the weeds of Jazz may be Burbanked into orchestral symphonies by leading American composers in another decade?

We do desire, however, to call our readers' attention to the remarkable improvement that has come in the manufacture of wind instruments of all kinds and to the opportunities which are presented for teaching these instruments. Jazz called the attention of the public to many of these instruments, but their higher possibilities are unlimited, and thousands of students are now studying wind instruments who only a few years ago would never have thought of them.

There is much to smile at in there, including the editor's idea of what jazz actually was. It is amusing to see George M. Cohan defined as a jazz composer—or Fred Waring's as a jazz orchestra.

Not one black musician is even mentioned. But the editorial does indicate, particularly in its last paragraph, how much impact on music education jazz had already had. And I remind you of the date: 1924.

Now let us look at comments of the people the magazine questioned. The composer and educator Felix Borowski, at that time president of the Chicago Musical College and music critic for various Chicago newspapers, said, "I do not see anything particularly pernicious in 'Jazz.' It would seem that the disapproval which has been bestowed upon it has been the result of the dancing which has accompanied jazz rather than the music itself . . . and in its own special department jazz is often as 'good' as a waltz by Strauss . . . . I find in this form of music something peculiarly American, our restlessness, for instance. Whether jazz could or should be used in what are generally considered serious compositions depends largely upon the composition and upon the person who writes it. Tchaikovsky, Borodin, Glazounow and others used Russian dances in their symphonies and chamber music; there is no reason why an American composer should not employ his own dances—if only he does it well."

Composer John Alden Carpenter, who had studied with Elgar, wrote, "All music that has significance must necessarily be the product of its time. . . . I am convinced that our contemporary popular music (please note that I avoid labeling it 'jazz') is by far the most spontaneous, the most personal, the most characteristic, and, by virtue of these qualities, the most important musical expression that America has achieved." Carpenter had used ragtime elements in his music as far back as 1917 and in his 1922 ballet *Krazy Kat*.

The Czech violinist and composer Franz Drdla, an associate of Brahms who had just finished touring in America, wrote, "Every time and every age has its characteristic music precisely as it has its characteristic dress. In the days of the madrigal, the very character of the words and the text reflected the architecture and the dress of the times. Jazz is the characteristic folk music of modernity because America is the most modern country of the world. It is . . . an expression of the times and it is not surprising that jazz should rapidly circulate around the globe like the American dollar."

The dramatist John Luther Long, whose play *Madame Butterfly* was adapted for the libretto of Puccini's opera, said, "One thing is certain: The world loves and will practice joy. And in jazz there is joy!"

John Philip Sousa wrote:

> My Standard Dictionary gives forth, "Jazz:—Ragtime music in discordant tones or the notes for it."
>
> This is a most misleading meaning and far from the truth and is as much out of place as defining a symphony when murdered by an inadequate and poor orchestra as "a combination of sounds largely abhorrent to the ear."
>
> Jazz can be as simple in construction and as innocent of discord as a happy child's musings, or can be of a tonal quality as complex as the most futuristic composition. Many jazz pieces suffer through ridiculous performances, owing to the desire of a performer . . . to create a laugh by any means possible. . . . (That) simply makes it vulgar through no fault of its own. . . .
>
> There is is no reason, with its exhilarating rhythm, its melodic ingenuities, why it should not become one of the accepted forms of composition.

A few of the people consulted denigrated jazz, but even they seemed a little uncertain in doing so, as if they suspected there was more to the music than met their ears.

Two years prior to the *Etude* survey, the *Atlantic* published an essay by Carl Engel taking up the cause of jazz. Engel too describes the disturbance in some social circles about the enormous popularity of jazz, again refuting the theory of an ignored music, and again—given Engel's own status—demonstrating the consideration and respect the music was receiving in serious music circles.

This example of what was being written and published about jazz in America during that period, instead of what British and French critics say was being written about it, is among hundreds James Lincoln Collier has uncovered that appeared in both large and small periodicals, including the *New York Times*.

As Collier's research has shown the extent to which jazz was being championed in the American intellectual establishment, die-hard defenders of the Europeans-appreciated-it-first dogma have taken to questioning whether these various writers in America knew what jazz was. (The Europeans, of course, knew, right?) Didn't the Americans in that period think jazz was Fred Waring and Paul Whiteman? Obviously the editors of *The Etude* did. But the emphasis of Engel's essay on improvisation and non-written music makes clear that he assuredly was not talking about Fred Waring. He seemed to know very well indeed what jazz was. He even perceives the problem of the piano in jazz, and jazz on the piano.

No doubt somebody in France will be quick to leap up, waggle a forefinger, cry "Tiens!" and point out that Engel was born in France. But Engel, a composer and musicographer by training, considered himself an American, as his essay reveals, and in any event the essay is indicative of what was being *printed* in America in that period. He emigrated to the United States in 1905, at the age of twenty-two, and proceeded to make a place for himself in American intellectual and musical circles. He became head of the music division of the Library of Congress in 1922, the same year this essay was written. Seven years later, in 1929, he became editor of *The Musical Quarterly,* a post in which he served for many years. So in this essay we learn what was the actual attitude of the editor of that pillar of the musical establishment—the very publication in which Louis Harap would again, in 1941, sing the praises of jazz. And Engel more accurately takes the music's measure than Borowski and Sousa would two years later in *The Etude.* Engel sees its importance as lying precisely in the fact of improvisation, not as a quarry for the materials of written composition.

> The contrapuntal complexity of jazz is something native, born out of the complex, strident present-day American life. Where did you hear, before jazz was invented, such multifarious stirring, heaving, wrestling of independent voices as there are in a jazz orchestra? The saxophone bleats a turgid song; the clarinets turn capers of their own; the violins come forward with an obbligato; a saucy flute darts

up and down the scale, never missing the right note on the right chord; the trombone lumberingly slides off on a tangent; the drum and xylophone put rhythmic high lights into these kaleidoscopic shiftings; the cornet is suddenly heard above the turmoil, with good-natured brazenness. Chaos in order—orchestral technic of master craftsmen—music that is recklessly fantastic, joyously grotesque—such is good jazz. A superb, incomparable creation, inescapable yet elusive; something it is almost impossible to put in score upon a page of paper.

For jazz finds its last and supreme glory in the skill for improvisation exhibited by the performers. The deliberately scored jazz tunes are generally clumsy, pedestrian. It is not for the plodding, routine orchestrator to foresee the unexpected, to plan the improbable.

Jazz is abandon, is whimsicality in music. A good jazz band should never play, and actually never does play, the same piece twice in the same manner. Each player must be a clever musician, an originator as well as an interpreter, a wheel that turns hither and thither on its own axis without disturbing the clockwork.

Strange to relate, this orchestral improvisation, which may seem to you virtually impossible or artistically undesirable, is not an invention of our age. To improvise counterpoint was a talent that the musicians in the orchestras of Peri and Monteverdi, three hundred years ago, were expected to possess, and did possess to such a high degree that the skeleton scores of those operas which have come down to us give but an imperfect idea of how this music sounded when performed.

A semblance of this lost, and rediscovered, art is contained in the music of the Russian and Hungarian gypsies. Just as that music is a riotous improvisation, throbbing with a communicative beat, ever restless in mood, so is jazz. Just as the gypsy players are held together by an identical, inexplicable rhythmic spell, following the leader's fiddle in its harmonic meanderings, each instrument walking in a bypath of its own, so is the ideal jazz band constituted—that is, the jazz band made up of serious jazz artists.

Franz Liszt could give a suggestion of gypsy music on the keyboard. He had a way of playing the piano orchestrally. There are few people who can play jazz on the piano. Jazz, as much as the gypsy dances, depends on the many and contrasting voices of a band, united in a single and spontaneous rhythmic, harmonic, and contrapuntal will.

Jazz, fortunately, can be preserved on phonographic records for our descendants. They will form their own estimate of our enormities. If we had such records of what Scarlatti, Couperin, and Rameau did with their figured basses, we should need fewer realizations, restitutions, and renditions by arranger and deranger.

A book of record reviews by three British critics, Max Harrison, Charles Fox, and Eric Thacker, *The Essential Jazz Records, Volume 1, Ragtime to Swing* (Greenwood Press, Westport, Connecticut), contains a section by Harrison, on "The Influence of Jazz on European Composers." He says, "The musical richness of the best jazz was bound to interest younger composers in the 1920s and beyond. Although the works they wrote in response to it are not in themselves jazz, knowledge of some of the relevant pieces is essential to an understanding of the impact jazz has had on Twentieth Century music."

Among the pieces he cites are Satie's *Jack in the Box* (1899), Debussy's *Golliwogg's Cakewalk* (1906), Auric's *Adieu, New York!* (1920), Hindemith's *Suite 1922* (1922), Schulhoff's *Rag-music* (1922) and *Esquisses de jazz* (1927), Burian's *American Suite* (1926), Copland's *4 Piano Blues* (1926-48), Stravinsky's *L'Histoire du soldat* (1918) and *Ragtime for 11 Instruments* (1918), Martinu's *Preludes* (1929), *Shimmy Foxtrot* (1922), *Three Sketches in Modern Dance Rhythms* (1927), *The Kitchen Revue* (1927), a ballet, *Le Jazz* (1928), *Jazz Suite* (1928), and *Sextet* (1929), Milhaud's *La Création du monde* (1923), *Caramel mou* (1920), and *Trois Rag Caprices* (1922), Weill's *Kleine Dreigroschemusik für Blasorchester* (1928), Constant Lambert's *Concerto for Piano and Nine Instruments* (1930-31), *Elegaic Blues* (1927), and *Elegy* (1927), Bliss's *The Rout Trot* (1927), and Walton's *Old Sir Faulk*.

In 1919, five years before *The Etude* addressed itself to *The Jazz Problem*, Ernest Ansermet, founder and first conductor of L'orchestre de la Suisse Romande and a mathematician, wrote an essay called "Sur un orchestre nègre," which the magazine didn't mention. Possibly it had not been translated yet. It is included in Ansermet's fascinating *Ecrits sur la musique*. Ansermet wrote:

> Today ragtime has conquered Europe. It is ragtime that one dances in all our cities under the name of jazz and hundreds of our

musicians apply themselves at this moment to accommodating this new art to a taste that is insipid and sentimental, to the coarse and mediocre sensuality of their clientele. Ragtime is even in the process of passing into what I will call, for lack of another word, *la musique savante*; Stravinsky has used the material in several works; Debussy has already written a cakewalk and I certainly believe Ravel will not be long in giving us a fox-trot. [Ravel "gave us" a foxtrot in *L'Enfant et les sortilèges* (1920-25), and the jazz influence is evident in his *Violin Sonata No 2* (1923-27). It is powerfully evident in the glorious *Concerto in G* for piano, which is drenched in its colorations.]

But there is, under the name of Southern Syncopated Orchestra, an ensemble of authentic musicians of the Negro race who have been heard in London. Instrumentalists and singers, they present pellmell all sorts of manifestations of their art, old and new, the best and the worst. . . .

The first thing that strikes us about the Southern Syncopated Orchestra is the astonishing perfection, the highest taste, the fervor of their playing. I cannot say if these artists make it their duty to be "sincere," if they are penetrated by the idea that they have a "mission" to fulfill, if they are convinced of the "nobility" of their task, if they have that holy "audacity" and sacred "valor" that our police of musical morals exact of our European musicians, or even if they are animated by any "idea" whatever. But I can see that they have a precise feeling for the music they love, and a pleasure in making it that communicates to the listener with an irresistible force, a pleasure that pushes them ceaselessly to outdo themselves, constantly to enrich and refine their medium. . . . They play generally without notes, and even when they have them, they are used only to indicate a general line, for few of their pieces that I heard twice were executed with exactly the same effects. I imagine that, knowing which voice is assigned to them in the harmonic structure, and aware of the role of each instrument, they can, in a certain way and within certain limits, let themselves go, according to the heart. They are so entirely possessed by the music they play that they cannot help dancing it within themselves, in such a way that their playing is a true spectacle, and when they surrender to one of their favorite effects, to return to a refrain at half speed with a redoubled intensity and figuration, a startling thing happens: it seems as if a great wind passes in a forest, or that doors are thrown brusquely open on an immense orgy.

Moreover, the musician who directs and to whom the constitution of this ensemble is due, Monsieur Will Marion Cook, is a master in every respect, and there is no orchestra leader I take so much pleasure in watching conduct. As for the music that comprises their repertoire, it is purely vocal, for one voice, a vocal quartet, or a choir accompanied by instruments, or again purely instrumental; it bears the names of composers unknown in our world or is marked: traditional. The music called traditional is of religious inspiration. It is the index of a whole religious way and a true religious art that merit a full study of their own. The entire Old Testament is recounted with touching realism and familiarity. There is much about Moses, Gideon, the Jordan, and Pharaoh. In an immense unison, the voices intone, "Go down, Moses, and tell old Pharoah to let my people go." And suddenly they clap their hands and stamp their feet with a joy like that of schoolchildren told that the teacher is out sick: "Good news, good news! heaven's chariot is descending to the earth. I don't want it to forget me!" Or else a singer gets up: "I got shoes . . ." pronouncing the s to make it pretty ". . . you got shoes, all God's children got shoes. When I get to heaven, gonna put on my shoes, gonna walk all over God's heaven . . ."

[Some of the songs] are about the sweetness of Georgia peaches, or the scent of flowers, the land, the mammy, or the sweetheart; the instrumental works are rags, or even European dances. Among the authors, some are Negro, but they are the exceptions. The others are of European origin, and even when this is not so of the author, it is of the music; most of the ragtimes are based on well-known works, or particular formulae particular to our art. There is one based on the *Wedding March* from *A Midsummer Night's Dream*, another on the celebrated *Prelude* of Rachmaninoff, another on typical Debussy chords, another quite simply on the major scale.

Lest Debussy-like chords seem an inspired naive discovery, let's briefly examine Will Marion Cook's background. He was studying violin at Oberlin College at the age of fifteen. He then studied the instrument in Berlin with Joachim, who had been closely associated with Mendelssohn, Schumann, and Liszt. On returning to the United States, Cook studied at the National Conservatory of Music, where Dvořák was one of his teachers. He later became a formative influence on Duke Ellington. "We would ride around Central Park in a taxi, and he'd give me lectures in music," Ellington said. "Some of the things he used to tell me I never got a chance to use until years later when I wrote the tone poem, *Black, Brown and Beige*."

The insights in the Ansermet essay are quite striking:

> In the field of melody, although his habituation to our scales has effaced the memory of the African modes, on old instinct pushes the Negro to seek his pleasure outside the orthodox intervals: he plays thirds that are neither major nor minor and false seconds and falls often by instinct on the natural harmonic sounds of a given note; no written music can give the idea of his playing. I have often remarked, for example, that (in their music) the A-sharp and B-flat, the E and E-flat, are not the sounds of our scale. It is only in the field of harmony that the Negro has not realized his own expression. Still he uses series of chords of the seventh, and ambiguous major-minors, with a sure hand that many European musicians should envy. But harmony is perhaps, in general, an element that appears in musical evolution at a point that Negro art has not yet reached.
>
> Perhaps we are going to see, one of these days, a Glinka of Negro music. But I am inclined to think that it is in the *Blues* that the genius of the race manifests itself most forcefully.
>
> The Blues, that is what happens when the Negro is in pain, when he is far from "home," far from his "Mammy" or from his "Sweet heart." He thinks then of a motif or a favorite rhythm, and he takes his trombone or his violin or his banjo or his clarinet or his drum, or else he sings or, simply, dances. And on the motif he chooses, he exhausts his fantasy. That makes the pain pass. It is the Blues. . . ."
>
> There is in the Southern Syncopated Orchestra an extraordinary clarinet virtuoso who is, it appears, the first of his race to have composed on the clarinet blues of consummate form. I heard two on which he elaborated at length, then played to his companions who responded with accompaniment. Though they were extremely different, one was as admirable as the other for the wealth of the invention, the strength of the accent, for their audacity of novelty and the unforeseen. They gave already the idea of a style, and the form of it was gripping, sudden, harsh, with an ending abrupt and pitiless like that of the Second Brandenburg Concerto of Bach. I wish to declaim the name of this artist of genius, because for my part, I will never forget it: it is Sidney Bechet. When one has sought so often to rediscover in the past one of the figures to whom we owe the advent of our art—those men of the Seventeenth and Eighteenth Centuries, for example, who from dance tunes created expressive works that thus opened the road on which Haydn and Mozart mark not the point of departure but the first milestones—it is such a moving thing to meet this large black boy, with white teeth and narrow brow, who

is so happy that you like what he does, but does not know how to speak of his art, save to say that he is following his "own way." His "own way" is perhaps the great road that the world will be swept along tomorrow.

The Ansermet essay is a remarkable document, more read about than read, unfortunately. And in a particular way, it is quite moving. It is not, however, helpful to a person trying to make a case for jazz as a music persecuted by a conspiratorial establishment. Bechet spent much of the rest of his life in Europe, where he was lionized, and even presented at court to King George V. (The event prompted his wonderful wisecrack that it was the first time he had ever met anyone whose picture was on money.)

For society to assign to the artist an exalted position is a comparatively recent thing. In Haydn's time, even the most celebrated artists were not served at the same table or even in the same room as the aristocratic patrons for whom they performed. Bach is referred to in a church document of the period as "our worthy Kappelmeister." Artists have always been held a little suspect in Western society—and not just in Western society. In some African tribes, musicians are looked on as lazy and useless because all they want to do is practice their craft.

Pulitzers and Tonys and Nobels and foundation support and all the rest are phenomena of recent times. True appreciation of artistic creation has always been limited to a minority of people, for, as Ray Brown says, "The better it gets, the fewer of us know it." Not everybody likes jazz. Not everybody likes opera. But a large and perceptive body of jazz appreciators demonstrably has come into existence.

Years ago, when I was classical music critic of the Louisville *Times*, I circulated professionally mostly in a "classical" music world, meeting many of the major "serious" composers of our time, pianists, conductors, and opera singers. I simply never encountered the condescension to jazz that is supposed to exist in that world, except now and then from one of the bluehaired ladies, as Alec Wilder used to call them, on the committees of symphony orchestras and chamber music societies. Among symphony players there was a widespread admiration for jazz. Many symphony brass players I have met have backgrounds as jazz or at least dance-band players. Miles Anderson, the principal trombonist of the Los Angeles Philharmonic, is a great jazz fan. So was the late cellist Edgar Lustgarten, who loved to play it if you'd write it out for him.

Vladimir Horowitz, Arturo Toscanini, and Sergei Rachmaninoff were all admirers of Art Tatum. When Sixten Ehrling was conductor of the Detroit Symphony, he could often be found after concerts and other evenings in Baker's Keyboard Lounge, listening to jazz. And the present conductor of the Los Angeles Philharmonic is André Previn, one of the most articulate champions jazz has had. Indeed, Previn is himself an accomplished jazz player.

Nor have things apparently been much different in Britain. Max Harrison told me, "As a person who's spent most of his life in classical music publishing and then as a—mainly—classical music critic, I can wholly endorse your Louisville experience. Apart, inevitably, from an occasional individual, I simply haven't encountered the anti-jazz prejudice which jazz people almost universally imagine to exist in that world. This is a prime example of jazz people convincing themselves, by repeating, à la Hentoff, over and over, something which is untrue."

This is not for a moment to suggest that jazz has encountered no resistance. Obviously it has.

But then that has been true of new music throughout history. Beethoven was fiercely attacked by critics, and one fellow composer said that the Fifth Symphony gave proof that he was mad. The Berlin critic Richard Wurst said Tchaikovsky's *Francesca da Rimini* was "a musical monster . . . an ear-flaying horror." The Boston *Evening Transcript* said his Fifth Symphony in turn was "pandemonium, delirium tremens, raving, and above all, noise worse confounded"—the same sort of thing detractors said of jazz. Debussy's *Pelléas et Mélisande* was booed cruelly and the French took to calling it *Pédéraste et Médisante*. The (London) *Times* in April 1924, four months before *The Etude* took up the jazz "problem," said, "To hear a whole program of Ravel's work is like watching some midget or pygmy doing clever, but very small, things within a limited scope. Moreover, the almost reptilian cold-bloodedness, which one suspects of having been consciously cultivated, of most of M. Ravel's music is almost repulsive when heard in bulk; even its beauties are like the markings on snakes and lizards." This of one of the warmest and most elegant composers of our century.

The blue-stockings of the 1920s hated jazz, and feared it. "The church also hated it," the classical music scholar and historian Robert Offergeld observed. "But they were more or less irrelevant. Jazz was deeply unnerving to the pedagogic community, and the music teachers associations set up what amounted to a national campaign against 'playing by ear,' a coded phrase that meant jazz. No respectable piano teacher had the faintest idea what jazz was, much less how to play it. Old maid piano teachers went out of business by the thousands."

Henry Pleasants adds:

> A great many professional and accomplished classical musicians have been familiar with the work of jazz musicians, both black and white, and respected it—but at a distance. And the establishment was instinctively hostile because it was, understandably, I think, fearful. In following the relationship between the establishment and our indigenous American music, I am constantly reminded of Robert Ardrey's book *The Territorial Imperative*. An alien (African) element had entered the mainstream of western (European) music. The tribe (establishment) closed forces to protect and perpetuate its territorial (ethnic?) integrity and keep the intruder out, or at least at a distance. One could respect him, but one didn't invite him to dinner. And not because he was black! Indeed, a black jazz musician had a better chance of being invited to dinner than a white!

It is not surprising, then, that jazz encountered hostility. What is far more interesting is that a music so new should have encountered as much understanding and admiration as it did among people who really mattered in musical circles. On this point that edition of *The Etude* is illuminating. And jazz still encounters a certain amount of resistance. People involved in the jazz education movement in the universities will, sometimes, tell you of a certain cool toleration they encounter from the "classical" department. But this is well within the frame of what we might call a normal human conservatism, an uneasiness with departures and the unfamiliar. By their very nature, universities are conservative organizations, for it is in them that we *conserve* our culture, to pass it along. Yet that kind of self-protective academic toleration of jazz is no longer general in the universities. You won't encounter it at Indiana University, certainly, not with Harvey Phillips, whose official title is Distinguished Professor of Music, so influential in its proceedings and policies. In his vacation time, he is off touring with the Tuba Jazz Consort. He notes that there isn't a college of consequence in the country that doesn't have a jazz course.

We are not talking here of the racial discrimination experienced by black jazz musicians. That is a separate matter. The discrimination they have encountered is based on color rather than music and would be the same no matter what the individual's profession. If you are, say, a black investment banker in Los Angeles, your chances of being shot by a cop are notably higher than they would be if you were white. The issue is a discrimination supposedly visited on the music from its origins into the present by a contemptuous classical establishment. And there *has* been some of it, but nowhere near what all too many writers about jazz would have you think.

Finally, the subject has to be viewed against a background of condescension toward *all* American music that was the long lingering consequence of an immoral American copyright law that permitted the use without payment of music by foreign composers, which caused publishers throughout the nineteenth century to steal it and exploit it as superior to American composition. This held back the entire American musical culture to a degree we can only imagine. Even without the law as it was, such was European prestige in America that this condescension would no doubt have existed to an extent anyway. It was only in the 1950s that the United States began to escape the utter domination of the French in fashions. Even now, the great majority of American symphony orchestras are led by foreign conductors. Only a few American conductors have been allowed to rise in this field, Michael Tillson Thomas, Leonard Bernstein, and André Previn among them. And if you want to split a hair, Previn was born in Berlin.

That the upstart musical art called jazz should have received so much acceptance in serious artistic circles, which turns out to be the case, is surprising. The notion that jazz has experienced unceasing scorn from the cultured world throughout its existence turns out on examination to be far from the truth. Its creators were anything but the ignorant intuitive "naturals" of jazz mythology, and they didn't all live lives of anguished obscurity.

After all, Louis Armstrong and Duke Ellington were among the most famous Americans of their time.

4

THE ENIGMA:
DUKE ELLINGTON

ON APRIL 19, 1982, on the stage of the New York theatre where *Sophisticated Ladies* was playing, a party was held to observe the eighty-third anniversary of Duke Ellington's birth. Its purpose of course was publicity for the show; the television coverage was extensive.

There were ironies in the situation which eluded the notice of the TV commentators. One was that the honors devolved on Duke's son, Mercer Ellington, who had been at times estranged from his father. It is not easy to be the scion of a famous parent, and Mercer Ellington no doubt had a worse time of it than, say, Bach's sons, who at least were able to persuade themselves that their old man was a square, or Johann Strauss Jr., who became a far better composer than his father. Mercer Ellington has lived his life in the sound of his father's acclaim. And so there was a second irony, I mused as I watched the television images of Mercer smiling and accepting congratulations on the show. When Duke finally got something he had wanted, a hit Broadway musical, he was not there and Mercer was.

Duke Ellington died May 24, 1974, at seventy-five, of the pneumonia that is usually the final insult of lung cancer.

I did not know him well, though well enough to know how shrewd he was. He was, I think, a far more interesting man, with complex dimensions, than the hagiography of jazz has made him out to be. He had a Buddha smile, and there was an amused light in his eye.

A substantial amount of nonsense was written about him at the time of his death. One disk jockey said, "He was the most important composer of the Twentieth Century—more important than Shostakovitch or Stravinsky." So much for you, Igor, and you too, Bela, Maurice, Alban, Claude, and the rest of you cats, including Sibelius and Charles Ives. As for Shostakovitch, he is hardly considered the summit of twentieth-century composition. In any event, such comparisons are foolish, generated by the assumption that art is some sort of contest. Duke Ellington's importance did not lay in comparisons of that or any other kind, since what he did was unique. He was an original.

In the obituaries, it was stated that Duke had written nine hundred or a thousand songs. That is not a lot, considering the length of his life and the intensity of his activity. And a lot of his tunes began as head arrangements, composed in effect by the band—and source of the complaint that Duke developed bits of material improvised by others and put his imprimatur on them as composer. If quantity is a criterion, which it is not (Paul Dukas left only twelve works), Duke's output did not begin to compare with the seven hundred-odd opuses of Bach, or the works of Schubert which, in reduced-score book-form, fill several feet of shelf space—including among other things fourteen operas, eight symphonies, fifteen string quartets, and six hundred songs. And Schubert died at thirty-one.

When Duke died, the commentators, not knowing what to say, then, compared him improbably to Shostakovitch or counted the number of his songs. And this phenomenon haunted his life: to be extolled for the wrong reasons. The praise of Duke Ellington had the odor of an attempted expiation of American guilt over the treatment of blacks. As if to hide this great national shame, sweep it under the carpet, deny its existence, everyone from presidents to television commentators seemed to be saying, "No, no, it's not true. Look how we honor Duke Ellington." I think Duke knew how jive the praise was. I cannot imagine that he did not. When Count Basie urged Artie Shaw to come back to the business because it needed him, Artie said, "I hated it, and so do you. Why don't you quit?" Basie said, "What could I be? A janitor?"

Having attained an exalted position in American society, Duke, I think, perceived that it was the better part of valor not to question it, even though it had been bestowed for dubious cause. Whether or not he had genius—I think he had; and more to the point, I think he thought he had—he was for those people at the Kennedy Center and in the State Department and the White House and all the other branches of the Establishment the right black man in the right place at the right time, one who spoke well and had manners and posed no apparent threat, and so they held him up for all to see not as the artist he was but as evidence that America is really not what those marchers and malcontents say it is. I don't think they had the slightest idea who or what Duke Ellington was. In any event, the way a society treats its celebrities has nothing to do with how it treats its common people, and the honoring of Duke Ellington in no way compensates for the abuse because of his color of even one black farm boy. Duke knew all that. And maybe that was the cause of the sadness that slept in his Buddha smile and the wellspring of his mocking "We love you madly."

Duke's father was a butler to the Washington, D. C., wealthy. And since the mighty are inclined to look on servants as self-propelled furniture, they converse indiscreetly in their presence. So we can only guess what table talk Duke heard at second hand in his home. And we can assume that his father was a master of the niceties and taught the son fine points of social behavior that were the foundation of Duke's unshakable poise and impeccable manners.

Late one night, watching on television with a kind of morbid fascination one of those 1930s Three Mesquiteers westerns that starred John Wayne, I was boggled by the racial stereotype of a black bellman, bowing and scraping and terrified of big old broad-shouldered Wayne, and rolling his eyes and saying, "Yazzuh, yaz-zuh." Was it really like that? And so recently? Yes it was. Let us not forget that Duke Ellington emerged into fame in the time of Mantan Moreland and Steppin Fetchit. It is doubtful that many of us, including younger black musicians who have tended to think of Louis Armstrong as an Uncle Tom, can grasp, except as an act of the imagination, what it was like to be a black man in that time. And a gifted one. You did what you had to do, and you smiled with big white teeth if you were in show business, and entertained the idiots and took the money home. Some, like Fats Waller, let a certain sly contempt creep into their work, which accounts for those hilarious performances of the utter junk he was often required to record. Even Fats Waller's lousy records are weird masterpieces.

Duke handled things in a different way. Having grown up in a sophisticated ambience, he used his learning well. Duke built a space around himself. He spoke to the white world in its own language, with his perfect diction and elegant enunciation. But Duke never let any white man think that he necessarily wanted to live in the same neighborhood. The question with Duke was always: did he want you to live in his neighborhood? He proclaimed not his equality but, in subtle and silent ways, his superiority.

In his book *Beneath the Underdog*, the late bassist Charles Mingus, who once played with the band, tells a hilarious story of how he came to leave it:

[Juan] Tizol wants you to play a solo he's written where bowing is required. You raise the solo an octave, where the bass isn't too muddy. He doesn't like that and he comes to the room under the stage where you're practicing at intermission and comments that you're like the rest of the niggers in the band, who can't read. You ask Juan how he's different from the other niggers and he states that one of the ways he's different is that HE IS WHITE. So you run his ass upstairs. You leave the rehearsal room, proceed toward the stage with your bass and take your place and at the moment Duke brings down the baton for *A-Train* and the curtain of the Apollo Theatre goes up, a yelling, whooping Tizol rushes out and lunges at you with a bolo knife. The rest you remember mostly from Duke's own words in his dressing room as he changes after the show.

"Now, Charles," he says, looking amused, putting Cartier links into the cuffs of his beautiful handmade shirt, "you could have fore-warned me—you left me out of the act entirely. At least you could have let me cue in a few chords as you ran through that Nijinsky routine. I congratulate you on your performance, but why didn't you and Juan inform me about the adagio you planned so that we could score it? I must say I never saw a large man so agile—I never saw *anybody* make such tremendous leaps! The gambado over the piano carrying your bass was colossal. When you exited after that I thought, 'That man's really afraid of Juan's knife and at the speed he's going he's probably home in bed by now.' But no, back you came through the same door with your bass still intact. For a moment I was hopeful you'd decided to sit down and play but instead you slashed Juan's chair in two with a fire axe! Really, Charles, that's destructive. Everybody knows Juan has a knife but nobody ever took it seriously—he likes to pull it out and show it to people, you under-stand. So I'm afraid, Charles—I've never fired anybody—you'll have to quit my band. I don't need any new problems. Juan's an old prob-lem, I can cope with that, but you seem to have a whole bag of new tricks. I must ask you to be kind enough to give me your notice, Charles."

The charming way he says it, it's like he's paying you a compliment. Feeling honored, you shake hands and resign.

Stanley Dance, Ellington's biographer and friend, said Mingus greatly exaggerated the incident. Stanley said that he asked mem-bers of the Ellington band about the confrontation, and "none of them could remember anything so exciting happening at all. Tizol did, however, take out his knife to Cat Anderson at the joint ses-sion of the Ellington and Basie bands."

But Mingus had a remarkable ear, and if he made up that speech by Ellington, or exaggerated it, he uncannily captured the tone of Duke's suave, ironic, convoluted manner of speech, his elegant "verbal arabesques," as Whitney Balliett aptly called them.

In the news reports of Duke's death, I did not encounter one mention of Billy Strayhorn, the gentle and gifted arranger and composer who died seven years before Duke, also in New York, also of cancer. Theirs was an unusual arrangement. Strayhorn was more than Duke's arranger and amanuensis, and their work was as close, probably, as we'll ever get to joint composition. No one will ever know how much of the Ellington music Strayhorn was responsible for, and indeed many compositions commonly supposed to be Duke's, such as *Take the A Train* and *Johnny Come Lately*, were, as one finds on reading the record labels, Strayhorn's.

The Ellington band was often sloppy to the point of sounding seedy. I once made the mistake of saying that sometimes it was mediocre. "Wrong," Johnny Mandel said. "That band was wonderful, or it was awful. But it was never mediocre." Another time, I said to Ted Williams, the noted photographer of jazz, that the band sometimes sounded as if a couple of the saxophone players had got drunk and not shown up. "No," Ted said. "It sounds as if they got drunk and did show up." Once in Chicago, Ted was shooting some pictures of Duke during a recording session. The band tried several takes on a tune. Paul Gonsalves kept botching it. Duke, in the control booth, said, "Oh shit." And he pushed the talk-back switch on the console and said, "Paul Gonsalves. You're wanted on the telephone in the hall." Gonsalves left the studio, and Duke called to the other musicians, "Lock that door!" And then he kicked off a tempo, and the band got its take. He did not of course fire Gonsalves. As he said to Mingus, he never fired anybody.

Sometimes he would begin a performance with only six or seven men on the bandstand. The others would come drifting in as they felt like it until a full complement, more or less, was reached. It is notorious that there were some imperious and difficult men in that band. One of the musicians—trombonist Quentin Jackson, if memory serves me—told me once that he was in the band eight months before anybody spoke to him.

They were a strange sort of traveling circus that Duke somehow knew how to handle, men who in some cases couldn't fit anywhere else in musical society but whose idiosyncrasies of sound Duke could use as colors in his own highly personal tapestries. He said he stayed on the road because it gave him the privilege of hearing his own music every night, but it is reasonable to suspect he also did it to provide employment for his orphans. His ASCAP earnings from his songs must have been enormous, so he didn't have to do it for the money.

His band was a sort of secret society whose members did as they pleased, and Duke let them get away with it. "But when it really matters," he once told Freddie Williamson, his agent with Joe Glaser's Associated Booking office, "they come through for me." Indeed they did. "If you caught that band on a hot night," Johnny Mandel said, "there was nothing like it. It was history, coming right out of the Cotton Club and Harlem in the 1920s, and it was alive."

No doubt everyone who listened attentively to that band would mention those nights that were forgettable and are forgotten. But its high nights stay bright in the memory. For me, the two occasions that flicker in that darkened movie theatre of the mind are the first time I saw the band and the last.

The first was in Niagara Falls, Ontario. I must have been ten or eleven. I was visiting my grandmother, and on a weekend summer evening I was out tooling around on my grandfather's bicycle (he never did learn to drive). I was returning from the Falls, at whose foot I would play among the rocks in the flying spray and awesome roar of the waters, when I saw a crowd gathering in front of the arena on Lundy's Lane. I paused to consider this and heard music. So I took my bike around to the back of this vast barn, put a padlock on the back wheel, and managed, by that sneaky skill with which small boys are endowed, to slip into the building through a rear exit. And there were these men, black, brown, and beige (as Duke put it in a suite), with their shining brass instruments, and a drummer with a great Oriental gong behind him (which immediately identifies him as Sonny Greer) and this suave man with a pencil mustache at the piano, collectively emitting a roar of music that put Niagara Falls to shame. I had never heard anything so exciting in my life. I worked my way through the crowd near the bandstand until I stood at the very feet of a black man with a trumpet in his hand who moved with a piquant cocky bantam-rooster strut, his shoulders back and his back arched, and sang laughingly into a microphone with such fervor that he was spraying spit on the crowd with every P and B of the song. No one seemed to mind. In memory, one recognizes Ray Nance. And vapor was coming from the bells of the trumpets and trombones. And I was so close that I could smell the slide and valve oil. I must have stayed there all evening. No doubt my grandmother was frantic with worry. No doubt she raised hell when I got home. But I don't remember that. I remember only the music. I soon learned there was a band at the arena every Saturday night, and so I went back the next week, found the same door ajar, and saw Jimmie Lunceford. My Uncle Harry, who was a trombone player and arranger, told me that this music was called jazz.

The last time I saw the band was as memorable as the first. It was at the Newport Jazz Festival eight or ten years before Duke died. Ellington and his weird ragtag go-to-hell we-couldn't-careless crew went on stage and started to play. Their power grew, and they became the meaning and embodiment of swing, of sheer surging musical strength. The crowd was going crazy. I heard a voice cheering and screaming and realized it was my own.

And so those two concerts are book-ends, as it were, on my memory of the Duke Ellington band. Between them, I heard many performances that were, well, awful. And one wonders about serendipity, and the antique claim that necessity is the mother of invention, and whether Duke's way of orchestrating was not in part an evolution from happenstance, a style of writing that evolved because some of his guys got drunk and didn't show up and he made remarkable use of those who did. The band itself, not score paper, was Duke Ellington's palette of colors.

One might speak of Basie and Ellington as the two main streams of big jazz-orchestra style. A lot of men contributed to the development of what we think of as the Basie way of orchestrating and playing, particularly Don Redman and Fletcher Henderson. Woody Herman, in his characteristically self-abnegating fashion, used to say Basie took care of one thing and Duke took care of another, "and we went for what was left over." That seriously understates Woody's own contribution to jazz, and particularly big-band jazz, but there is a point to the remark. Redman and Henderson organized the sections in the way that is common to big bands—rhythm section, trumpets-trombones, and saxophones, voiced by and large to work antiphonally as separate choirs. The sections led independent lives, except insofar as they would accompany each other or sometimes come together tutti.

Duke didn't work that way. He put his colors together up through the sections, as it were, mixing and matching them in all sorts of odd ways. He was the first man in jazz (Debussy had already done it in the "Sirènes" section of *Nocturnes*) to use the wordless female voice as an instrumental color. *Mood Indigo* used a trumpet on top, a muted trombone as the middle voice, and clarinet in the chalumeau register (later bass clarinet) below them. That gave it its haunted sound. Whether Duke did it because one night he had only this possibility available to him or whether he planned it, I cannot say. Chances are that Duke found some of his combinations because of the vagaries of the band's behavior and then saw possibilities, as Dizzy Gillespie did the night somebody sat on his trumpet and he picked it up in fury and tried playing it with its uptilted bell and said to himself, "Damn! I think I like that!" Many a great discovery is tripped over.

Gil Evans, Charles Mingus, Gerry Mulligan, Bob Brookmeyer, Oliver Nelson, Clare Fischer, Eddie Sauter, Rob McConnell, and many superb writers learned in Duke's school. Robert Farnon admires Duke, and other arrangers and composers admire Farnon. And the influence of these men has permeated American—and world—music, including film scoring. Thus through his disciples Duke has infused the world with his way of writing.

Thad Jones was trying to describe the character of the Basie band, trying to describe what it was like to play in that band, with its great fraternal sense of shared identity. Words were failing him, as they would anyone, and he was using his hands. He held them in front of him, waving them back and forth in parallel, describing a sort of walled highway in the air. "It's focused," he said. "The sound comes straight out at you." And you know what he means. The Basie band had force, even when it was loping lazily over

Freddie Green's guitar, which was the nexus of it all, and then, casually, it went wham!, blowing you out of your socks.

The Ellington band was totally different. It had a wide sound, a sort of Cinerama effect in color. When it came off, as Johnny Mandel says, there was nothing like it. To be both diffuse and intense at the same time was the thing that the Ellington band could on occasion accomplish. That is what they were doing that night at Newport. And it was no doubt what they did that night I first heard them. When it was all working, the band was exotic.

Duke did all sorts of things before anybody else did, including use of the brass section as a sort of rhythm instrument. He was incorporating Latin American touches into his music long ago. When he would discover something strange, like the sound of Puerto Rican valve trombonist Tizol, he would use it—as in the recording with Tizol of *Caravan*. Instead of saying to a musician, "Do it this way because that's how I want it," he would say to himself, in effect, "That's how this man plays, and I'm going to use it just the way it is."

His band was like a brilliantly strange assemblage of *objets trouvailles*. Juan Tizol, Tricky Sam Nanton, and Lawrence Brown in the same trombone section? In Ellington's world of color, the answer was "Why not?" And these distinctive musicians, interestingly, almost always sounded better in the Ellington band than out of it. Some really couldn't work anywhere else. Where else could you fit the odd, slushy drumming of Sonny Greer? "We used to say," said Johnny Mandel, "that nobody but Sonny Greer, who had strange time, could play with that band. We did not foresee how good it would sound when Sam Woodyard or Louis Bellson was with it."

Only a few men—Clark Terry and the late Ben Webster in particular—were as effective out of the Ellington band as they had been in it. Some of his musicians left for a while and then, like lost sheep, came back.

For all these things and more, Duke Ellington is a major figure in American musical history, if a creature quite different from the paper hero described by the wire services when he died.

Among the other inaccuracies expressed at that time was a remark by John Chancellor, the NBC newscaster and jazz fan. He said Duke didn't look a day over forty. It was a gracious thing to say, but it wasn't true. In the latter years, the suave handsomeness had given way to a lined and weary puffiness. There were great sacs under the eyes. Duke didn't like growing old. Who does? But I think he hated it more than most men. He dyed his hair, and it had a henna tint that people pretended, sometimes even to themselves, not to notice.

For, as everyone in the music business knew, Duke had a taste for the ladies. Married and separated in his young years but never divorced, he later traveled on the more elevated planes of society, that world of lofty hedonism inhabited by the likes of Tallulah Bankhead, Noel Coward, and Cole Porter. He was not, shall we say, averse to the pleasures of the boudoir.

Because of his position and perhaps too because of what he had learned from his father, Duke knew plenty. Duke once told someone, during a discussion of politics, "Trust nobody. Nobody." Duke kept his cool and his own counsel and seemed content, if sad, to know more than anybody knew he knew. He took the world as he found it, both in life and in music, tolerating discrepancies and contradictions in men and circumstance. That is how he was able to make a functioning unit of men with such disparate sounds and personalities. Therein lies one difference between classical and jazz composition. Classical music assumes, within a certain narrow variability, a "correct" trumpet sound or a "correct" trombone sound. Jazz tolerates all sorts of peculiarity, and Duke went beyond toleration: he celebrated difference. He turned idiosyncrasies to advantage and accommodated Ray Nance's violin; Cat Anderson's paper-thin high-note trumpet; the swooping golden-sad alto saxophone of Johnny Hodges; the big throaty baritone saxophone of Harry Carney, ever since the 1920s the solid cement foundation of that band, a kind and good man who himself lay in a hospital with terminal double pneumonia even as Duke's cancer was producing its pneumonia; and the smoky autumnal trombone of Lawrence Brown.

Duke knew how to handle them, producing order out of their chaos. He knew how to handle the world. And he could do it all at the same time and find a distant laughter in the very act of it. He was putting us all on, and that very put-on was perhaps his most brilliant performance.

This is an instance:

Paul Gonsalves, who was afflicted with heroin addiction, died a few days ahead of Duke, which was a mercy—it is doubtful that he could have functioned in a world without Duke. A few years earlier, the man had been picked up by two federal narcs in Las Vegas. They booked him and then spoke to Duke. How, Mr. Ellington, they asked, can someone of your international repute, who has received every honor, keep a man like that in your band?

"Gentlemen," Duke said in a way that anyone who knew him can hear in the mind's ear, "he has two of the most beautiful little girls."

The two narcs went to court and testified in the saxophonist's behalf. And got him off!

Quite aside from his gifts as a composer, Duke Ellington was a far better pianist then he was usually given credit for. *The Single Petal of a Rose* is enthrallingly lovely. There is an album on Atlantic called *Duke Ellington's Jazz Violin Session*. It contains a track in which Stephane Grappelli plays Duke's *In a Sentimental Mood*, accompanied by Duke on piano, Ernie Shepard on bass, and Sam Woodyard, drums. It is one of the most gorgeous tracks in jazz. Grappelli will make you cry, and not with sadness but with an exaltation that fills his startling solo. Duke plays no solo on the track but his accompaniment for Grappelli is so constantly surprising that one wonders, as one does with Mozart, how he ever thought of certain things. And he subtly prods Grappelli. If Duke could command and direct other musicians from and through the piano—and he could—this track perfectly reveals him in the process of doing it.

Duke functioned in an insane world. He made his music and managed not to let the madness drive him mad and still got wry amusement and some life out of life. And the girls. Always the girls.

Duke was a complex, clever, highly intelligent, articulate, restless, ironic, worldly, superior, tolerant, amused, hurt, and, in the last analysis, intensely private man. I know a lot of people who saw him frequently but few people really knew him well—Stanley Dance better than most. Duke and Benny Carter were acquaintances over a period of many years. Benny traveled with him with Jazz at the Philharmonic and says he knew him "hardly at all." Gene Norman too traveled with him at one time and hung out with him extensively, and says he too knew him hardly at all.

The final irony is that Duke probably would have hated *Sophisticated Ladies*, made up of various of his tunes but not composed as a unit intended for the stage. Indeed, Mercer Ellington has said in an interview that he feels that, had his father been alive, he would not have allowed it to be produced.

No one who knew Duke's music well seems to have liked the show. "It was like visiting the Hollywood wax museum," Johnny Mandel said. "I don't think anybody connected with that show understood Duke's music."

The tunes, at least, are wonderful, though the lyrics—this was true of many of his songs—are well below the standard of his music.

If few people knew Duke Ellington, I must say that I did not go out of my way to know him better. The reason is that I am uncomfortable in the kind of sychophancy, the abject acclamation and supine worship, that surrounded him. But I admired him greatly, and more than he knew. But perhaps he did know. He was that perceptive.

Duke Ellington had his secrets, and he took them with him. I sometimes wonder what ever happened to the autograph I obtained from him when I was twelve. I still can see it, as elegant and rounded as his way of speaking, seeming to glow there on the paper.

5

THE ROMANTIC:
ARTIE SHAW

ON ONE OF those folding chairs designed no doubt by the same
misanthrope who invented the wire coat-hanger and those modern
medicine bottles that only a child can open, I was enduring a
chamber-music concert with a friend who, at that time, had a full
beard. This was in the ornate white marble rotunda of the city hall
of Ventura, California. Perhaps a thousand yards away lies a strip
of sand beyond which the Pacific Ocean begins its long march to
China, Japan, Polynesia, and India. My friend and I, both of us far
from the crimson autumns and white winters of our respective
childhoods, were listening to European music on the final frontier
of Western civilization.

The orchestra comprised eleven musicians. The audience,
despite casual California attire, had the air of earnest interest
(concealing many a wandering thought on other subjects) common to chamber-music recitals, and I tried to keep a certain
amusement from showing in my face. Then the orchestra turned
to a piece by Charles Gounod. The respect of twentieth-century
audiences for nineteenth-century composers has anesthetized us
to Gounod's mediocrity. The piece opened with a long major
chord that for some reason I recognized to be E-flat, which is the
opening chord of P.D.Q. Bach's *Schleptet in E-flat Major*. That's the
piece where the orchestra plays an interminable tonic triad followed by an even longer dominant chord during which the musi-

cians begin to faint and crash to the floor. My friend chose that moment to whisper in my ear, "You have to admit, this is pretty dull music," and in my effort to maintain the proprieties I nearly choked.

The Gounod, fortunately, was followed by a nice Dvořák piece and then some Stravinsky. During the course of both works, my friend drew my attention to the two young clarinetists in the orchestra. After the performance he made it a point to speak to one of them. I paused for a moment to talk to someone else, then joined him. He told the young man, who must have been about twenty-two, "Anyway, I just wanted you to know how much I liked your playing." And he walked away. The young man went on disassembling his clarinet and putting it into its velvet-lined case. His equanimity piqued my curiosity, and I went back and said to him, "Did the man with the beard tell you his name?"

"No," he said. "Who is he?"

"Artie Shaw," I said.

He looked as if he had been hit with a brick. He abandoned his clarinet and hurried to find other woodwind players, and soon they and some of the string players had Artie surrounded and were begging him, as musicians always do, to start playing again.

Artie chatted with them for a while. Then we left for a nearby restaurant with some friends of Artie's. One of them asked, "How did they know who you were?"

"This idiot," Artie said, jerking his thumb toward me, "told them."

"Arthur," I said, "there was no way that I was going to let that young man go through life never knowing that once, when he was very young, his playing received a compliment from Artie Shaw."

Arthur Arshawsky, writer, of New York City, via New Haven, Connecticut, and a long detour through a music he loves and a fame he detested, was at this point seventy-two years old and bald on top. The beard disappeared soon after that evening, though he still retained a full mustache. He quit smoking when he reached five packs a day and was in such good form and health that he looked about fifty-five.

He could now visit restaurants without causing a stir or tool around Newbury Park (a suburb of Thousand Oaks which is in turn a suburb of Los Angeles) on his bicycle, wearing his jogging clothes and, usually, a cap resembling those you see in Holland, without drawing attention. He had the anonymity he once craved. But it was a conditional anonymity. You had only to mention his name to anyone over forty-five in America to make eyebrows rise. And he was so well known in France that there once was a joke on his name: "Why do Americans name their bandleaders after vegetables?" (They pronounce his name *artichaut*, which means artichoke.) And clarinet players everywhere know his work.

Early in 1983, Yoel Levi, conductor of the Cleveland Orchestra, decided to perform Shaw's *Concert for Clarinet* with Franklin Cohen, the orchestra's principal clarinetist, performing Shaw's part, which had been transcribed from the record. (Shaw's solo had been largely improvised.) "When I got the music," Cohen said during rehearsals, "I thought it looked easy. After I heard the tape, I told Yoel he was crazy."

"Shaw was unbelievable," Yoel Levi added. "He could improvise endlessly, on and on. He was an amazing talent. Shaw's the greatest player I ever heard. It's hard to play the way he plays. It's not an overblown orchestral style. He makes so many incredible shadings."

Jerome Richardson, himself a fine saxophonist, clarinetist, and flutist, said: "I was a Benny Goodman fan until I heard Artie Shaw, and that was it. He went to places on the clarinet that no one had ever been before. He would get up to B's and C's and make not notes but music, melodies. He must have worked out his own fingerings for the high notes, because they weren't in the books. To draw a rough analogy, Artie Shaw was at that time to clarinetists what Art Tatum was to pianists. It was another view of clarinet-playing. A lot of people loved Benny Goodman because it was within the scope of what most clarinet players could play and therefore could copy. But Artie Shaw took the instrument further."

Barney Bigard said, "To me the greatest player that ever lived was Artie Shaw. Benny Goodman played pop songs; he didn't produce new things like Shaw did." Phil Woods, one of the finest sax-ophonists jazz has known, says he modeled his clarinet playing on Shaw's. Saxophonist Billy Mitchell said, "I'll bet I can still play his clarinet solo on *Star Dust*. I ought to. I spent weeks learning it when I was a kid." For most jazz musicians, and countless laymen, that solo is part of the collective memory.

Writer Jon McAuliffe said, "Shaw's shading, tone, and phrasing were singular, and unlike any other, before or since. Listening to Shaw, one can imagine that one is hearing not an instrument so much as an alien human voice. No clarinet player has ever created such an aura of command on the instrument."

Shaw's elegant smooth glissandos always amazed me. One day I asked him how he'd done them.

"I don't know," he replied.

"You must know," I said. "You did them. Is it a matter of squeezing the reed or what?"

"I truly don't know. You think it, and if you know what you're doing, the instrument does it."

Superlatives are always dangerous, but these few are safe:

Artie Shaw was the most celebrated and the most glamorous of the big-band leaders, and he made the most headlines, in part because of marriages, eight in all, to famous beauties such as Ava Gardner, Lana Turner, and Evelyn Keyes, and in part because he did what in America is unthinkable: he walked out on success. The headlines have yellowed by now, but what he left behind, in a business that still regrets his leaving it, is a persistent legend, four hundred recordings many of which are still selling forty years after they were made, and a reputation for peerless musicianship.

The trouble with Artie Shaw, to paraphrase the title of his first book, is that his glamorous image (he was in movies; and he and Charlie Barnet were probably the handsomest of the bandleaders) obscured the fact that he led one of the most beautifully polished and swinging of all the big bands and one that played some of the most intelligent charts of the era. And his image as a bandleader in turn has overclouded the fact that the man up there in that spotlight was one of the finest jazz players America has produced.

And back when classical music and jazz were considered mutually exclusive and inimical tastes, he was also a superb classical clarinetist. Book of the Month Club Records has issued a three-disk package of his last performances and some of his very earliest. Some of the sides are jazz, others classical, including a rediscovered 1947 performance of a difficult clarinet concerto by Nicolai Berezowsky.

The further trouble with Artie Shaw was that we all knew his music only too well. Most jazz musicians and a lot of laymen over fifty can whistle not only his solo on *Star Dust* (except where it goes above one's pucker register and also the legitimate register at that time of the clarinet) but the entire arrangement, from beginning to end. A fish, it has been said, is unaware of water, and Shaw's music so permeated the very air that it was only too easy to overlook just how good a player and how inventive and significant an improviser he was. Only when, at Artie's home, I heard tapes that had never been issued—such as a performance in which he and Lionel Hampton and Tommy Dorsey and Ziggy Elman jammed with the Count Basie band—did I begin to appreciate the man as a jazz musician.

Artie had no idea where or when that improbable performance occurred—the cassette had been sent without explanation by an admirer—but since an announcer referred to Ziggy Elman as a sergeant, we deduced that it must have been toward the end of World War II, probably on a military base. Part way through this tossed salad, Artie said, "What tune are we playing?"

"I haven't the slightest idea," I said, "and neither does anybody in that band." We laughed at the scrambling (during which, by the way, Tommy Dorsey played some surprisingly hot hard-toned trombone) and I said, "This may be a historic recording but it's terrible."

However, there is on that tape a blues in which Artie solos at length while Basie weaves fluent lines around him and Freddie Green paves the highway smooth and straight.

It was in such moments of hearing him in unfamiliar settings that I began to perceive him not as a bandleader but as a superlative player.

The sporadic reissue of his recordings by RCA also helped put him into historical perspective. *The Complete Artie Shaw* eventually got up to seven volumes, each containing two LPs with as many as eight tunes to a side. Some of these tracks were previously unissued—Shaw has been fighting RCA for years to get all his masters released—and they are valuable precisely because they are unfamiliar. One of these is a tune Shaw wrote and Ray Coniff arranged, *Who's Excited?*, a riffy thing with strings playing the harmonic pads that previously would have been assigned to saxophones. Shaw plays a radiant solo, filled with those fluid glissandos, smooth rapid runs, and the rich lyrical tone that was one of the several glories of his playing.

Another value of these recordings is that some of them contain two takes of the same tune. These alternates—a blues called *Mysterioso* by the Gramercy Five, for example—put to rest a rumor you occasionally heard that Shaw wrote his solos in advance, a denigration that pays an inadvertent compliment to their compositional perfection. His solos in *Mysterioso*, recorded probably minutes apart, are distinctly different. The rumor may have had its source in the fact that on his major hits, Shaw would play in personal appearances the solos he had recorded. So did the side men.

What Shaw did do was to write out saxophone choruses, even marking the breathing places, and turn them over to his arranger, who in the early years was usually Jerry Gray. "Jerry came very close to being to me what Billy Strayhorn was to Duke," Artie said. "He was a pupil and he was a friend. I taught him how to arrange. Remember, I was an arranger before I was a bandleader. Jerry started with my string band in 1936. He was my first violinist. And he played some jazz accordion. Later, in 1939, when I broke up that band, I called Glenn Miller and told him I had a few people he ought to listen to. He hired Johnny Best on trumpet, and he hired Jerry. Jerry did Glenn a lot of good. Jerry wrote *A String of Pearls* for him."

Because, then, of the close relationship between Shaw and Jerry Gray and because of his habit of writing out the sax choruses (and Artie was a sought-after lead alto player before he was an arranger or a clarinetist), there is a stylistic continuity in what he plays and what the band plays. The sax-section choruses, in effect, are orchestrated Shaw solos.

Even Artie can't remember whether he or Jerry Gray wrote certain things during the 1938-'39 period. "I didn't write too much for that band," he said with that touch of sarcasm that sometimes comes into his voice when he is talking about his former self. "I was too busy being a celebrity."

In addition to the RCA reissues, there are five albums on the Hindsight label containing as many as nineteen tracks each, drawn from radio broadcasts. These are casual performances, and some of the tracks stretch out to nearly six minutes.

"When you went into the recording studio in those days," Artie said when we were listening to some of the Hindsight test pressings, "there was no tape and you knew it was going to have to be perfect. The tension got terribly high. And often you wouldn't take chances doing things that might go wrong. But on radio broadcasts, you could do anything. It didn't matter. You never thought of anybody recording it and forty years later releasing it! The recordings were done under better conditions. You had better balance. But you didn't get anything like the spontaneity you have here."

The Hindsight records reveal what the band played like in the late 1930s but cannot reveal what the band actually sounded like. Recording technique was too primitive. The bass lines are unclear and the guitar chords all but inaudible. What you get, really, is the upper part of the harmony, and you cannot follow the separate lines in the voicings.

For a sense of the band's true sound you have to hear a Capitol stereo LP (unfortunately out of print) for which Shaw put together a band containing a number of his former side men. As we listened to it, I caught a glimpse of the inner Artie Shaw and something I don't think even he knew about himself.

Shaw had quit playing by then and his solos were recreated by Walt Levinsky. His attack lacks the chilly bite that Shaw's had. There is a sound that many superb pianists have in common, a click that occurs on the leading edge of the tone, as the hammer connects with the strings. Nat Cole's playing had it. It is a particular kind of clarity, a coldness that expands immediately into a round warmth. A similar quality inhered in Shaw's playing.

Listening to Levinsky, I said, "Well, he's not you."

And Artie immediately said, not so much defensively as with a hint of hurt, "He's an excellent clarinetist, don't you think?"

"Absolutely. But he was asked to do an all but impossible thing. He's not being allowed to play in his own style and he can't quite get into yours."

"Well, that's true enough," Artie said. "But he's a very fine clarinet player."

His respect for the dedicated musician is enormous. He thinks Phil Woods is one of the finest saxophonists jazz has ever known, adding, "and I've heard them all, including Charlie." Artie may have quit playing in 1954, but he didn't quit listening. He had great admiration for Art Pepper, and someone told Pepper about it. He was flabbergasted. He immediately contacted Artie and told him he was going to send him all his albums. A few days later Pepper died.

In the first flush of success, Artie made about $55,000 in one week, equivalent to $550,000 today. The superlatives were flying, including the statement that he was the best clarinetist in the world. As he was leaving a theatre in Chicago, aware that he was becoming rich at an early age, a thought crossed his mind. So what if I am the best clarinetist in the world. Even if that's true, who's the second best? Some guy in some symphony orchestra? And is there all that much difference between us? And how much did he earn this week? A hundred and fifty bucks? There's something cockeyed here, something unfair.

It is at such moments in conversations that one sees, behind all that rationalism and adamant logic, a hidden gentleness in Artie and a sense of brotherhood with all the world's musicians.

It is occasionally said that some musicians who worked for him hated him. It may be true. He was a strict disciplinarian and would not, and still won't, tolerate the lazy, the careless, the second-rate. But I have never been able to find one of these detractors. "Great dude," said Johnny Mandel, once one of his arrangers. "I love him." Neeley Plumb, who played saxophone in one of the Shaw bands, said, "He always knew exactly what he wanted, and you cannot imagine what a joy it was to work for a man who'd rehearse four new charts in three hours, get them straight, and never bother you about them again."

The Book-of-the-Month Club albums are titled *A Legacy*. The jazz performances are by Shaw and the Gramercy Five, which at that time included Tal Farlow on guitar, Hank Jones on piano, Irv Kluger on drums, Tommy Potter on bass, and Joe Roland on vibes. "We had been working together and the group sounded so good," Artie said, "that I thought it should be recorded. So I just took them into the studio and recorded them myself." After that he stopped playing. That was in 1954.

The collection contains a *Star Dust* that is startling. For one thing, recording technique had advanced to the point that you can hear all the parts, and the true nature of Shaw's own tone is evident. He had at that time taken a year off to play "classical" music—or "long-form music," as he prefers to call it—and this had altered his approach to the instrument. Indeed, he had even begun playing a different clarinet. On the old records, you rarely hear Shaw play more than eight or sixteen bars, due to the necessity of limiting performances to about three minutes. But on this final and farewell version of *Star Dust*, he is able to lay back and develop his material. The solo is absolutely gorgeous, one of the most beautiful things I have ever heard. It had me on the edge of the chair at his house, mouth agape. "Play it again," I said.

"There are some other things I want to play for you."

"Please. I really want to hear that again." And he played it three or four times. Its beauties only grew with familiarity.

The further trouble with Artie Shaw is that he never did suffer fools gladly. In her autobiography, Helen Forrest said that Shaw was the most intelligent man she ever met. He not only has read seemingly everything but he has known many of the major intellectual figures of the twentieth century. Even when he was very young, he was an omnivorous reader, hungry for knowledge. One musician recalls that when he joined Artie in a New York sax section in the early 1930s, he was reading Thorstein Veblen during the breaks.

Arthur Arshawsky was born on the Lower East Side of New York City and spent an impoverished childhood in New Haven, Connecticut. Abandoned by his father, he grew up being teased about his "strange" name, out of which he later carved Art Shaw. That is the name on his first recordings. RCA Victor hung "Artie" on him; it stuck, and in time he surrendered to it. It is one of the few accommodations he ever made. Another was hiring girl singers to perform the pop songs of the day. Curiously, all his hits— *Star Dust, Frenesi,* and *Begin the Beguine*—were instrumentals. (By 1965 his top five records had sold 65,000,000 copies.)

At fourteen Arthur got his hands on a C-melody saxophone and won a five-dollar prize for playing *Charley My Boy.* He was amazed that money could be earned so easily and decided to make music a career. But he couldn't read music. Nor did he know anything about keys and transposition, and when he acquired an alto saxophone, which is tuned in E-flat, the notes came out all wrong. He quickly learned the craft, however, and a year later he was a working road musician. By the age of nineteen he was back in the city of his birth, and only a few years later he was the top lead alto player in the New York radio and recording studios.

His career as a bandleader began by accident. Joe Helbock, owner of the Onyx Club, a former speakeasy frequented by musicians, was planning the first "swing" concert at New York's Imperial Theatre. In the spring of 1936 he asked Artie to put together a small jazz group to play in front of the curtain while the setup was being changed. Artie did, but as usual he did it in his own way. He assembled a group comprising a string quartet, a small rhythm section without piano (which he thought would be too strong for the texture of such a group) and himself on clarinet. He wrote for it a piece that he didn't bother to name, calling it what it was— *Interlude in B-flat.* He and his colleagues went onstage the evening of April 7, 1936, and played it to an astonished murmur from the audience, which included musicians. When the piece ended, the audience roared its approval. But Shaw hadn't written any more music for the group, and all he could do for an encore was to play the piece again.

Somebody made an acetate recording of this performance. Many years later a fan sent Artie a tape of an Australian radio broadcast containing, to Artie's bafflement, the *Interlude in B-flat*. He telephoned the broadcaster in Australia. The man said he had obtained the recording from someone in Seattle, who turned out to be a collector. Artie tried calling him; the man didn't return his calls. We can imagine how apprehensive the man was—he could presume the recording had been made illegally. Finally, Artie left a message: "Look, I'm not trying to make trouble for you, I just want that recording. And if you don't answer my call, I'm sending the police." The man returned the call and told Artie he had found the recording in a stack of old acetates he'd bought. He was a long-time Shaw fan, recognized the style, knew this piece was not among the known Shaw recordings and, having read *The Trouble with Cinderella*, realized what he had. And of course he was only too happy to send Artie a copy of the record. It was very worn, but Artie ran it through digital recording equipment and with the aid of a skilled engineer managed to clean up the sound considerably. This documentation of his first venture as a bandleader is in the Book-of-the-Month-Club collection.

Artie Shaw was from the beginning, intellectually and emotionally, ill-suited to deal with the primitives who dominated the business end of the popular music world. Shaw did not set out to be a public figure, did not even want to form a band. He wanted to become a writer, and his studio work was financing his studies. But nature had given him an X-ray ear, infallible taste, and a steely will about developing musical technique. After the *Interlude in B-flat* performance, a booking agency approached him about forming a band. He said he was interested only in finishing his education at Columbia University. He was asked how much money that would take. He took a deep breath and blurted the largest figure he could think of—$25,000. He was told he could earn that in a few months if he organized his own band. And so he formed a band, but hardly the one the agency had in mind. Following the pattern he'd set for the *Interlude*, the group contained a small jazz front line, a rhythm section, and a string quartet. It failed. So he broke it up and organized a big band with conventional saxes-and-brass instrumentation. "If the public wanted loud bands," as he put it, "I was going to give them the loudest goddamn band they'd ever heard."

But as Buddy Rich always said, there is a way to play musically loud and a way to be unmusically loud, and the Shaw band was from the start very musical.

A confrontation with "the business" was inevitable. Artie had a prickly integrity and complete faith in his own musical judgment. "I never really considered myself part of the entertainment business," Artie said. "I recognized that people had put me in that business. That's where I worked. That is, the ambience I played in had to do with entertainment. So I had to make the concession of having a singer. But that's the only concession I ever made—aside from occasionally playing so-called popular tunes. Mostly I was doing this to meet some inner standard of what I thought a band or I should sound like."

That faith in his own judgment was at least part of the cause of his reputation for arrogance. Arrogance is requisite to the creation of any kind of art. The fact of assuming that what you have to say will be of interest to so many people that you will be able to make a living from it is implicitly arrogant. "As a matter of fact," Artie said, "the arrogance goes so far that you don't care whether it's of interest."

"The only thing," I said, "that humbles the real artist is the art itself."

"That," Artie said, "and his own fallibility."

Shaw's problem is clearer in retrospect than it must have seemed at the time. While most people, including many musicians, were still thinking of jazz as entertainment or simply dance music, Shaw was already seeing it as an art, something that should be regarded as a concert music. As soon as he could, he added a good-sized string section—sixteen men; the band traveled in two buses—and further enhanced his reputation for pretension. Now, of course, string sections are common in jazz recordings, but Shaw used one first, not out of aspiration to status but because, as every musician knows, there is no more gloriously transluscent harmonic texture against which to play than fine-tuned and well-voiced strings. (Tommy Dorsey picked up Shaw's entire string section when Artie joined the Navy.)

There was something new in the air when Shaw formed his first band. There had always been more influence of classical music on jazz than many of its fans and critics realized. The bebop era was seen as having its harbingers in Charlie Christian and Lester Young. But there were earlier signs of the music that was to come. If Bix Beiderbecke was interested in the French Impressionist composers and in Stravinsky, so was Artie, who roomed for a while with Bix when he first arrived back in the city of his birth, New York. And Artie says he was deeply influenced by Bix, trying to play like him, but on saxophone.

Once your attention is drawn to it, you can hear the influence of Bix in Shaw's early recorded solos, which go well beyond the diatonicism of much early jazz. So did Louis Armstrong's, Artie said. "You are too young to know the impact he had on all of us in the 1920s," he said. "By the time you were old enough to appreciate Louis, you had been hearing those who derived from him. He defined not only how you play a trumpet solo but how you play a solo on any instrument. Had Louis Armstrong never lived, I suppose there would be a jazz, but it would be very different." The chromaticism in jazz increased as musicians absorbed the harmonic and melodic material of twentieth-century classical music. Artie said, "I was listening to the same things that Dizzy Gillespie and Charlie Parker were listening to a little later on—the dissonances, as we thought of them then, of Stravinsky, Schoenberg, Bartók. Another factor was that I was not thinking in two-bar and four-bar units. The lines would flow over bar lines. That's simply being musical, of course. In the Mozart A-major quintet, I can show you a phrase that's eleven bars long followed by one that's nine, and they're completely organic. We have been so trained to think of music in even numbers. Have you ever noticed that the things of nature—the number of kernels in a corn row, the number of peas in a pod—occur in odd numbers?

"Incidentally, while we're on the subject of Dizzy and Charlie, can you answer a question for me? Why hasn't Dizzy, one of the greatest trumpet players we've ever had, been given the recognition Charlie has?"

"Because," I answered, "he isn't a junkie who died young and tragically. Haven't you ever noticed that America immortalizes those who live screwed-up lives and die young? America makes legends of such people. Lenny Bruce, Hank Williams, Bix."

"Billie Holiday, Bunny Berigan, Lester Young," Artie added.

"It's an American pattern, a corollary of puritanism. Dizzy has been successful, he's gregarious, he likes laughter, he was the great teacher, and for that reason full approval is withheld. If Bill Evans hadn't lived a tortured life, he might never have been given the recognition he's received. There is a kind of condescension in the phenomenon. So long as you can look down on someone with pity, it's okay to praise him."

"I think you're right," Artie said.

Those who thought they were going to get a conventional smiley bandleader in Artie Shaw should have paid more attention to his theme, *Nightmare*, which he composed. It was no promise of romance, no *Moonlight Serenade* or *Getting Sentimental Over You*. "And no *Let's Dance*," Artie added in pointed reference to Goodman. *Nightmare* was a stark piece, consisting of a four-note chromatic ostinato over a pedal point and gloomy tom-tom figure, joined by a falling major third in which the clarinet plays lead to trumpets in straight mutes. It screams a kind of shrill terror, a dark Dostoyevskyan vision of the world, a clairvoyant look into the horrors to come. "*Guernica*," Artie says, and it does indeed have something of the Picasso mural about it.

Artie was to encounter some of the horrors personally. He joined the Navy early in 1942 and formed a band. He was offered the rank of lieutenant commander but turned it down. "As soon as you took a commission," Artie said, "you got into another world." And he wanted to play for the enlisted men. Eventually he was given the rank of chief petty officer. At first he was stationed at Newport, Rhode Island. He soon chafed under the easy assignment. He knew Secretary of the Navy James Forrestal, and he pulled wires. An admiral said to him, "Son, you're the first man I've met who didn't want to stay here and hang onto the grass roots. Where do you want to go?" "Where's the Navy?" Artie said. "In the South Pacific," the admiral said. "And that's where I want to go," Artie said.

Glenn Miller joined the Army Air Corps and became a captain, then major, and went to England, to broadcast to the troops on the BBC from somewhere outside London. Artie took his men, designated Band 501 by the Navy, to the Pacific. There are a few mementoes of those days in his house, including a bullet-torn Japanese battle flag inscribed to him by Admiral Halsey; a model of a P-38 fighter made from brass shell casings by Seabees, who gave it to him; and, on the wall of the landing of the stairs, a painting done by a wartime artist for *Life* magazine that shows Artie playing his clarinet in front of the band for troops on Guadalcanal. The background is a wall of jungle. In the picture Artie is wearing a black Navy tie tucked into the front of his khaki shirt. This detail bugs him. "Halsey had banned ties," he said. "No tie. That was the uniform of the day." But there is something else that is somehow off. Artists rarely portray musicians accurately, and the stance of the figure in the painting isn't quite right.

The band was in the South Pacific from mid-1942 until late 1943. It played in forward areas, some still harboring snipers, and at times being bombed almost nightly. Once, with all its members under ponchos, it played for thousands of young paratroopers, themselves under ponchos and stretched up the slope of a hill in a pounding tropical rain. When the band finally came home, the men were exhausted, depleted by what they had seen and by disease. Several of its members were immediately given medical discharges. "Davey Tough was just a ghost," Artie says. And Artie had been having crippling migraine headaches. When the Navy learned of this, he too was discharged. Several months later he formed a new and superb civilian band.

This was the band that recorded *Lady Day, Jumpin' on the Merry-Go-Round*, and *'S Wonderful*. But Artie still was not comfortable with fame, and that band, for which Ray Coniff did some fine writing, lasted only a year. Artie says he wasn't simply indifferent to fame: he actively loathed it.

"It is a very strange thing to realize you are no longer a person," he said. "You have become a thing, an object, and the public thinks you belong to them.

"A guy yelled at me, 'We made you!' I said, 'Well, break me, man. If you're powerful enough to make me, break me. I'm waiting. Do it.' They look at you, baffled. Another line is, 'Who do you think you are?' And I'd say, 'I know who I am. Who are you?'

"You can't believe the things that happen. A guy once came up to me and said, 'Remember me?' I said, 'No.' At first I used to say, 'Yeah,' but that can get you into trouble. The guy said, 'Remember the Cornell prom?' I said, 'I don't remember. It was just one more one-nighter.' For me at that time, one out of maybe two hundred a year. The guy said, 'I was there.' I said, 'No kiddin'. But even so, why should I remember you?' He said, 'I asked for *Begin the Beguine*.' 'Oh, well sure. You're that one. Now I know who you are.' So help me Jesus. I make that up not."

Artie chuckled. "Another guy—oh, God!—said, 'Remember me?' And I said, 'Nope.' And he said, 'I used to sit behind you at Dwight Street School.' I left Dwight Street School when I was nine. At the time he did this, I must have been fifty. Which makes it forty-one years. He told me he sat behind me in English or something. I said, 'Do you expect me to remember that?' He said, "'Well I remember you.' I said, 'Would you have remembered me if I'd become an insurance man?'

"It's crazy," he said. "I guess lots of people are conditioned to be stupid."

"Do you think it's as bad in Europe?"

"It's just as bad, but there is one good thing about it: they have respect. They have a certain respect for people who are no longer big stars. They seem to recognize that in order to have become a big star, you had to have had something going for you.

"I used to get a lot of criticism for being 'nasty' to fans. But I don't think I was being nasty. I remember walking out of the Stanley Theatre in Pittsburgh one time, and this kid came up to me and was very aggressive about getting my autograph. I finally said, 'Wait a minute, what do you want this for?' And he said, 'Well, I admire the way you play.' So I said, 'Well get a clarinet and learn to play,' and walked away. That's what I think you should do if you really admire something.

"I just remembered something. When I was about ten years old in New Haven, some kid came up to me and said, 'Hey, come on,' and I said, 'Where we goin'?' and he said, 'The Rialto Theatre,' or whatever the hell the name of the place was. They were playing *Son of the Sheik*, or one of the old Valentino movies. He said, 'Valentino, Rudolph Valentino, he's gonna be there. Let's go and watch him come out of the theater.' And so we went. We stood in the alley leading to the stage entrance and, by God, here came Rudolph Valentino. Surrounded by people. And I looked, and there he was—the Sheik. Well, the kid grabbed me and said, 'Come on,' and I said, 'Whatya doin'?' 'I'm gonna get his autograph.' And I said, 'Well jeez, I don't wanna talk to him.' I pulled back. So you see, even then, I felt that way. If there's someone you look up to, well, leave him alone, man. Don't invade his privacy.

"The point is that I learned that I had lost my privacy. And you know, it's taken me forty years to get it back."

"Some people like fame," I said.

"I wonder if they'd like it if they had it long enough. Johnny Carson hates it. Johnny told me he hardly ever goes anywhere because someone is always trying to pick a fight. I'll tell you another guy. Mohammed Ali. People are always taking a poke at him. What can they lose? He can't hit them back."

"Julius LaRosa," I said, "played a gig in Dallas last year. A couple of ladies came up to him and one of them pulled his cheek and said to her girlfriend, 'You see? I told you it isn't a face lift.'"

"I believe it," Artie said. "You're public property. People are always asking me, 'Don't you miss playing?' Well of course I miss playing. But not enough to give up what I've got now. It's like having a gangrenous arm. The only thing you can do is amputate it. Obviously you're gonna miss the arm, but if you don't cut it off, you'll die."

"I guess if you decided to do it," I said, "you could get your chops up in six months."

"No way," Artie said. "Closer to a year."

Shaw's book *The Trouble with Cinderella* was published in 1952. It was not so much an autobiography as an unsparing and self-searching essay on the life of one troubled man living in a fame-crazed America. Probably no country on earth has ever placed as high a premium on conspicuous public success as the United States. This preoccupation amounted, and to a large extent still amounts, to a national disease, embodied in the cruelly misleading myth that anyone can grow up to be president, anyone can be discovered sipping a milkshake in a drugstore and become a movie star overnight. The movie industry nurtured and magnified the myth but did not invent it: it was embodied in the nineteenth-century Horatio Alger novels. In the 1940s or '50s, Glenn Ford appeared in a movie in which he played a bus driver. You knew as the film unfolded that there was something amiss. Hollywood didn't make movies about bus drivers, bus drivers were not people with stories worth telling. Movies were made only about the rich and famous, or the likes of test pilots and soldiers of fortune and outlaws. And sure enough, toward the end of this picture, Glenn announces that he is really a writer, and that his first novel has just been accepted; he has made the great leap into doing the only thing considered worth doing in America, namely being rich and famous.

This is not to suggest that the aspiration to upward mobility did not exist in Europe: it is inherent in fairy tales such as *Snow White* and most notably *Cinderella*, which is of course the reason for the title of Artie's book. But Europe's was largely a stratified and inflexible society in which these sudden elevations into power and fortune were accomplished only by the intercession of improbable accident if not the supernatural. Europeans were sensible enough to let the dream repose in wistful stories for children. The trouble with the Cinderella myth in America was that, in a flexible and open culture, one that is alas now becoming stratified along economic lines, as in Europe, the dream came true just often enough to encourage the dreamers and lead them to numberless heartaches and suicides.

It would be inconceivable that Artie, in his youth, did not aspire to making a lot of money. His painful Jewish childhood in New Haven was too impoverished for him to have been devoid of that ambition. He is a man of deep cultivation, who speaks Spanish well and some French, who collects and knows a great deal about art, is endlessly and penetratingly observant of politics and history, and who is in sum, and in the largest sense, a citizen of the world. There are, however, two things about him that I find to be quite Jewish, and particularly Russian Jewish. One is his passion for education. The other has to do with music, and it requires a little explanation.

Under the czars there was a law that a Jew could not live in Moscow unless he or she was an artist, a ballerina or a fine musician— a wind-up toy to entertain the rich. And so in Jewish families in such cities as Odessa (the breeding ground of an astonishing number of great violinists and, coincidentally or not, the birthplace of Artie's father), there was emphasis on becoming a musician in order to live in the great city of the czars. It was a way up and a way out. In America, among Russian Jewish families, the tradition lingered. And so in Arthur Arshawsky, a Lower East Side Jewish boy transplanted to WASPy New Haven and later abandoned by his father and always teased about his "peculiar" name, there must have been a tremendous drive to get out of that poverty whether through literature or music or whatever variant of the Cinderella-Alger myth. Sometimes, when I am talking to Artie, sometimes when I hear him laugh or see some trace of an old sadness, I think

I catch a glimpse of that boy, the boy standing in the alley watching Rudolph Valentino.

And I think his permanent aversion to signing autographs may have a cause quite different from what he considers it to be.

When *The Trouble with Cinderella* was published, it caused a stir but sometimes for the wrong reasons. It is an extremely well-written and literate book on an interesting subject, which should have been enough to commend it, but the attitude toward it was often one of surprise, as if one had come across a bear riding a bicycle. The reaction in these instances was not one of pleasure that Artie Shaw had written a good book but of amazement that he had written one at all. This bespoke underlying assumptions that jazz musicians were illiterates and bandleaders only baton-waving clowns. More than that, it implicitly expressed a peculiarly American belief that no one can do more than one thing well—an article of faith whose father was probably Henry Ford.

If anybody thought Shaw's first book was a fluke, his second, *I Love You, I Hate You, Drop Dead*, three novellas dealing with American marriage, proved him to be a skilled writer of fiction. He has not published another book since then, but he has worked on and off for years on a vast novel about the evolution of a musician. The character's name is Albie Snow. If it bears a certain resemblance to Artie Shaw, that is not by coincidence. "It's fiction, though," Artie says. "I'm having fun making this guy a genius." And fiction of course allows a writer to take liberties with time and sequence, to elide several characters into one for the sake of story organization—and, not incidentally, to avoid libel suits. Artie writes carefully and slowly, constantly revising, always seeking what Flaubert called *le mot juste*, that perfect word. With a touch of self-mockery he says, "I've got twelve hundred pages of manuscript and I've just got the guy up to the age of twenty-three."

His 1944-45 band was followed by a 1949 band, one that contained Al Cohn, Zoot Sims, Herbie Steward, Dodo Marmarosa, Don Fagerquist, and Jimmy Raney. Its writers included Johnny Mandel, Tadd Dameron, Gene Roland, George Russell, Eddie

Sauter. It was, by all accounts, an advanced and adventurous band. Its only recordings were transcriptions, and it never found a large audience.

After that Artie put together—almost contemptuously, it would seem—a band that played the hits of the day. To his dismay, it was a success. He folded that band in 1950. Senator Joseph McCarthy was running around like a rabid dog, causing heartache and heart attacks and leaving a trail of blighted lives. McCarthy told at least one journalist I know that he was going to be the first Catholic president of the United States. And he obviously didn't care whom he killed in pursuit of this ambition. This vicious political performance contributed to Artie's disgust with the public and its manipulators. After playing some Gramercy Five gigs with Tal Farlow and Hank Jones, he quit playing completely. He moved to Spain, there to finish *I Love You, I Hate You, Drop Dead*, whose acerbic content to some extent reflects his state of mind at the time.

After he returned to the United States in 1960, he tried his hand at several things. He started, of all things, a rifle-range and gun-manufacturing business. At one point he set out to become a marksman and got so good that he placed fourth in national competition. He established, and did well at, a film-distribution company. It was while he had this company that I first met him. That would have been about 1966. When I encountered him again in California, in 1981, I found him changed—still a dominating talker, to be sure, but somehow more accessible. And witty. And funny. And his anger had softened into a kind of resignation. He was living alone in the house at Newbury Park with his books and his typewriter and a big friendly English sheepdog named Chester Chaucer and a Hindsberg grand piano at which he would occasionally sit in solitary musing—"I've done some stupid things in my life," he said recently—playing Debussy or Scriabin. Now and then he would have friends in for dinner and, to judge by his protestations, he finally had his life in the rational control he had so assiduously sought to impose on it. But a certain loneliness, like a fine gray rain, seemed to have come over him. He never said so, and I never asked, but I could sense it.

There were traces of the old Artie Shaw, to be sure. He was teaching a course at Oxnard College not so much about music as about aesthetics in general. At the end of it, he asked the class if they had any questions. A young man stood up and said, "I play three instruments, piano, tenor, and bass."

"You've got a problem right there," Artie said. "What do you consider your primary instrument?"

"Bass, I guess."

"Because you can get away with more on bass, right? People can't hear pitch that well down in those registers. But what's your question?"

"I hate to practice," the young man said.

"Is that a question?"

"Well, yeah."

"Practicing goes with the territory, man. But I still don't know what the question is."

"What do I do about it?"

"Quit playing," Artie said.

He asked the class if they'd got anything out of the course. One elderly man said, "You seem to be saying: We pass this way but once, so pay attention."

I swung off Highway 101 and wove through the winding streets to Artie's house, which, at the end of a short lane lined by oleanders, is hidden from the street. I rang his bell. As he opened the door he said, "Hey, man, I got a book you should read."

"What's it called?"

"*The Aquarian Conspiracy.*"

"Just read it."

"Well, that takes care of that."

"What else have you been reading?" I said as we settled on the sofas of the living room.

"It's kind of interesting. I've been re-reading Hemingway. I was astonished to see what had shaped me in many respects. Hemingway shaped our whole generation, of course. He stood there like a block in the road. You couldn't ignore him. It interested me to find that the kinds of values he espouses in certain stories—*The Short Happy Life of Francis Macomber, The Snows of Kilimanjaro*—are essentially the stiff-upper-lip we-don't-speak-about-that upper-class British thing: like looking down on some poor bastard who runs from a charging lion. Not done, dear boy. Right? Man, if a charging lion comes at me, you're gonna see me under the nearest couch, and I don't care about anybody saying, 'That's just not done.'

"Which takes me right back to old Socrates, where he says in *The Apologia*, 'The unexamined life is not worth living.' When you go back to re-reading something that helped shape you, you can examine why you feel a certain way, why you think certain things that aren't logically sound. Why do we feel in our bones that to be afraid is a very bad thing? You're not necesarily a coward to bow to superior force, and a wounded charging lion is something I would definitely call superior force.

"And you're not necessarily foolish to examine what music is—music, not popular entertainment. There's a big difference between the artist and the entertainer. When we talk about Elvis Presley or John Denver or Fleetwood Mac, we're talking about entertainment. Now there's nothing wrong with entertainment. But we ought to make a distinction between that and art.

"Take Phil Woods—or anybody who's an artist. The man has a serious purpose, which is basically to do what he does to his utmost limits. If the audience doesn't like it, that's too bad. He naturally wishes they did. But he can't stop himself. Where the entertainer says, 'Give the people what they want,' the artist says, 'No, I'm gonna give the people what I want. And if they don't like it, *tant pis*, that's tough, but I gotta do it.' Isn't that the basic distinction? And don't we overlook it?

"I keep telling people, 'If you want to play your own kind of music, get yourself a livelihood. If you want to write your own kind of music, do something like what Charles Ives did—run an insurance company, or take up carpentry, whatever.' I read something somewhere recently. If you cheat on your own ability, for instance by writing less than your best, in order to make money, you're doing something that'll vitiate your abilities forever.

"It's too bad most people can't seem to see these distinctions. When you're a young man just getting out in the world, one or your biggest problems is, 'How am I going to make a living?' In order to do it, you must please a certain number of people so they'll pay you the money you need. When you get past that—that is, if you grow—you can then ask yourself, 'Now. What do I want to do? Rather than, 'How do I make more money?' And the more they make, the more some like it, and they laugh, as they say, all the way to the bank. Man, what a phrase. But they've stopped growing. I prefer to invert the old phrase, 'If you're so smart, why ain't you rich?' and make it, 'If you're so wise, why ain't you poor?'

"A few weeks ago I was at a writers' conference in Santa Barbara. Joey Bushkin was playing piano, and he talked about Bing Crosby. When he was working with Bing, he played something and Bing liked it and the audience liked it. The next time Joey played it differently. Bing said to him—and Joey quoted this with some admiration—'If you do it right and the audience likes it, why change it?' Joey looked at me and said, 'Don't you agree?' And I said, 'No. If you're an artist, you have to change it. How can you keep doing the same thing over and over without being bored to death? And the boredom, if you're someone who's capable of growth, eventually communicates itself to an audience.' Point is, the reason Lawrence Welk has been so successful is that he does what would bore me to tears and does it with great enthusiasm. Guy Lombardo did what he did very well. But it was Model T music, of course. He was a sweet guy, and the band played Model T music. We used to laugh at them when I was a kid. When I was seventeen, I worked right across the street from him in Cleveland. I was listening to Bix and Tram at the time, and the Goldkette band and, occasionally, even the Dixieland Five. Guy's was a perfectly okay sweet band, like Jan Garber, Paul Specht. Paul Whiteman, mostly, was a sweet band.

"But it's a strange thing to look at the business forty years later and realize, 'It's going backwards.' That bothers me. It seems to be a mirror of what's happening to the entire world."

We talked some more about the nature of improvisation. "I'm reminded," I said, "of something a friend of mine, a symphony conductor, said about Mozart. He said Mozart would be developing his material logically and then suddenly he'd come up with something so unexpected and off the wall and yet so right that you wonder how he thought of it."

"The point is that he didn't think of it."

"Which clarifies something Bill Evans argued. He said that any kind of music that was not somehow in touch with the process of improvisation was likely to be sterile."

"Of course. If music is all left-brain, it comes out cold. If it's all right-brain, it comes out chaos. When I was playing, if I got into a good solo, my right brain was doing it. My left brain was translating it into fingers."

"There's a remark attributed to Charlie Parker: first you learn the instrument, then you learn the music, then you forget all that shit and just play."

"Right. Learn enough technique, develop enough ability that you can then ignore it. Use a boat to get to the other side of the river. Then you don't need the boat any more. You turn the switch that says, 'Improvise.' Technique is something you learn so you can throw it out. Charlie was dead right."

I used to hope that Artie Shaw would one day pick up the clarinet again, and that hope quickened when he told me he had sent his several clarinets out for cleaning and servicing.

Then he told me on the phone he was thinking seriously about forming a new band. He said that, if he did, he would limit himself to hiring and rehearsing it. Then he would send it on its way with someone else as its leader. That struck me as being like deciding to get a little bit pregnant.

And then one day he told me he was indeed forming a new band. It would be led by clarinetist and saxophonist Dick Johnson. Artie was doing the hiring in conjunction with Johnson, and rehearsing the musicians. From time to time he would enthusiastically describe the young players—including Joe Cohn, the guitarist who is Al Cohn's son. He said they were the best group of players he had ever worked with.

He went back East to debut the band, playing the initial engagement at the refurbished Meadowbrook ballroom. Someone who attended the opening said that it was fascinating to watch him. At first he watched the audience suspiciously, but as its perceptive attention and warm applause continued, he gradually unwound and finally said to them with a grin, "Where were you when I needed you?"

Everywhere the band went people said it was a superb organization. Sometimes Artie led it; much of the time it was led by Dick Johnson.

Then he told me he'd had it; he'd let Dick Johnson continue with the band, he wanted nothing further to do with public appearances. "I was right the first time," he said.

Early in 1982, Artie phoned to urge that I see a showing in Los Angeles that evening of a documentary film about his long-dead friend Bix Beiderbecke, made by a German-born Canadian filmmaker named Brigitte Berman. I made the trip, and saw the picture, a very sensitive and illuminating piece of work. Artie is one of those who discusses Bix on camera. Afterwards I attended a party with a number of elderly musicians who had known Bix and who discuss him, as Artie did, in the picture.

Two days later Artie called to be sure I'd seen the film. He sounded slightly annoyed. "I thought you were going to call me back and tell me what you thought about it," he said.

I told him that I'd found the film so powerful I could hardly bear to talk about it. I said, "It left me with a terrible sense of melancholy. I feel as if I had known him, almost as a close friend, and I am overwhelmed by a sense of loss."

"Melancholy," Artie said. "That's a good word for it. I saw the picture again yesterday, and it left me in a peculiar state of mind. Full of rue."

A few months later Brigitte Berman called him. She'd decided on her next film project: a documentary about him. She began shooting.

In February of 1987, Artie was hospitalized for emergency prostate surgery. He was on the operating table for five hours and nearly died. Little over a month later, on the night of March 30, 1987, Berman's film *Artie Shaw: All You Have Is Time* won the Academy Award for documentaries. Artie attended the ceremony with her. They ran a gamut of clicking cameras, photographers grabbing pictures of the celebrities. Not one of the cameras was aimed at him. A reporter asked how he felt about this. He said, "It took me thirty years and I had to grow a beard and lose my hair to achieve this condition."

A few weeks later, he stumbled and badly broke his right arm. It was slow to heal and remained in a cast for weeks. "Did you ever try to clean your teeth with your left hand?" he said. I have seen him angry—and two of his ex-wives, Evelyn Keyes and Lana Turner, have testified in their autobiographies to his sulfurous temper—but never depressed. Now he was depressed. After many months the arm began to heal.

"I was half awake at five o'clock this morning," he said, "and trying to work out the clarinet fingering on *All the Things You Are* in F-sharp, which presents some serious problems on that instrument, and then I woke up and thought, 'What are you doing? You don't *do* that any more. You don't have to solve that problem.' This is thirty-five years after I gave up playing.

"But my career as a serious dedicated player of a musical instrument really came to an end before that. It ended in 1941, when the war started. I was playing a theatre in Providence, Rhode Island. The manager of the theatre asked me to make an announcement. I went out and asked all servicemen in the crowd to return immediately to their bases. It seemed as if two-thirds of the audience got up and left. We hadn't realized how many people had been going into service. With the whole world in flames, playing *Star Dust* seemed pretty pointless. After the show I sent out the word to the guys, two weeks' notice. In the South Pacific I saw death face-to-face. It was never the same after that."

This was a day after the death of Woody Herman. He said, "There are three things I have promised myself I will never be: poor, dependent, and sick. I've got a gun for that. I'm seventy-seven," he reminded me, and then chuckled. "I'm too mean to die. I won't give the sons of bitches the satisfaction.

"I don't know, though. I don't want to live forever. I don't like what the world has become. Goddamned idiots with pit bulls . . . "

Artie Shaw was in full cry. His health, obviously, was returning quickly.

6

THE FATHER:
WOODY HERMAN

"YOU KNOW," I said on sudden impulse, "you are a very great man."

"No," said the man in a face I first knew from photos in magazines when I was a boy. "No, I'm not."

What prompted the statement was a certain flash I had on the scope of Woody Herman's whole career, and perhaps too the keen awareness that Charlotte was no longer in this house. If I could feel her absence, what must Woody Herman be feeling on this day soon after Christmas in 1984?

"It's tough at times," he said when we talked of her. "I'm all right as long as I keep moving."

He met her in San Francisco when she was dancing in a musical called *The Nine O'Clock Review* and he was playing saxophone in Tom Gerun's band. They were seventeen. Tony Martin at that time also played saxophone in the band. When Woody turned fifty, Martin sent him a telegram saying, "You may be admitting it but I'm not." And now Woody, who was born May 16, 1913, was seventy-one. And Charlotte had been gone more than two years.

She was one of the nicest—there is no other word for it—women I ever knew. She must have been an arresting beauty when he met her. Even in her last years, when her Norwegian redhead's skin had taken on a fine crepe texture, the classic bones in that face kept her quite striking, someone you noticed when you

86

entered a room. And she had a dancer's classic posture. She was kind and soft-spoken, with a dry sense of humor.

Woody had brought her to this house in 1946. He bought it from Humphrey Bogart. It is poised high in the hills above Sunset Strip on one of those narrow roads that twist improbably up the arroyas. From the street it looks like a tiny bungalow but it descends a steep declivity, so you enter it, actually, from the top. You glance to the right into the kitchen, then down a curved flight of stairs into a living room that seems taller than it is wide. From the bottom of those steps you see out across a railed deck over Los Angeles, a sea of small buildings washing around curious islands of skyscrapers that were not there when Woody and Charlotte came here. Ingrid, their daughter, was new-born then. Now, after a career of her own as a folk musician in Nashville, Ingrid lived here with her husband. Her son and daughter were themselves grown. And Woody still was still coming home from the road to this house.

Woody broke up the so-called First Herd that year, 1946. Various explanations have seen print, but none of them, Woody told me in some late-night conversation years ago, was correct. He gave me the real reason.

"Is it all right if I tell it now?" I said.

"Sure," he answered.

In that earlier conversation he said, "It had nothing to do with dissension in the band or anything like that. I was destroying Charlotte."

On a December night, after a dance at Indiana University, Woody told his men—Chubby Jackson, Flip Phillips, Neal Hefti, Bill Harris, John LaPorta, Don Lamond, the whole fantastic exuberant crew—that it was over.

Some people date the end of the big band era from that December, for that month the bands of Benny Goodman, Tommy Dorsey, Harry James, Les Brown, Jack Teagarden, Benny Carter, and Ina Ray Hutton all broke up, along with Woody's.

He was at the peak of his fame as well as his young manhood. He was thirty-three years old. Bandleaders then were movie stars.

Woody had made the sudden discovery that there were other women in the world besides the girl he had married so young. And Charlotte was stuck here in this house with a new baby. She became what they now call cross-addicted to pills and liquor. "You start mixing Nembutol with booze, baby," he said, "and you're on your way home." Woody had a gift for colorful metaphor. Years ago he said nightclubs gave him the clausters, a graphic expression to anyone who has worked in them.

And so he folded the band and came home. Charlotte joined Alcoholics Anonymous. "She didn't have as many problems as she thought she did," Woody said, with that kind of benign tolerance he extended to the foibles of our species. "She thought alcohol was the problem, but she was really hooked on the pills." Later, when she had it all under control, she would now and then have wine with dinner. In time she gave even that up, and Woody cut his own drinking back to an occasional Heineken's. Woody said to me a few years ago, laughing, "I went to an A.A. meeting with Charlotte and my old band was sitting there."

Woody and Charlotte put the pieces of their marriage back together, and in later years, whenever she could, she would travel with him, all over the world. She accepted the life of hotel rooms and the endless runs down America's long highways. Woody liked traveling by car. I never saw a husband and wife more devoted to each other. There was something special about her attitude to his work. Every musician is only too familiar with the phenomenon of the bandleader's wife, the lady who is hipper than hip and knows how everybody should play and live their lives and who should be hired and who should be fired. Charlotte was the antithesis of that. She had a subtle sense of how close to let people get to her—close enough to make them comfortable, not close enough to jeopardize Woody's authority as leader. She had a way of being warm and distant at the same time.

Woody's retirement after the First Herd lasted seven months. By the time the itch came over him again, the marriage was in good condition, so he organized what came to be called, accurately or no, the Second Herd. Of all the great jazz bandleaders of the

1930s and '40s, four continued touring more or less without interruption into the 1970s: Count Basie, Duke Ellington, Stan Kenton, and Woody Herman, though Les Brown maintained a tasteful
dance band with jazz colorations that worked mostly in California.
Basie, Ellington, and Kenton were now gone, and Charlie Barnet
lived in retirement in Palm Springs. Dizzy Gillespie and Benny
Carter remained active, but mostly with small groups. There was
currently an Artie Shaw band, but it was led by Dick Johnson,
although Artie supervised and rehearsed it. Woody coined the
term "ghost bands" for those, like the Glenn Miller and Tommy
Dorsey orchestras, led now by someone else. The Shaw band was
an anomaly—if it was a ghost band, it was directed by a very live
and vigorous ghost. Shaw's semi-emergence from semi-retirement
precluded neat historical packaging, in accord with his wont, but
in any case only Basie, Ellington, Kenton, and Herman continued
more or less *uninterruptedly* (to put a slight strain on the point) into
the recent past. And now only Woody, of the four, was left. Of the
"sweet" bands, only Fred Waring's, which was really a concert
organization, with choir, and Guy Lombardo's, lasted. Both men
were gone.

"Why do you keep on?" I said, knowing full well that he must
get this question constantly.

"Two reasons," he said without hesitation. "The first is my love
of music. The second is that I have an overwhelming need to make
a living."

"The I.R.S.?"

"Yes."

"Are you still paying that?"

"Yes, and it gets bigger. My lawyer is trying to get a settlement
for once and for all, and I am hoping he will."

"Can I tell that story too?"

"Sure."

Woody's manager for years was a corpulent diabetic ex-
marine—he had been badly shot up on one South Pacific atoll or
another—named Abe Turchen. Abe was what used to be called a
character.

He would sit there in Woody's office in New York, his desk a great mound of paper, watching a football game on television, playing solitaire, carrying on a conversation with some drop-in, then grabbing the telephone and booking the band with consummate ingenuity, coming up with such things as supermarket openings in places you never heard of. He looked not unlike the late Jack E. Leonard, with whom he was friendly, and even talked a lot like him. Abe was a fountain of pessimism whose response to any promising situation was (use Jack Leonard's voice to hear it): "It'll never happen, it'll never happen." To the point where one of his friends said one day, "But Abe, we have to believe in something!" We all loved Abe and said he had a heart of gold. And we all knew he gambled. But after all, it was his money. Or was it? For three years during the late 1960s, Abe gambled away the money Woody thought had been paid to the government for his income taxes. When the government stepped in, it was discovered that Abe hadn't filed withholding on the musicians, either. Woody was held responsible for all of it. He came close to going to prison. And he had been paying those taxes ever since. He told Artie Shaw, "I'll be on the road the rest of my life." And Artie said later, "What was done to Woody is cruel."

On another occasion, one of the band's players, who functioned also as its road manager, dropped the payroll on the gambling tables in Reno. At the time I was astonished that Woody not only didn't prosecute him, he didn't even fire him. He said, "If I fire him, I'll never get my money back." That was of course a plausible explanation of his own behavior, but the truth is that it wasn't in him to take a spiteful action. He was the most forgiving of men, though if he did take it into his mind at last that he disliked someone, he was immovable about it. Not surprisingly, you did not dare say a word against Woody Herman to the man who dropped the payroll and was allowed to pay it back. He was another member of the phantom Woody Herman Alumni Association whose attitude bordered on the reverent.

"How do you maintain such equanimity?" I asked.

"Well," Woody said, "I think I learned it from Tom Gerun. It was during the Depression, the end of the Wall Street crash. He got a telegram, right while we were on the bandstand, telling him that he had been wiped out financially. He went white, and said, 'Boys, tonight we're going to have a party.' And we had a band party. I think that had something to do with shaping my philosophy."

The first time I saw the Woody Herman band—probably in 1946, probably just weeks or months before he packed it in and went home to Charlotte—I was struck by his shoes, beautiful black and white loafers. They had a look of levity, almost of flight, and they were for the period very avant-garde footwear. Woody's father made his shoes for him. By hand. Otto Herman, whom I met once or twice about 1962, was a small and (it seemed to me) sweet-natured man, a German-American shoemaker who was in charge of quality control at Nunn-Bush in Milwaukee. Woody's mother was Polish—born in Poland, in fact, and brought by her parents to America as an infant. When Woody took the band to Poland some years ago, the Polish jazz fans knew all about his mother and claimed him as one of their own, as the Russians claim Bill Evans. He was like royalty to them. (American Polish jokes fall flat in Europe. The European image of the Poles is of a quick, intelligent, cultivated, good-looking people.)

One of the first things that happened to Woody on the road, after he left Milwaukee, was getting shot. The Gerun band was playing the Grenada Cafe in Chicago, a front for the Al Capone mob. Every nightclub in Chicago was a mob front. It was the Grenada Cafe that Guy Lombardo had played only a few years before when gunsels entered with Thompsons and wasted the place, sending Guy and the other musicians diving for cover. On the bill at the Grenada with Gerun was Fuzzy Knight, a comedian who would make a name in movies. When they finished work at three in the morning, they would go over to the Grand Terrace Ballroom to hear the Earl Hines band, which worked later than they did.

"One night," Woody said, "we were in the Grand Terrace, feeling no pain. Somebody spotted that Fuzzy had a big diamond on his finger. And we were tipping everybody like it was going out of style. So they figured us for live ones. It was winter, and when we came out of there at five or six o'clock in the morning, it was still dark. We got into my little car and headed back to our hotel. We got about a block when we were stopped by a traffic light. A big black sedan drove up, and when that happened in those days, you thought something was going to happen to you. Three guys jumped out. One of them had a gun. And they kept opening the door of my car. It was a roadster, and the side curtains weren't up. So they were scuffling with us, and they wanted us to get into the big car. Well, that was the thing that put us in shock, man. We weren't going to go for a ride, right? So everybody starts flailing around with their arms."

"You were fighting them in the car?"

"Yeah, which is the hard way. And finally, seeing that nothing was happening, these guys figured it was taking too much time, and so the one with the gun shot into the floorboards, and my leg happened to be in the way."

"Which one?" I said with an old journalist's concern for detail.

"The *right* one," he said.

"Do you still have the scar?"

"Yeah, where it went in and where it came out."

"It went right through?"

"Yeah."

"Then what happened?"

"We got out of the car, and they started to frisk Fuzzy. The only reason I didn't get knocked out is that I was wearing a Homburg hat. They kept hitting me with something, and the Homburg saved my head. A crowd began to gather. And I began to get bored with the whole thing and I walked off."

"With a bullet wound?"

"Well I was dragging the leg a little. And I ran into this big black cop."

"They had black cops in Chicago as far back as the 1930s?"

"On the South Side anyway."

"Then?"

"He said to me, 'What's the matter with you, boy?' I told him what was happening and said that if he looked he could still see them. He said, 'You're drunk, boy.' But by then the crowd was growing, and those guys took off."

Any musician who has ever thrown up the original tape of a recording session on the machine and heard the between-the-takes chit-chat, the laughter of forgotten conversations, knows the odd feeling of looking down a telescope into time gone. We are confronted suddenly with a curious image of the past: a seventeen-year-old boy in a Homburg, drinking in gangster speakeasies, and driving his own roadster. The fact is, however, that Woody was already an eight-year veteran of the road.

"When I was a little kid," he said, "working in presentation theatre, the vaudevillians had one expression for all audiences. They called them the Great Unwashed. And that's where I gained my first philosophy of the business, at nine years of age."

"You were already playing professionally at nine?"

"No. I was a song and dance kid. I was on the road when I was nine. When I came back from that trip I bought the saxophone and then a clarinet. And started studying."

"How did you get into the business so early?"

"Actually I started before that, in kid reviews in Milwaukee. It was my father, really. He was the one who was crazy about show business."

"So after the shoot-up in Chicago, you went out to San Francisco and met Charlotte, right?"

"Right."

"But you weren't married immediately."

"No. After *The Nine O'Clock Review*, Charlotte was in another show, which traveled across the country from San Francisco to New York, with Barbara Stanwyck and her husband, Frank Faye, who was a very funny man. But he wanted to take a show back to New York, to prove he was a great director and producer, I suppose. And of course, Miss Stanwyck paid the tab. They finally got to New York, and the show lasted a week or so.

"Charlotte and I had been romancing over the telephone and by letter. She finished a radio show or something in New York, and she stopped in Chicago when I was still with Tom Gerun, and I arranged for her to meet my mother, because I was trying to prepare her. I was going to ask her to marry me. I was doing my midwestern type family business.

"It went on for three years. We were married when we were twenty."

Woody's next band was that of Gus Arnheim, after which he moved to the band of Isham Jones. That move was to set his direction forever.

The Isham Jones orchestra was classed as one of the "sweet" bands, but it was a sort of hip sweet band. It made use of a clarinet section in ballads in a way that would turn up later in the Tommy Dorsey orchestra. "Oh yes," Woody said, "I think you heard that with Tommy's band. Our chief arranger when I was with Isham was Gordon Jenkins." It was a very good band, with good charts and good players. But Isham Jones, a saxophonist, pianist, and composer with a big ASCAP rating—he wrote *On the Alamo, Swingin' Down the Lane, There Is No Greater Love* (which Woody would later record), *You've Got Me Crying Again*, and *It's Funny to Everyone but Me*—decided in 1936, when he was forty, to quit the business. "I think Isham was at heart just a country boy," Woody said. "He opened a little music store in one of the Los Angeles suburbs. He would go into Hollywood and visit the music publishers and get free sheet music—you know, professional copies. Then he would sell them in the store. With all his money."

Woody and five other members of the band decided to form their own band, as a co-operative. They approached some other musicians, who joined them, and Woody was elected leader. He was twenty-two. This was the so-named Band That Plays the Blues, which recorded for Decca. Arranger Joe Bishop wrote its first hit, *Woodchopper's Ball*, as well as its theme, *Blue Flame*, a conspicuous pun on a notorious locker room prank.

The band lasted nine years. In fact it did not break up but evolved during World War II into what came to be known as the First Herd. Woody said, "As each member was drafted—I don't think anybody enlisted—I bought his stock in the band, and eventually I had all of it. I wanted to do something different with the band. I loved the voicings of the Duke Ellington band, and I got Dave Matthews to write for us. And I got Dizzy to write for us. He wrote one piece called *Down Under* and another called *Swing Shift*. Dizzy also played with us for a short time. I think it was a week we did at the Apollo."

Dizzy also wrote *Woody 'n' You* for the band, but by happenstance they never recorded it. It is noteworthy that Woody admired Dizzy's work as far back as 1943, before the bebop-versus-traditional fuss had really begun. That admiration is reflected in the 1945 Herman hit *Caldonia*. The soaring trumpet-section passage that electrified the band's young fans is actually a transcribed Dizzy Gillespie solo. In the Decca years, Woody made some records with guest soloists Johnny Hodges, Ben Webster, and Ray Nance from the Ellington band—further indication that he was not interested in having simply another commercially successful orchestra. The transition from the Band That Plays the Blues to the First Herd was, then, more evolutionary than revolutionary. What made it seem revolutionary is that during its period of most rapid metamorphosis, it did not record. The American Federation of Musicians was enforcing Petrillo's folly, the deeply destructive recording ban. By the time it ended, Woody had moved to Columbia Records and he quickly recorded a backlog of material that had built up during the silence, the stuff that startled the fans, not to mention young musicians coming up: *Apple Honey, Happiness Is a Thing Called Joe, Northwest Passage, Caldonia, Goosey Gander*, and *Your Father's Mustache*. The band was wild and yet disciplined, loud, completely musical, irreverent, and very funny to hear and to see, with bassist Chubby Jackson laughing and shouting encouragement to his colleagues and lead trumpeter Pete Candoli leaping on-stage in a Superman costume to play his high-note solos. "Ah your father's mustache" was a catch phrase of the 1920s, an expression of skepticism that for some reason seemed funny, and when the band sang it in unison during the tune of the same name, it was wonderfully silly. There was a touch of Dadaism to the band, and to the young people who caught it, it was irresistible.

To an extent, the band's success was a matter of timing. But the timing was probably not a matter of chance. World War II was drawing to a close that year; Germany surrendered in May, Japan in August. And the band's giddy exuberance was no doubt what the public was in a mood to hear. At the same time, the band's spirit was surely a reflection of that general euphoria—the musicians were feeling it too. Indeed, Dave Tough was fresh back from that grueling trip to the South Pacific with the Artie Shaw Navy band. Woody made the first record for Columbia, *Apple Honey* (the name of an ingredient supposedly in Old Gold cigarets, which sponsored the band in network radio), on February 19, 1945, only weeks before the German surrender that was already known to be imminent, with a personnel that included Sonny Berman, Pete Candoli, Chuck Frankhauser, Carl Warwick, and Ray Wetzel, trumpets; Bill Harris, Ed Kiefer, and Ralph Pfeffner, trombones; Sam Marowitz and John LaPorta, alto saxophones, Pete Mondello and Flip Phillips, tenors; Skippy DeSair, baritone; Billy Bauer, guitar; Margie Hyams, vibraphone, Chubby Jackson, bass; and Dave Tough, drums. With that record, Herman became, although no one knew it at the time, one of the major figures in the history of jazz.

Later Conte Candoli, Ray Linn, and Neal Hefti came into the trumpet section, and Tony Aless replaced Ralph Burns when Burns devoted his full time to writing for the band. Shorty Rogers joined them, and Don Lamond replaced tiny Dave Tough, a very intelligent man who had a drinking problem and was found on a street, injured by a fall or a beating, and soon thereafter died. After he dissolved that band near the end of 1946, Woody tried loafing and playing golf in the California sun and recording with pickup groups. The life soon palled, and, with his marriage seemingly restored to stability, he formed a new band in the fall of 1947, with Burns, Lamond, Rogers, Markowitz, and Marowitz held over from the previous band. The saxophone section included not two but three tenors, the players being Herbie Steward (later Al Cohn), Zoot Sims, and Stan Getz. The baritone saxophonist was Serge Chaloff. Jimmy Giuffre used the three tenors and baritone to get a distinctive sound in a composition he called

Four Brothers, and Woody would later cut the sax section to that size.

This was the band of *Keen and Peachy*, *The Goof and I*, and the Ralph Burns suite *Summer Sequence*, from which *Early Autumn* (with Johnny Mercer lyrics) was derived. It was another superb Herman orchestra, but it was a band with troubles. "I was so naive," Woody said once with his chuckle, "that I couldn't figure out why the guys were falling asleep on the bandstand."

The heroin fashion was in full grim flower. And that band was extremely strung out. It was also a cocky and smart-assed band. Gerry Mulligan remembers it well. "I wrote a piece for that band," he said, and described the collective attitude. Some of its members looked smug when Woody soloed, because his style was rooted in an older tradition and he wasn't a hip bebopper as they were. And they all awaited their turns to solo. They played clever solos, too. "But Woody's," Gerry said, "was the only solo that had anything to do with the piece."

Eventually, Woody—who somehow combined the deepest naiveté with a shrewd perception of people—began to be aware of what was wrong with his collection of sleeping beauties. And he found that Serge Chaloff was the band's druggist, as well as its number one junkie. Serge would hang a blanket in front of the back seats of the bus and behind it would dispense the stuff to colleagues. This led to an incident in Washington, D.C. "Can I tell that story too, now?" I asked Woody.

"Sure, why not?" he said, and laughed at the memory. "But the funniest part of it is Joe Venuti's reaction." And he retold the story.

The band not only looked bad, it sounded bad. And Woody, furious at what had happened to it, had a row right on the bandstand with "Mr. Chaloff," as he called him, emphasis on the first syllable.

"He was getting farther and farther out there," Woody said. "And the farther out he got the more he was sounding like a fagalah. He kept saying, 'Hey, Woody, baby, I'm straight, man, I'm clean.' And I shouted, 'Just play your goddamn part and shut up!'

"I was so depressed after that gig. There was this after-hours joint in Washington called the Turf and Grid. It was owned by a couple of guys with connections, book-makers. Numbers guys. Everybody used to go there. That night President Truman had a party at the White House, and afterwards all his guests went over to the Turf and Grid. They were seven deep at the bar, and I had to fight my way through to get a drink, man. All I wanted was to have a drink and forget it. And finally I get a couple of drinks, and it's hot in there, and I'm sweating, and somebody's got their hands on me, and I hear, 'Hey, Woody, baby, whadya wanna talk to me like that for? I'm straight, baby, I'm straight.' And it's Mr. Chaloff. And then I remember an old Joe Venuti bit. We were jammed in there, packed in, and . . . I peed down Serge's leg.

"You know, man, when you do that to someone, it takes a while before it sinks in what's happened to him. And when Serge realized, he let out a howl like a banshee. He pushed out through the crowd and went into a telephone booth. And I'm banging on the door and trying to get at him, and one of the owners comes up and says, 'Hey, Woody, you know, we love you, and we love the band, but we can't have you doing things like that in here.' And he asked me to please cool it.

"Well, not long after that, I was back here on the coast, working at some club at the beach. Joe Venuti was playing just down the street, and I was walking on the beach with him after the gig one night, and I told him I had a confession to make, I'd stolen one of his bits. Well Joe just about went into shock. He was horrified. He said, 'Woody, you can't do things like that! I can do things like that, but you can't! You're a gentleman. It's all right for me, but not you!'"

Serge Chaloff, an inventive soloist whose playing had a sweeping balletic kind of phrasing all his own, eventually gave up dope only to die of leukemia. Musicians in Boston, Chaloff's home town, remember him performing in a last concert, seated weakly in a chair but playing beautifully to the end. In time all the addicts in that band gave up dope, becoming collectively a notable refutation of the bleak statistics of heroin recidivism. I once asked one of them how he did it. He said that he and the girl he was going with got into a car and headed out from New York across the country. When the withdrawal got too bad, they would check into a motel and she would hold him until the worst sweats and spasms passed. Then they would go on. And then one day he became aware of the sky and clouds and green fields, and of the stars at night, and by the time they got to California, he was clean.

The band recorded some of its best work in California, and did so in a comparatively short time. James Caesar Petrillo, president of the American Federation of Musicians, imposed yet another recording ban, a second body blow to the band business when it was facing other problems. Travel costs were rising. The ballrooms were gradually going out of business. And television would soon phase out the network radio broadcasts that were critical to the bands if they were to build and retain an audience.

The public never really accepted the Second Herd—not, in any event, as it had accepted the First. "It was a very musical band," Woody said. "But the public doesn't want you to change. If you do it enough, of course, you confuse them and sometimes they relent and let you get away with it." Then, too, it was not, as one can see in retrospect, that perfect reflection and expression of a public mood, as the First Herd had been. And in time that band too faded away.

Yet Woody never really left the business. Throughout the 1950s, he either led small groups or put together big bands using the libraries of the two Herds and even the earlier band.

Why did Kenton, Basie, Ellington, and Herman survive out there on the road when more obviously commercial bands, like that of Kay Kyser, went the way of the passenger pigeon? Because they were jazz bands, Woody says, devoted to their own music rather than the ephemera of commercial pops, and such bands commanded a perhaps diminished but knowing and serious audience.

"This is a grim question," I said, "and you've probably heard it a hundred times, but it's an inevitable one: How do you feel about being the survivor of an era?"

He laughed. "Well, it's led to some rather dubious honors in the last year or so." Behind him, a further flight of stairs descended from the living room to the lowest of the three tiers of the house. All down the walls and on shelves were the symbols and statuettes of a long list of honors he had received: honorary citizen of New York State, honorary citizen of Maryland, honorary Kentucky colonel, citations from jazz societies, along with the small brass gramophones of NARAS and two or three figurines from an award now forgotten, the little bemustached character Esky, the one-time symbol of *Esquire*, holding a trumpet high in the air and silently blowing his brains out. Off to the right, beyond the wide windows, the afternoon was almost gone and the carpet of lighted beads was coming up in the Los Angeles basin.

"Stravinsky," I said, "made the remark that growing old was just a matter of one indignity after another."

"I'm at the stage," Woody said, "if I wake up in the morning, I figure I'm ahead of the game. I've had the 'flu once this year. You have to keep warm. That's when you know you're no longer a boy."

"It's crossed my mind that if you don't make younger friends along the way, you could end up one day with none at all."

"I don't have any trouble there, of course, because of the ages of the young men in the band. It keeps me in touch, and it's a stimulus. We get along just fine—as long as we stick to the subject of music. If we get on anything else, the generation gap starts to get very wide, man."

The average age of Woody's bands was about the same, ever since he headed that first band at twenty-two, a short five years after he went out with Tom Gerun. "The team stayed the same," he always used to say. "The coach got old."

It must have been in 1959 that I first actually met Woody. It was in Chicago. I had already spent enough time among actors and other performers to be aware that the public image may have little to do with the private personality. Woody turned out to be unlike my image of him.

He was one of those people who light up, rev up, turn on when they step into the spotlight. And his public personna would impress you as cocky and confident. But take him off the bandstand and you had a quiet, if sharply humorous, man, even a very shy one, until he got to know you. He was in his late forties then, and he was still a pretty good drinker, and I got hammered with him one night. All I remember of that evening is his melancholy—a wolf he normally kept at bay—and his humility. Nor was the modesty an affectation. Some months later, in New York, I went with Marian McPartland to hear him in the upstairs room at the Metropole. He was leading a septet, and a vibrant one, that included Nat Adderley and Zoot Sims. It had all the fire of his big bands. ("All my small groups have sounded like bands," he said at the Christmas of 1984. It was the nearest I ever heard him come to boasting.) Marian and I sat with him after a set, and he said, in I do not remember what context, "I never have been much of a clarinet player." Actually, I liked his clarinet playing, although I liked his alto playing more. But that was when I got the measure of the man and knew how much I liked him.

I do not wish to convey an impression of a milktoast. Woody was capable of scathing wisecracks, although they only seemed to come from him if he'd been goaded. One incident involved Benny Goodman, who was also unlike his onstage personality, which was that of the friendly bespectacled old uncle. But he was notorious for his contemptuous and even cruel treatment of musicians. One night Goodman came by to hear Woody at Basin Street East in New York. After a set he made some patronizing comment about Woody's clarinet. Woody just smiled and said, "Well, that's how it goes, Benny. You could always play that clarinet and I could always organize a band."

Stan Kenton, on the other hand, was much like his bandstand personna. Stan contributed less to jazz than his devotees believe but more than his detractors admit. His bands screamed but didn't swing, a point on which you will get an argument from his fans but not from most of the band's alumni. His bands were stiff because Stan was stiff. He was a friendly and kind man, and I liked him very much. But he was also a grandiloquent man, and about some things very foolish, and he brought himself great pain in the end.

At one point, Stan married a singer much younger than he. And he had lunch with Woody shortly afterwards. He talked of his happiness and told Woody that he should follow his example and get a younger girl. Woody indicated that he wasn't interested. And Stan said, "Do you *love* Charlotte?"

"Love?" Woody said. "Love? When we were young we loved, very deeply. Now we're getting old, and we understand each other. And yes, I do love Charlotte."

I always had the impression that that conversation had, if not destroyed, at least seriously undermined Woody's respect for Stan.

(Later, a musician traveling with Kenton heard the girl screaming at Stan, "Love you? You're *old*. I married you for my career!" Still later I saw Duke Ellington give her a freeze treatment at a festival. There are two sides of course to any story, and I know people who liked her. In fact I liked her. She committed suicide.)

The Third Herd simply evolved. And I went to work for Woody at that time, not long after I arrived in New York in 1962. I was broke, and Woody could sense it, and he asked me to go to work for him as his publicist. He said it would give me a sustaining income, and I could have the use of his office at 57th Street and Seventh Avenue.

The band was fantastically good. This was the band with Bill Chase, Jake Hanna, Henry Southall, Phil Wilson, Nat Pierce, Sal Nistico. Their home base in New York was the Metropole, the room at street level. There was no bandstand, only a precarious long shelf behind the bar. There was no place for music stands, and they played from memory, standing up, stretched out in a straight line in a sort of strange super-stereo. How they could be cohesive under the conditions was incomprehensible. But they were, and that band burned. Advances in musicianship since the 1940s were manifest in the fact that they performed *Caldonia* at about twice the tempo of the original recording (you can hear it in an album on Phillips), so fast that Woody stumbled over the time when he sang, "Caldonia, Caldonia, what makes your big head so hard?" When that Dizzy Gillespie unison passage came up, Bill Chase would take the trumpets through it with enormous bite and then, in its second part, jump the lead up an octave. Bill was a superb player who later had his own successful group, called Chase. He died in a plane crash.

I have no particular talent for publicity, but I believed in that band, and I got it a lot of publicity. I like to think that I made a contribution to putting Woody back on the map after the comparative doldrums of the 1950s.

People began to record my songs. A book of mine was published. I was writing for several magazines. Driving into town one day, Woody heard one of my songs on Mort Fega's radio show. He came into the office and said, "Why didn't you tell me you could write lyrics like that?"

"You didn't ask me," I said.

Woody picked up the phone and called Howie Richmond, the music publisher. Within a day or two I had a contract to write songs for The Richmond Organization on a livable weekly retainer.

I worked for Woody for a year. In late 1963, I told him in a restaurant that I was getting busy, thanks in large measure to him, and pressed for time. Like almost everyone who had ever worked for him, I had formed something akin to a filial attachment to him, one I would never lose. By now I knew of a lot of kindnesses done quietly for a lot of people, including a disk jockey who told me Woody had unquestioningly handed him several thousand dollars when the man was about to lose his home.

"Well what's the problem?" Woody said.

"I have all these things to do, and you really don't need me any more."

"But what?"

"But I have torn feelings. I don't want to leave."

"Oh. If that's all the problem you have, I'll make it easy for you. You're fired."

And we had lunch. And that is how I have gone around ever since making the boast that I am the only man Woody Herman ever fired.

"It's the way he rehearses a band," Al Cohn said. He was replying to a question I asked of various people who had worked for Woody over the years. How is it that whatever the group, whatever the personnel, even his small combos, a Woody Herman band always, or almost always, sounds like a Woody Herman band, fiery and free, and full of laughter? And several other people, including Nat Pierce, confirm Al's opinion.

When a new chart went into the book, he would let the band play it down their way, without him. When they had found the groove of the piece, he would step in and edit.

"I'm just an editor," he said to me once. Just? It is a rare ability. And, after the Christmas of 1984, he said, "I concern myself with being a fair editor. I may take letter B and put it where letter A is and put letter C somewhere else. And I may change solos, because it will suit that particular chart better.

"The reason I got that, in the early days, was Ralph Burns, who I thought was one of the greatest talents of all, ever. And the first chart he brought in to me, which was about 1944, was *I've Got the World on a String*. He said, 'Here's this thing I made for you to sing.' It was a tune that I liked and used to sing anyway. Ralph said, 'If there's anything you don't like or anything you feel could be changed, go right ahead.' He said, 'I've done the best I can, but if you can make it better, great.' I didn't even touch that one, nor did I very often with Ralph, but it gave me the courage so that if I could make something better—mostly by pacing—I would do it. Ralph had given me this freedom to do that, and if *he* did that, then I believed I could do it as well as anyone else. It was Ralph who encouraged me, and he was much younger than I."

"It's a mysterious phenomenon," I said. "I understand how a different feeling is developed from the same piece of material by a symphony conductor, carefully rehearsing, telling them what he wants, then actually conducting the music with his hands. But in jazz, there's comparatively little manual conducting. Yet if you took the same chart to Basie or you or someone else, it would come out sounding different each time."

"Yes," he said.

"I don't know how it's achieved, how the leader's personality gets into the music. A Basie groove is a Basie groove, absolutely distinct."

"Well, Nat Pierce was really into the Basie sound. The whole thing. When he was writing for me, I'd say, 'You can make it sound like whomever you want, I'll fix it so it identifies with *this* band.' That's the way we worked on many things." But he hadn't answered my question: how is it achieved? And I'm not sure he knew.

He had a kind of sixth sense about talent. Once I asked how he kept finding his gifted young people, and he said, "I don't find them, they find me."

But that begs the issue, which is selection, his unerring perception of which ones to choose from all those who applied or were recommended to him. He could detect the real thing in its most formative stages. He was always touting this young man or that, and he never seemed to be wrong.

Woody's bands were never showcases for Woody, although his Hodges-like alto playing was lovely. He was not jealous of his own young employes. On the contrary he was very solicitous of them. When a young man came into the band, Woody usually took him aside and told him not to sweat it, just relax and get the feel of the charts. He took the fear out of the boy. And after the young man had been with the band for a week or two and had begun to unwind, Woody would hold up a finger one night, meaning, "Take one chorus," and he would listen to the boy's jazz playing, without putting pressure on him. And then, later on, he might, toward the end of that one chorus, hold up a finger again, meaning, "Take another one." And the young man was gradually broken in as both soloist and ensemble player.

The Woody Herman band was the great finishing school of

American music, and if the economics of the band business and Woody's tortured thralldom to the I.R.S. did not permit him to pay as much as he would have liked to, and the young men, when they came to the time of making families, dropped out of the band to play in the studios or teach on some school faculty somewhere, there were always the others, waiting in line to travel with Woody—the road father, as he came to be known.

"I love bringing them along," he said. "I love seeing them develop. I'm the Vince Lombardi of the bandleaders." It was when I heard him say that, with a quiet pride over all his young men (some of them now in their sixties), that I told him he was a great man. Without the alumni of splendid musicians he helped develop, American music would be very different indeed. His mark on the American and indeed the world's culture is hard to estimate.

"How do you do it, Wood?" I said. "Losing Charlotte, the road, all of it."

"Well, I was raised a Catholic . . . "

And this astonished me. All the years I had known him, and I had never known that! But of course; a Polish mother, and chances are the German father was also Catholic. The reason I did not know it is that Woody never laid his personal life on you, never laid his heavies on you. He would listen to yours but he didn't burden you with his. "Are you still?" I said. "A practicing Catholic?"

"Yes," he said, further surprising me. "I have my faith, and I pray. I went to church the other day."

I thought then about his early days. With him in the Tom Gerun band was a young man named Al Morris, the one who would change his name to Tony Martin and become one of the big singing and movie stars of the 1930s and '40s. He would go through marriage and divorce and end up married to Cyd Charisse, whose ex-husband, Nico Charisse, owned a dance studio where Judy Garland would rehearse. In that show, *The Nine O'Clock Review* was another young dancer named Betty Grable, who would go through marriage and divorce and end up married to Harry James. Three years after Woody met Charlotte, Betty Grable and Tony Martin would be in a movie together, *Pigskin Parade*, in which the young Judy Garland would make her film debut. Garland's sister would marry Bobby Sherwood and then divorce him to marry another musician. Garland wanted to marry Artie Shaw, but at that time Shaw married Lana Turner and Garland married David Rose (and four others) and Artie married Ava Gardner, who had been married to Mickey Rooney, Garland's friend from childhood at MGM, and Gardner later married Frank Sinatra . . .

La ronde.

Charlotte and Woody alone, it seemed, got through it all together and did not participate in this vast erotic rite. Amazing.

"Was Charlotte Catholic too?"

"Yes. She was a convert." That would figure too. With a Norwegian background, she would have been raised Protestant.

"Is that the reason you stayed together?"

"I think the reason Charlotte and I were survivors," he said, "is humor. We could always laugh at each other." He paused, looking inward, then told me something that will tell you a lot about Charlotte, that lovely woman whose poise after the mastectomies was impressive. She beat the disease for a few years, too. "She was lying in there," he said, his hand indicating a bedroom off the living room, "a few days before she died, and I was sitting on the bed. And what can you say to anyone in those circumstances? And I put my face in my hands and I started to cry. And she raised her hand . . . " he imitated the gesture, a slow and hesitant lift of the arm . . . "and who knows how much it cost her, and she put it on my shoulder, and she said, 'Straighten up, boy!' "

For a moment then I saw him and Charlotte at seventeen.

The next day he was gone, off on the road again, to play a gig through New Year's Eve in Sparks, Nevada, with the Nat Pierce-Frankie Capp big band, then to New York for ten weeks at the St. Regis with a small group.

Some time after that, Woody played a job with a small group at the Vine Street Bar and Grill in Hollywood. He told me his teeth were bothering him. He was playing badly, and everyone knew it, and had it not been for the Internal Revenue Service he would not have been playing at all. That was the heartbreak for all of his friends, to hear him shrieking out high notes that were no longer secure and flamboyant all for the I.R.S. In the *Los Angeles Times*, James Liska wrote one of the cruelest reviews Woody received in his whole life, diligently and meticulously cataloguing every defect in an old man's playing; the musical community was incensed, and John Heard, the bassist in the group, said indignantly, "This man is a national monument!"

I didn't see Woody for a while after that. Then came his fiftieth anniversary as a bandleader. Two of his bands played the Hollywood Bowl, one of them made up of his veterans, older players such as Med Flory who had been with him over the years, and one of them the current band of youngsters. Afterwards there was a party at his house, arranged by his daughter Ingrid.

The house and balcony were so crowded that you could hardly move. Yet many of his oldest friends, such as Tony Martin, and younger friends such as Alan Broadbent, had not been invited; and many people had been invited whom Woody did not even know. He wandered around looking lost, and finally settled in the kitchen, a plaintive gentle figure on a wooden chair. He said to my wife, "I'm tired of it all. I just don't want to go on." And then, "Who are all these people? I don't know a lot of them." And the spark returned. He grinned at her: "Let's get out of here."

"Where do you want to go, Woody? Shall we go to the south of France?"

"Naw," he said. "They don't know me there. Let's go to Poland. I'm very big in Poland."

He went on working, because the I.R.S. kept after him, this exhausted and feeble old man. The government of Finland put Sibelius on a pension for life. Woody Herman's government hounded him right to the grave. His friends talked about benefit concerts, but there was no way they could give him the proceeds: the I.R.S. was waiting to seize any penny that came his way. Artie Shaw attempted to put together a syndicate of people to buy

Woody's house and let him live out his life in it. The deal fell through.

So Woody stayed on the road until, in Detroit, he was hospitalized in critical condition. The doctors nursed him back from the brink and sent him home, and he went back to work. In early 1987, his health crumbled again, and in March he gave his last performance. He was in and out of hospital with congestive heart disease and emphysema. His boys, all the musicians he had nurtured, kept vigil. Nat Pierce and Jake Hanna spent an afternoon with him and left knowing he had not been entirely sure who they were. I called one day, and Ingrid put him on the phone with me. I did not know the cracked old voice on the line; and he really didn't know me either. One day I went by the house, but he was asleep and unable to see anyone.

The Internal Revenue Service seized his house and put it up for auction. Though it was worth close to half a million dollars, a real estate speculator picked it up for just under a hundred thousand. He rented it back to Woody. But by now Woody was beyond earning anything. He fell four months behind on the rent. His landlord ordered him evicted. Though he was bed-ridden and helpless and not always conscious of what was happening around him, his landlord arranged with marshals that at 5:00 p.m., Tuesday, September 8, 1987, he was to be put out of the house onto the street.

The news media picked up the story and spread it in newspapers and on television tubes across the country. Woody was brought out of his bedroom in a wheelchair to face the camera. He had a small white beard and his head looked like a skull, a pathetic little figure as helpless as a baby. Saul Levine, the owner of the Los Angeles jazz radio station KKGO, paid back rent of $4,600 on the house. The station became a center for donations, which soon amounted to $18,000. Les Brown led Woody's band in a concert in Ventura, California, to raise money. On October 23, Tony Bennett, Rosemary Clooney, Doc Severinsen and his band, and a Herman alumni band directed by Nat Pierce, gave a benefit concert in West Los Angeles. But by then Woody was back in Cedars-Sinai Medical Center. His heart had already stopped two or three times, only to be started up again by amoral medical virtuosity. He was on a life-support system, a fragile skeleton without awareness. His friends began saying, "For God's sake, why don't they pull the plug?" And the I.R.S. told the press it would not give up; it was going to get its last few dollars out of this vegetable.

"Why," journalist Peter Keepnews asked in *Billboard*, "is the I.R.S. hounding Woody Herman, a tireless and gifted exponent of home-grown music, while institutions dedicated to the preservation of European music enjoy tax-exempt status?"

On the afternoon of November 26, 1987, Woody Herman died. On Monday, November 30, All Souls' Day, which is to Mexicans the Day of the Dead, Woody's funeral mass was held in St. Victor's Church, just below Sunset Strip in Hollywood, not far from the house he had lost. He'd been coming here for years. It is a bright airy church, and modern, though not aggressively so. It was crowded with friends from his childhood and his later life, among them Howie Richmond, the publisher to whom he had introduced me so long ago in New York, and Les Brown, and with musicians whose careers he had nurtured, such as Alan Broadbent and Nat Pierce and Pete Candoli. The service was quiet, and tasteful. Afterwards everyone stood around on the sidewalk in the sunlight and talked, as if they were in no hurry to leave, and there was a notable lack of melancholy. Maybe it was because they were aware that his death was a release. As Nat Pierce put it, he was out of the Frankenstein laboratory where strange machines sustained a sad semblance of life in a fragile depleted body.

He was right about almost everything he ever told me. But on one point he was wrong and I was right: he was a very great man.

The gray metal coffin with silver handles was lifted into a Cadillac hearse, which drove off. The road father was gone, gone where the I.R.S. could not reach him. And best of all, he was gone—I'm sure this is what he believed with utter simplicity in the waning days before the power of thought glimmered out—to join Charlotte.

7

THE JOKER:
FRANK ROSOLINO

THERE ARE THOSE, the fine saxophonist Don Menza among them, who long afterwards found it all but impossible to talk about what happened in those early hours of November 26, 1978. By one of those bits of mental prestidigitation with which we protect our sanity, we all succeeded in not even thinking about it. We pushed the event into some closet in a back room of the mind, and then we all shut the door.

I cannot to this day explain, and neither can the Van Nuys homicide detectives, why it happened. I'll tell you, as I told them, what I know.

Frank Rosolino was among the best-loved men in jazz. One of the finest trombone players in the history of the instrument, he had a superb tone, astonishing facility, a deep Italianate lyricism, and rich invention. Frank was, very simply, a sensational player. In addition he had a wonderful spirit that always communicated itself to his associates on the bandstand or the record date.

He was one the funniest of men, with a wit that literally would not quit. He bubbled. Quincy Jones remembered touring Japan with a group that included Frank and drummer Grady Tate. "With those two," Quincy said, "you can imagine what it was like. The band was always in an uproar."

Frank was one of a number—Donald Byrd was another—of fine jazz musicians to come out of Cass Tech in Detroit, a superior

high school which drew its students from all over the city. Only
the exceptional could even get into it. Frank always had the air of
a mischievous kid looking for some hell to raise or trouble to get
into, and this trait had emerged by the time he went to Cass Tech.
Giggling in that way of his, he would in later years recall swiping
cars for joyrides. It was always a serious mistake to get into a poker
game with Frank. He was one of those men who, but for a soaring
and compelling musical talent, might well have ended up in jail.

Like everyone who knew him, I remember vividly the last times
I saw Frank. We were at Dick Gibson's jazz party in Colorado, one
of those events that have sprung up in recent years in which aging
rich jazz fans invite brilliant musicians to come and play for them.
At one point he played with Carl Fontana and Bill Watrous, and
the three-trombone music was gorgeous. In another unforgettable
set, Clark Terry and Frank did several scat-singing duets. They
kept making each other laugh, and afterwards I urged them to
record together, not playing so much as scatting. Frank was one
of the few people who could scat on the same bandstand with
Clark Terry.

The main events of the long weekend were held in the Broad-
moor Hotel in Colorado Springs, noted for exciting scenery, dull
food, and sullen service. After the last performance at the Broad-
moor, we all traveled by bus back to Dick Gibson's house in Denver. Frank and the girl he was living with, Diane, were in the seat
behind my wife and me.

We did not know it at the time, but Frank's third wife, the
mother of his two sons, had gone into their garage, shut the door,
turned on the car's engine, and sat there in the fumes until she
died. I do not know her motive. Frank, in the seat behind us, was
talking about following her, killing himself and taking the two boys
with him, since he could not bear the thought of leaving them
behind in this world. Were we hearing him correctly? Diane said,
"Don't talk that way, Frank. Let's pray together."

That evening in Denver there was a final informal party at Gibson's house. Frank seemed cheerful, making my wife and me

doubt the accuracy of our hearing in the noise of the bus. She and I had to leave early to get back to Los Angeles. So did Frank, who had a gig the next morning. We took a cab to the airport together. Frank was as funny as always. The conversation overheard on the bus seemed like the morning memory of a nightmare.

We were told at the airport that the flight would be boarding late. My wife and Frank and I wandered around with little to do. Frank shattered the impersonal tedium that hangs in the atmosphere of all airports: he had us laughing so hard that a salesgirl in the bookshop, watching us with suspicion, pointed us out to a security guard, who kept an eye on us.

Part of it was Frank's delivery. It has been said that a comic says funny things and a comedian says things funny. Frank was both. He had a lazy low-key way of talking, the epitome of cool, that was either the archetype or the mockery of the classic bebop musician. You never knew who Frank was putting on, the world or himself. Or both. And he had a loose-jointed rag-doll ah-the-hell-with-it way of walking. Frank could even move humorously. He seemed to relish the idea of the bebopper, even as he made fun of it.

Having exhausted the airport's opportunities for amusement, we went into its coffee shop. It had a U-shaped counter and a terrazzo floor that someone had just mopped with a hideous disinfectant. The air was full of flies, drifting back and forth in lazy curves. We slid onto stools. A waitress about thirty years old approached us. Frank said in that unruffled-by-anything drawl of his, "I'll have a bowl of those *flies*, please."

With unexpected sang-froid, the waitress tossed the ball right back at him. "We only serve them on Thursdays," she said.

"Then I'll come back Thursday," Frank said, and we all laughed, including the waitress.

Finally, late, we were told that we could board the plane, a TWA flight on stopover between Chicago and Los Angeles. On the plane, returning from an engagement, was, to our delighted surprise, Sarah Vaughan. Red Callender, the bassist, and his wife were also with us. We all sat together and talked, waiting for the take-off. The pilot's disembodied voice told us that there was fog in Los Angeles and the flight would be further delayed. Frank got funnier, Sass got helpless with laughter. Frank asked a pretty stewardess if we could have drinks. She said it was against regulations for her to serve them before takeoff. But Frank soon had her laughing too, and she left to get us the drinks. Frank said, "I have to be careful. I wouldn't want her to lose her gig over it, 'cause then I might have to marry her."

At last the plane took off. Sass wanted to sleep but Frank kept up his jokes, and she said, "Frank, *stop* it!" Finally, shaking her head, she moved further back in the plane to escape him.

At last weariness overcame him, and Frank too fell asleep, sprawled across two or three seats of the nearly empty aircraft.

I awoke in daylight to the sound of the pilot's voice telling us to fasten seat belts for the descent into Los Angeles. I peered around the back of the seat ahead of me and saw that Frank was still asleep. By this time in his life, his thick dark curly hair had become almost white and he had a full iron-gray mustache. And yet, asleep, he looked like that bad boy at Cass Tech, trying to find a little action. I shook his shoulder and said, "Frank. Frank. Wake up, we're home."

I turned on the television that morning to watch the news, then drifted back into that soft state between sleeping and waking. Then there was a voice saying, "The internationally celebrated jazz trombonist Frank Rosolino took his own life last night. Police in the Van Nuys division say that Rosolino shot his two small sons and then turned the gun on himself. One of the children is dead, the other is in critical condition, undergoing surgery. Rosolino, who became nationally known with the bands of Gene Krupa and Stan Kenton, was . . . "

"No!" I shouted, waking my wife. She asked what had happened. I told her. She burst into tears. We remembered his words on the bus.

I got up and, after staring at the floor for a while, telephoned the Van Nuys police and asked first for homicide, then for whomever was handling the Frank Rosolino "case." After a while a man took up the telephone and gave me his name. I gave him mine and asked if he could tell me any more than I had heard on the news.

"Did you know him, sir?" he asked.

"Yes, I did."

"Then perhaps you can help *us*," he said. "We're just puzzled."

"So am I," I said. "But not totally surprised." I told him about the bus trip in Colorado.

"Is it possible that drugs were involved?" the detective asked carefully.

"I don't know," I said. "Although nowadays, you always wonder that." I told him what kind of person Frank was, how loved he was. But even as I said it I questioned how well any of us had really known him. I had realized there was a dark side of Frank but had never dreamed that it was this dark. And, as Roger Kellaway said later, "When somebody cracks four jokes a minute, we all should have known there was something wrong."

The conversation with the detective at last ended, as unsatisfying to him as it was to me.

In the course of that day and the next I learned a little more. Diane had wanted to go to Donte's to hear Bill Watrous. Donte's is a nightclub in North Hollywood, a hangout for musicians and one of the few places in Los Angeles where the best studio players can go to play jazz and remind themselves why they took up instruments in the first place. Frank said he wanted to stay home with his two boys: Jason, who was then seven, and Justin, nine.

I met those boys once, at a party at the home of Sergio Mendes. They were full of laughter and energy and mischief, like Frank. They were wonderfully handsome and happy little fellows, scampering like puppies amid the hors d'oeuvres and among the legs of people, having a high old time.

Diane went to Donte's with a visiting girlfriend. They came home toward four o'clock in the morning and were sitting in the car in the driveway when they saw a flash of light in the boys' bedroom. Thinking the boys were awake, they got out and went into the house. As they entered they heard the last shot, the one Frank put into his brain. He was still alive. I do not know and do not want to know the further details. In any case, he soon died.

Frank had gone to the bedroom where Jason and Justin were sleeping and shot each of them in the head. Justin was dead. Jason was not. That night and long into the next day he underwent surgery—fourteen hours of it.

The autopsy deepened the mystery. The coroner's report said that there were no significant amounts of alcohol or drugs in Frank's system.

A service was organized for Frank's friends. His two brothers, Russell and Gaspar, had flown out from Detroit to take Frank and Justin back with them for burial. I do not remember the name of the funeral home, but I can see its polite and muted decor. A lot of us, including Don Menza, Shelly Manne, and Conte and Pete Candoli, were standing around in little groups in the lobby, watching our friends arrive. It seemed everyone in town was there. I don't think any man ever had fewer enemies and more friends than Frank Rosolino. J.J. Johnson and Herb Ellis came in together; I can still see their bleak faces. Med Flory said, "Well, Frank sure took care of Christmas for all of us."

Finally, because it seemed the thing to do, I wandered into the chapel. The two coffins were in the expected place at the front of it. Roger Kellaway and I walked apprehensively toward them. The cosmeticians had done well. Beautiful little Justin truly did look as if were merely sleeping on the velvet cushion. Frank too looked asleep, as I had seen him on the plane over Los Angeles.

Roger said something softly as he looked at Justin. Later he told me it was a prayer. Then he looked down at Frank and said, "You asshole," expressing the strange compound of love and grief and anger we were all feeling toward Frank.

I couldn't face sitting through a service. What was there to say? Roger and I headed for a nearby tavern and had a couple of Scotches. For, as Roger put it, "I've had friends who killed themselves before, but I've never had one who killed his kid." He stared into his drink. The bar was lit softly. The upholstery was red. He said, "You can make that decision for yourself, but you have no right to make it for anyone else." After a time we went back to the chapel. The service, which had been short, was over, and our friends were standing quietly in the lobby.

Later there was a wake at Don Menza's house in North Hollywood. Menza and I talked for a while about Verdi. And about Frank.

Frank had fought his share of the jazz wars. He had been through financial hard times and lived to see himself and other musicians of brilliance and in some cases genius struggling to pay their telephone bills, while grungy illiterate singers rode around in limousines, with expensive whores, and demolished hotel rooms and recording studios and told their underlings to put it on the bill. He had even lived to see their likes earnestly analyzed as artists in the *New York Times* and the *Los Angeles Times* and *Rolling Stone* and *Newsweek*.

But things had been improving for him, Menza told me, including Frank's financial situation. Frank had wanted to play more jazz, and he was doing it. Don said that he and Frank had been scheduled to make an album, and there was more work of that kind on Frank's calendar. He and Frank had been very close.

Med Flory was right. Christmas was dreary that year.

At first we heard that Jason would be both deaf and blind. For a long time he was in a coma. We heard that he would come out of it and scream and then lapse back into unconsciousness. You found yourself thinking some strange thoughts. What would happen to him if he should indeed be both blind and deaf? What communication would he have with the world? Would he be a vegetable? Or, worse, would he be a sentient conscious being trapped in a black silence with memories of sight and sounds and never knowing why and how they had suddenly ceased? Had he been the second one shot? Had he seen his brother killed?

After a while we heard that Jason could hear. He was living by now with relatives of his mother. Gradually I stopped thinking about him. And about Frank. Every once in a while, though, something would happen to remind me.

Roger Kellaway and I were on our way to an appointment in Tarzana, an area of Los Angeles at the west end of the San Fernando Valley. We saw a little boy, about three, crying in the street. We stopped the car. The boy was lost. Roger and I decided that he would go on to our appointment while I tried to learn where the boy belonged. I asked passing people if they knew the child. Gradually a crowd gathered. A tall handsome man in his late fifties introduced himself. He was a cop, a lieutenant. He lived in a nearby building. We went up to his apartment, where he gave the boy something to eat. The child stopped crying. The man picked up the phone, dialed, and identified himself. He was head of the Van Nuys homicide division.

While we waited for a police car—which in due course did find the boy's home—I asked the lieutenant if he had handled the Rosolino case. He said that two of his men had. I found myself going over it all again. So did the lieutenant.

He told me that in his line of work one inevitably becomes inured, but the two detectives who had gone to Frank Rosolino's house that night had come back to the office in tears.

"Yeah," I said. "They were beautiful little boys."

After that I banished Frank from my thoughts. I never listened to his records.

But Jason Rosolino didn't cease to be. He was adopted by a cousin of his mother, Claudia Eien, and her husband, Gary. Caring for him exhausted the family's resources, emotional, physical, and financial. Jason was sent to Braille school, but he was suffering from psychological problems. Surprised? "But he's beautiful," Don Menza's wife, Rose, said. "He's smart as a whip. He has all Frank's fire and energy." He was also, she said, very musical. He had tried trumpet and trombone and piano, but he had no patience.

Five years passed. The strain on Claudia and Gary of caring for him had proved enormous. Don and Rose Menza and other musicians and their wives planned a concert to help Jason and some other people in need. It ran from 5:00 p.m. to midnight on the evening of October 30, 1983, at the Hollywood Palladium, a grand old ballroom from the 1930s filled with the ghosts of van-ished bands. It seemed everyone was there: the big bands of Bill Berry and Don Menza, Supersax, Steve Allen, Jack Lemmon, Shelly Manne, Ernie Andrews, the *Tonight Show* band . . .

And Jason. He was there with his adoptive parents and a young psychologist who had been working with him. At first I stayed away from them. A lot of people did. Finally my wife said, "We can't all ignore him."

I thought, What is it? Am I afraid of a twelve-year-old boy? Or am I afraid of seeming to manifest a morbid curiosity? Or are you, I said to myself, afraid that *you* can't handle what *he* has been through?

"Go and talk to him," my wife said.

"You go and talk to him!" I answered. But in the end I did it. Very timidly, I introduced myself to the Eien family, and soon found myself caught up in conversation. My wife then joined us.

"I used to know you a long time ago, Jason," I said.

"Before I was seven?"

"Yes," I said. "Before you were seven."

He was a handsome boy, tall, dark, and strongly muscled. There was a scar on his temple but it was not all that conspicuous. The eyes were in deep shadows, unseeing. The bullet destroyed the optic nerve but it did not touch the centers of intelligence. The psychologist told me Jason had a genius I.Q. And you could see, as you watched him listen to the music, that he had elephant ears.

An uncanny thing happened then—two uncanny things. He touched my wife's hair. Not her face, just her hair. He said, "I know what you look like."

"And what do I look like?"

He gave a wolf whistle, then said, "You have blonde hair and a full mouth." All of it accurate.

I was not too severely unnerved by that. Dave MacKay, the pia-nist, is also blind. I have known Dave, at a social affair, to describe the color of a sweater worn by someone just entering the room.

And Dave has a remarkable ability to fathom character merely from the sound of a voice.

"How do you know that?" I asked Jason.

"From her voice," Jason said.

But the next one was even stranger. My wife mentioned a friend in Santa Barbara who grew flowers. Jason said he knew what the man looked like. He said the man was tall and fair-headed. This was accurate. But how many tall sandy-haired Japanese have you met?

Don Menza's band was performing. "Who's playing the trumpet solo?" Jason asked me.

"Chuck Findley," I said, and then thought, Why misinform him? "Actually, it's not a trumpet, it's a fluegelhorn."

"What's the difference?"

"It's a somewhat bigger instrument, it plays in a slightly lower register, and it has a darker sound."

"What do you mean by *darker*?"

That stopped me. One of those moments when you realize that music cannot be described. And in the attempt we usually resort to visual analogies, which did not seem appropriate in the present instance. "It's fatter, it's thicker somehow," I said.

Then Bill Berry played a solo. "That's a trumpet in a harmon mute," I told Jason, and explained the use of mutes.

"It sounds a little like a saxophone," Jason said. And not many orchestrators have noticed *that* resemblance.

Shelly Manne was playing with Don Menza's band. Two weeks earlier Shelly had been hurt in an encounter with a horse on his ranch and one leg was now immobilized by a cast. This meant he was working without a high hat. I explained this to Jason. "What's a high hat?" he said.

"Give me your hands," I said, and put them palm to palm horizontally. I slapped them together on the second and fourth beats of the music. "Two cymbals facing each other, like that. You work them with a foot pedal."

"Oh, yes, I know," Jason said. "I used to play drums."

We listened to the music for a time. "I think a lot of people are trying to help you, Jason," I said. "A lot of people in this room love you."

"Why?"

"Just because. Take my word for it," I said.

"Do you know who really loves me?"

"Who?"

"God loves me," he said.

8

THE PAINTER:
JOHN HEARD

JOHN HEARD suffers from a speech impediment so severe that sometimes his jaw will lock open, the word he is trying to get out frozen into a silence that produces anguished suspense in whomever he is talking to. Then a broken bit of the word will emerge, a phoneme repeating itself like a sound coming from a stuck record, d- d- d- . The aspirated h seems to give him particular trouble. As suddenly as a sentence stops, it will resume, often broken by a burst of exuberant laughter. He is unselfconscious about his stammer and soon puts anyone he has decided to accept as a friend as much at ease with his problem as he is. When John, along with Frank Morgan and Tootie Heath, was interviewed on a TV news brief about jazz clubs in Los Angeles, friends called to chide him that he hadn't stammered once.

"I got a lot o' balls," he said, laughing about it.

So he does. This is evident in his playing. John Heard is a magnificent bass player of the modern school, one of the heritors of the Charles Mingus-Scott LaFaro tradition of playing. But for all the speed and fire in his fingers, he is able, in ensemble passages, to walk the instrument right into the ground, after the manner of George Duvivier and Ray Brown. Matched with an appropriate drummer, he is the living embodiment of what rhythm sections are supposed to do: swing.

John Heard sneaked up on everybody. There was no sudden

prominence in magazine polls, no flurry of interviews—partly, to be sure, because the speech impediment has usually caused him to decline interviews. He slipped into our awareness through his work with Jon Hendricks, Ahmad Jamal, Count Basie, and Oscar Peterson. One day there he was. Where did he come from?

From Manchester, a district of Pittsburgh sufficiently dangerous that many Pittsburgh people decline to set foot in it. He was born there July 3, 1938. His mother, who came from Mississippi, left school after the second grade to work. She taught herself to read from the Bible. His father, who also had a second-grade education, was born in Georgia. Both his parents liked to sing. He would wake up mornings to the sound of his father's cheerful blues, whose words were made up on the spot.

Pittsburgh lies in the valleys that have been cut by the Allegheny and Monongahela rivers, which converge at this point to form the Ohio, the major tributary of the Mississippi. By the late 1960s, legislation had forced its famous steel mills to put scrubbers on their smokestacks, and its air was cleaner than that of most major cities. Now many of those mills are out of business, rusting away in silence. But when John was a boy, the street lamps would sometimes be alight in the daytime. "That's how little sunlight got in," he said.

"My father was an alley cat. He was just built that way. He was probably the smartest man I ever met. He could do anything. He could tear a house down and put it up. I used to have to help him. He had a garden that fed the family. He would get an old model T Ford and he and his friends knew how to work on cars and they'd fix it up. We were all poor, but it was real close. My mother never really had to worry about me outside, because they knew if I did something too wrong, a neighbor would kick my ass and tell them later, and I'd get another spanking. All the families around there had six or seven kids. Everybody knew everybody else. I still stay in touch with a lot of those people. One of the kids I grew up with, who was a Yugoslavian, is an oceanographer. We all did well.

"My father never wanted anything, outside of taking care of his family. I don't know anything about my grandparents. He left

Georgia when he was quite young. And he would never go back. We think he probably offed somebody there and got out. But he would never tell us. He used to take me fishing on the Allegheny.''

John was the second youngest of the Heard children, six of whom were girls. One sister, Freddia, became secretary to the district attorney. John's only brother, now deceased, became a Pittsburgh policeman. He was a self-taught boogie-woogie pianist and, John says, ''he was really tough. He was the only man I was ever afraid of.'' John takes a certain pride in being tough himself. He stands a sinewy five-foot-eleven, wears a beard, is balding now, and has flecks of gray in his tight wiry hair. Speaking of one musician he worked for and who gave him a hard time, he said, ''I told him I would remove his ass from this earth, and I meant it, and after that he didn't bother me.''

John has a strong sense of Pittsburgh about him, as many of that city's sons and daughters do. He is keenly aware of people in the arts who were born or grew up in Pittsburgh or the surrounding communities, particularly jazz players, and he will, with civic pride, rattle off their names at the drop of an excuse—Art Blakey, Ahmad Jamal, Maxine Sullivan, Billy Eckstine, George Benson, Ray Brown, Al Aarons, Erroll Garner, Roy Eldridge, Earl Hines, Mary Lou Williams, Eddie Safranski, Joe Pass, Joe Harris, Dodo Marmarosa, Kenny Clarke, Paul Chambers, Stanley and Tommy Turrentine, Henry Mancini.

''It was hip,'' he said. ''There's a lot of money in Pittsburgh for the arts. I grew up getting a lot of exposure to the arts. They had the Civic Light Opera, they had grand opera, they had one of the major symphony orchestras. We used to go on field trips from my high school to hear it. And they had the Pittsburgh Playhouse, where Gene Kelly came from—and Frank Gorshen and Shirley Jones. We had field trips to that, too, if they were doing something like *The Petrified Forest*. It was kind of nice.

''When I was about twelve, I wanted to join the Boy Scouts. My part of town, the north side, had a YMCA, but it was white only. I went in there one day to talk about joining the Boy Scouts, and they told me I had to go over to another part of town. I didn't particularly care for that, so I vandalized the building one night. I don't remember what I did, but it was something. In junior high school, I wanted to take a photography class. I walked in to register, and the teacher just kind of put his arm around me and walked me out to the hallway, and booted me and said, 'Don't come back in here.' I've been laying for him for a long time. If I saw him now, I'd cold-cock him. As a matter of fact, when I got out of the Air Force, I went back, but he was gone from the school. I think that's the only guy I'd really like to run into."

I reminded John that he had once commented to me that so-called race relations in the United States were better at the turn of the century than they were later, because of the director D.W. Griffith, a racist from Kentucky who also happened to be a great film maker. Hollywood—and John is far from being the first person to make this observation—reinforced this impression of blacks with Mantan Moreland, Steppin Fetchit, and a procession of eye-rolling cooks and maids. Furthermore, Marlon Brando insists, Hollywood created the general image of the American Indians.

"That's right," John said. "What D.W. Griffith did with *The Birth of a Nation* was to stereotype *us*. Watch that film some time. And then there are the blacks who are influenced by upper-class white behavior. They're ashamed of being black. As a result, they won't eat watermelon in public, or whatever.

"In Nice one time, when I was there with Count Basie's band, they had this buffet laid out. And they had these seedless little round watermelons that looked fantastic. I walked over there and I copped. I just grabbed one and sat down and chopped it up and was eating. And some of the guys in Basie's band—" he began to laugh "—got up and walked away! They were saying, 'Man, you know you're embarrassing us, eating that.' I just hollered after them, 'You don't know what you're *missing*!' But all of that's because Griffith made a movie."

"You know Les McCann's remark about wo-dee-melon, as he calls it? 'I'm not going to give it up because *they* say I like it.'"

"Perfect!" John said, and laughed.

"British social stratification," I said, "was maintained only through the acquiescence of the lower orders, as they put it. You cannot have an army big enough to suppress an entire social class, particularly in view of the fact that armies are always drawn from the suppressed class itself, excepting the officers who command them. So you must have their complicity in their own suppression. My grandfather, who was a Lancashire coal miner, used to say of anything that seemed fancy, 'That's not for the likes of us.' And he believed it. He co-operated with the very people who put him in the coal mines when he was only a boy."

"Right! It was easier to fall in place. That's the position people saw you in. If you fall in place, you're a good nigger. You're a 'credit to your race.'" He used the expression in audible quotation marks. "If you behave the way we want you to, you're a credit to your race. Well, my folks brought me up different—to have a sense of pride. Every Sunday morning when I was a little boy, we had to walk about eight blocks from where we got off the trolley to the church. During that eight blocks, I had to walk out in front. My mother said, 'Don't slope your shoulders, hold your head up, don't drag your feet.' Eight blocks every Sunday morning, I had that regimentation. My mother wanted you to be aware of yourself. Love yourself.

"Now I reflect back on conversations I had with my parents. When I left home to go on the road, my mother said, 'Read the Book of Proverbs.' Those were her parting words. Just read the Book of Proverbs, and chances are you'll be okay. And I did it sometimes too. I'd meet somebody, an interesting kind of character, and I'd see if I could find that kind of person in the Book of Proverbs.

"And I remember what my old man used to say, 'Watch your friends, 'cause you know what your enemies are up to.'"

John, who took up the bass in a Manchester junior high school orchestra, plays with the precise and correct left-hand technique that modern bass players use, the two center fingers close together, the index and pinky fingers outspread. The close-together middle fingers accommodate the half-step between the third and fourth degrees of the major scale. The position is derived from "legit" symphonic bass playing. Earlier jazz and dance-band bass players for the most part used all four fingers in a closed grip, moving the entire hand up or down the neck to make the next note. Some of them did this with amazing dexterity, like those old-time two-finger newspaper reporters who got around on a typewriter the way Lionel Hampton plays piano. But they couldn't really dance over the instrument like Steve Swallow or Clint Huston. After LaFaro, the "legit" technique became almost universal. And it freed the bass from its rudimentary function of walking simple lines, usually made up of roots and fifths.

No instrument in jazz has advanced in the last twenty-five years the way bass has. One of the ways to get more speed on the instrument is to lower the bridge. But you sacrifice that big tone when you do that. Heard and a few others get the speed without loss of the big sound.

It is all the more surprising, then, that John Heard cannot read a note of music. This puts him in that small and remarkable group of jazz players that includes Bix Beiderbecke, Erroll Garner, Wes Montgomery, and Lenny Breau. But Heard's case, like Breau's, borders on the miraculous because of the classical sophistication of his playing. His tone is big and beautiful, and he can sustain notes for great lengths. It seems almost inconceivable that anyone could achieve so much without formal training or theoretical understanding. Oscar Peterson was thunderstruck to learn Heard couldn't read. Finally accepting the fact, he would tell John in rehearsal what chord he was playing at a given point. "I didn't know what he was talking about," John said, laughing at the memory. So Oscar would simply play what he had to play, and John's ear would instantly strip the harmony into its component parts. Oscar then decided to teach him some theory. The effort was futile and he finally gave that up too. John's been working with him on and off for the last eight years. "But I'm phasing that out now," he said. "I won't be working as much with Ahmad or with Kenny Burrell either."

Why? Because John Heard intends to withdraw from music. By the end of 1988, he insisted, he planned to put the bass aside forever. This is another of the odd things about him: he has achieved his present stature in jazz only to walk away from it—or at least to claim he's going to. It is a decision he made long ago.

What is he giving it up for? "This," he said, waving his hand around the garage he uses as a studio. It is attached to a low white brick house in North Hollywood, where he lives with his wife, Carolyn, and eighteen-year-old daughter Nicole.

The gesture took in several paintings in various phases of completion, including a striking acrylic portrait of Ella Fitzgerald, some of his pencil drawings, and three busts, a completed study of Duke Ellington and two works in progress, Louis Armstrong and Billy Eckstine. He was about to begin a bust of George Shearing, who commissioned it, a sculpture being the only form of portrait that Shearing can "see." John won awards for his art work in high school and continued to work as an artist during four funny years in the United States Air Force, a series of con-man adventures that recall the antics of Yossarian in Heller's *Catch 22*. Examining Heard's pencil portraits of jazz musicians made over the past twenty years or so, one notes the growing assurance of the style. The earlier pictures—one of Bessie Smith, for example—are rather cautious, the pencil markings rubbed smooth to produce an approximately photographic effect. But by the time of his 1984 portraits of a grinning Zoot Sims and a Frank Rosolino whose laughter you can almost hear, done from photographs, the technique is at once rougher and more polished, and certainly more confident. The sculpture is something new. He began working in clay only in 1987, and shows every indication of developing the proficiency he already has in other media.

John is also a capable photographer. Often he will shoot a subject extensively before beginning a portrait. He took countless photos of Eckstine before beginning the bust. Since he can't photograph Louis Armstrong, he had affixed to a board photos of Armstrong culled from newspapers and magazines, the face seen in the many angles prerequisite to the attempt at a rounded reconstruction. John also has a copy of the film *High Society*, and although he dislikes the picture and detests the shabby scene in which a condescending Bing Crosby and a tomming Louis Armstrong sing *Then You Has Jazz*, he uses it to study Armstrong in motion. "Nobody has caught the essence of him yet," John said, and although the unfinished bust has the head back, the mouth open in that showboating smile, there is something dark in the expression. I told John to find, if he can, a print of the Danny Kaye movie about Red Nichols, *The Five Pennies*, which offers an image of Armstrong more as musician then jester.

Many artists have been fascinated by jazz musicians as subjects, the magnificent penman David Stone Martin among them. Heard's drawings and paintings have the virtue of being a jazz musician's vision of jazz musicians. There is an extra if indefinable something about them, a special insight.

"You'll see portraits of white people by white artists and of black people by black artists," John said. "But I'm going to break that barrier." In fact, he already has.

At the center of all this talent is the speech impediment. He was not born with it. Pennsylvania is coal country, and where there is coal there is often slate. Smooth flat chunks of it abound, and slate makes excellent missiles. The laws of aerodynamics cause the thin gray slabs to sail beautifully. John and a friend were having a horseplay fight. John was bending to pick up a piece of slate when a chunk of it thrown by his friend caught him in the temple. His mother said the stammer began with that accident.

"Manchester was really tough," John said. "I saw more people killed there. They'd throw them in the river. They'd just grab a club and beat the shit out of a guy and throw him in the river. They'd find him downstream about a mile."

"Is that why you learned to fight as a kid, because you had to protect yourself?"

"Yeah, and because of the speech impediment. It became a part of my life. It's the most important thing that ever happened to me. A blessing in disguise. Because when I go somewhere, the first thing I do is get off in a corner and just kind of check everything out. I would never talk to people. In high school, the teacher would ask me something. If I tried to answer a question, and I'd have a little problem, and somebody would start laughing, I didn't care whether they were bigger or not, they had to try me out. That's the way I grew up. I was about a hundred and sixty-five pounds, and I was always athletic. The speech impediment was a constant of my life.

"It made me go inside. And I observed things more. I didn't socialize, I didn't want to be bothered with it. But as a result, something else was happening. I was noticing people. I got to learn how people really are, just by being in a corner. In that sense it was a blessing. I never wanted to be an actor or a teacher. I always knew I was eventually going to paint."

"So music," I said, "was always something on the way to this?"

"Yes."

"Portraiture is a special thing," I said. "Even some very gifted artists can't capture the subtle proportions of faces. It's a special accuracy."

"It is," John said. "It's mostly in the eyes. The eyes and the hands are the hardest things to do. But I was always able to do it. Maybe the speech impediment had something to do with it. Getting off into a corner and observing people. I started when I was about eight years old. The eyes and the hands tell me more about a person than anything else. I'll look at someone and say, 'Maybe I'll stay away from this guy.'"

"You can judge a lot by voices, too," I said.

"I used to practice diction," he said. "After I got out of the Air Force, I'd call around, looking for a job. People could tell whether you were white or black by the way you talked on the phone, more or less. So I'd practice diction. And then I'd go out about the job and they'd see me and that would be that."

"I must have known you for at least six months before I ever noticed the speech impediment. What brings it on? Tension?"

"Yeah," he said. "I think so. People have told me I'm very intense."

"Does it ever disappear completely, like when you're really relaxed?"

"No. You see, I'm used to it. It's part of my life. I rely on it for different things." He started to laugh. "Like, when I first went into the Air Force—this is a funny story—down at basic training, they had us on guard duty. I was at the door, and a sergeant, a training instructor, was sneaking up on me, so I said, 'Wh- wh-wh-' and the guy's, like, trying to help me get it out, and I held that guy up there for about five minutes. I was gasping for breath, I was overdoing it so much. Man, that was the last time I pulled guard duty! So you can really use it to your advantage. Like, sometimes, when a cop pulls me over for speeding or something like that, I'll go into that, and they'll feel sorry for you and let you go. I will use it! But I don't like to talk into mikes, and as for talking to crowds, forget it! I'm not going to talk in front of a crowd in my *life*. So to me, it just became a part of life. And it's a hell of an instrument for observing people. Seeing what they're like. If someone is going to come up bugging me, in a nice way, I'll just go into that. And they don't know how to handle that. So they'll leave me alone. I can really listen to people."

"When were you in the Air Force?"

"From 1958 to 1962."

"Why?"

"Many reasons. Some of them I'm not going to tell you about. Someone told me that in order to play well, I had to shoot up. I am a religious person. I'm not into churches. As far as I'm concerned, they can get rid of all of them. But I am religious. And when someone you look up to tells you something like that, that I have to shoot up, a kind of conflict happens inside. So I said, 'No, I can't do that. I think I'm just going into the Air Force, there ain't nothing else to do.' Because I was becoming a hoodlum in Pittsburgh. Getting into a lot of fights and stuff. So the Air Force was a good out for me.

"When they gave me my aptitude test, the guy said, 'We can make you a mechanic or an air policeman,' and I said, 'I'm not interested in that. I'm not workin' on nobody's fuckin' car! I want to play my instrument.' He said, 'Well what do you do?' I said, 'I play music.' He said, 'What kind of music?' I said, 'Jazz.' He said, 'What else do you do?' I said, 'I'm an artist.' He said, 'Well, we may have something for you.' I said, 'Well if you don't, I'll leave right now, I'll go back home. Because if I'm an air policeman, I'll tell you right now, I'll shoot someone.' So they assigned me as an artist.

"When somebody had a brainstorm about, like, getting a picture from behind the pilot while he was on a mission, that's what I'd do. I'd draw it for them, and they'd mail it back to Washington. Easy job. I was AWOL five times, never got busted. I used to hang out in Amsterdam all the time. The Scheherazade Club. Rita Reyes was working with the Diamond Five. I used to go in there and play. I was stationed forty-five kilometers north of Luxembourg, in Germany. It was right on the Moselle in the mountains. I was there two and a half years.

"I used to go down to Paris a lot to hear Bud Powell. Benny Bailey was there. When I first went over there, I landed at Orly outside Paris. They took us to a hotel in the Bastille area where they kept military personnel. I went out walking one night, and there was a club, and there he was, playing—Benny Bailey. So I just walked in and said, 'Can I play?' 'Cause I was in Paris, I didn't have to impress anybody, they can't play over here anyway. That was my attitude then. There was a West Indian guy playing bass. They let me sit in on bass. So after one tune, Benny said, 'Play another one.' I went the whole set. Afterwards Benny said, 'You know, I need a bass player.' So I went AWOL the first time I landed in Europe. I was supposed to be headed toward Etaine in France, the air base there. I wound up playing with Benny Bailey for a week. The Air Force didn't even know I was there. I just went to the base and they processed me. At that time De Gaulle was telling the Americans to get out of France. So they shipped me up to Germany. So that's how I landed in Europe. I made money my first week, playing. In Paris, yet! I was having fun! Then I went up to that other base, an Air Force fighter wing. It was more regimented."

"You weren't exactly marching in step," I said. "I'm amazed you could handle it."

"Well, I got on the base, and I did a portrait of the base commander's wife. And from then on I had it made. I wouldn't salute officers, I had a beard, I wore civvie clothes, and I worked in the service club. I organized tours for the officers. They wanted to go to Bertchesgaden for the weekend, that kind of thing. A woman was in charge of this section, a GS 9, a civilian, and in the military they give those ladies a hard time. So I was a blessing to her. I used to go down to wing headquarters and con these guys out of everything, pinochle decks, pingpong balls, whatever. I was dealing my ass off. Getting her what she wanted. So in return, when I didn't have anything to do, I'd say, 'I'm going to Amsterdam,' and she'd say, 'Why don't you take my car?' And I'd be having fun and sometimes I'd just forget to come back, and I'd call her, and she'd say, 'Well, there's nothing going on here.' But the officers didn't like that. I was an airman second, I was doing paintings of all these guys who came over there. They'd have these old ladies and girl friends back home. And I'd do paintings of them and sell them to them for forty-five bucks. I was teaching officers' wives how to paint with the palette knife—paint the Matterhorn and things like that. Each of them was giving me fifteen bucks a month, and I had fifteen of them going. So I was raking in the money. All of it perfectly legal. And this made the officers mad.

"On top of it, I was playing the NCO clubs on the weekends. And that was pretty nice bread too. So I would just take off, I'd say, 'They don't need me, checking in every morning at eight o'clock.' So that's what it was like. I had a lot of fun.

"That two and a half years was an eye-opener for me, with both the art and the music. I had a chance to hang out in the Louvre in Paris and the Prado in Madrid. In Amsterdam I saw Rembrandt's *The Night Watch*. Europe opened up that world for me. And I used to hang out with a German guy who was going to architecture school. He also played drums. I got into this little tight German circle. Through them I was exposed to Mingus, for instance. I wasn't into Mingus when I went into the Air Force. I was into Ahmad Jamal, Monk, Art Blakey, real hard-core bebop. West Coast music to me at that time didn't mean anything. The East Coast guys I was hanging out with said, 'Fuck that gingerbread music out there, let's *sweat*!' So that's how I grew up, always playing hard. But over there, they introduced me to Bill Evans, at the time Scott LaFaro was with him. And Mingus. And Eric Dolphy and Ornette Coleman. John Coltrane I was into before I went into the Air Force. And Phineas Newborn.

"And I'm saying to myself, 'Gee, I had to come all the way over here to learn all this about *my* music.'"

"Who were the painters you got turned onto? El Greco, I presume, at the Prado."

"Yeah. El Greco. The cubists. German cubists were particularly fascinating to me. And Braque. He was a heavy in this close-knit group. They were always talking about Braque."

"What did you get out of going to the Louvre?"

"The Mona Lisa. The minute I saw it, I got goose pimples. It blew me away. Also in Paris, I was very impressed by the impressionists—Degas, Monet in particular. Not so much Renoir. And I loved Van Gogh. The color! I got involved in all of it.

"When I got out of the Air Force in '62, I went back to Pittsburgh. I went to the Pittsburgh Art Institute for one month. It's a commercial school. They would pile all this work on you, but I still wanted to play at nights. They'd give you homework, and you'd have to do five layouts. You'd have to do five airbrush things, and you'd go to life drawing, and you'd have to do five of those. So I gave it up, and went to work in a vulcanizing place, vulcanizing tires. The heat is something like twelve hundred degrees. They had me and a Polish guy working together. Those Polish guys can work their asses off. The molds were so hot, when you'd have to lift a tire out, sometimes I'd touch it, and I'd get hot silicone on my arms. Both of my arms got infected to the point where I couldn't move them."

"Great for a bass player," I said.

"Right!" John said, laughing. "So I left that job and went to Buffalo. I worked at a hotel with a piano player named Jimmy Manuel. All during that winter, I kept telling him, 'Hey, man, you better get somebody else for next year, 'cause I'm not going to be here another winter.'"

"The sky just unloads on that town in winter!" I said. "And the wind comes off the lake. It's almost as bad as Chicago."

"It is. But, while I was there, I met Sammy Noto, and Joe Romano, and some other cats. Sammy had an after hours club called the Boar's Head. I used to go over and play with those guys after I'd get off the other gig. Around April, after that winter, Jon Hendricks came in town, working at the Royal Arms. I worked with him that week, and he said, 'I'm going to Toronto, and I need a bass player. Why don't you come on the road with me? We're going back out to San Francisco.' Working with him was more than I bargained for, because he used to do Count Basie things, so eight months of that with Jon, traveling, was wonderful.

"After that I stayed in San Francisco. I used to play at the Half Note. George Duke was in the conservatory then, just out of high school. He copped the gig. And Al Jarreau was the vocalist. Al was a social worker at the time, moonlighting as a singer. Pete Magadini was playing drums, a hell of a drummer. That was the group in this club. We worked Thursdays, Fridays, Saturdays and Sundays. We were two blocks from the Both-And Club, where John Handy played a lot.

"I was learning the instrument by watching everybody play. I had just gotten married. I met Carolyn in Pittsburgh. She's from Duquesne, Pennsylvania, Earl Hines' home town. We lived in a boarding house with John Handy's rhythm section—Don Thompson on bass and Terry Clarke on drums and Michael White on piano. That's when John made the record of *Spanish Lady*. I used to listen to those guys all the time, and Don and I used to hang out every night. Don is one of my biggest influences. Handy brought Don and Terry down from Vancouver at that time. They were hot. They blew the Monterey Festival away that year.

"Before that there was a bass player from out here named Albert Stinson, who came through Pittsburgh. He was playing with Chico Hamilton's group, with Gabor Szabo and Charles Lloyd and George Bohanon. I went down to hear them. I was watching this kid Albert Stinson play with this facility, all those fingers going, playing his ass off, just a young cat. So I hung out with him a couple of times. He was turning me onto all these method books, which I hated doing, because I hated practicing. I never practiced. I'd get migraines from it. I'd go mow the lawn, wash windows, run errands, do anything but practice. But I always worked. Every night I played a gig somewhere. That was my practicing—on the bandstand. But Don Thompson and these guys, I learned the fingerings, the thumb positions, from watching them. Then I heard Eddie Gomez, who came out here to the West Coast, before he joined Bill Evans. He was playing melody with chords. I kept thinking, 'What is *this*?'

"Israel Crosby with Ahmad Jamal was my first big influence. Israel played the root plus all kinds of counter-melodies. And there was Slam Stewart singing with the arco. And then you got Major Holley who kind of plays the same way, but not exactly. Major sings an octave lower than Slam. That's how you tell them apart. And Andy Simpkins. I loved Andy Simpkins. I listened to him a lot.

"That period at the Half Note in San Francisco was very important to me. Once in a while they'd bring in Miles, bring in 'Trane, bring in Wes Montgomery. They used to come down to the Half Note. And Cannon, when he'd play the Workshop. Sundays they'd be off and they'd come over to the Half Note and play with us. So I was playing with everybody, and learning a lot.

"I came to L.A. after being up in the Bay Area in '68 and '69, and played around town here. I worked with Shelly Manne. And then I got a call to join Count Basie. I thought, 'Maybe I should pass on this.' But I went, and, as it worked out, I showed up out at Disneyland. The band was getting ready to hit. Basie was playing one of his intros. I asked Al Grey, 'Which tune?' Al said, 'Four twenty-five.' Somebody else said, 'Five ninety.' Somebody said, 'A hundred and twenty.' I said, 'Well fuck these guys.' But when the band came in, I knew the arrangement from working with Jon Hendricks. And the whole night went like that. I didn't read one note. And that's how I caught that gig. I was with Basie for about two years that time. Then I left and worked with Ahmad Jamal, then I went back with Basie. And then with Oscar Peterson. And Kenny Burrell."

"Aren't you going to miss music?" I said.

Again John waved a hand at his pictures. "This *is* music," he said. "It is the culmination of all the years I've been painting and playing. People have asked me, 'What do you think about when you're playing?' I think about color, form, line, texture. As opposed to playing C, E-flat, G and B-flat on this chord. I hear a chord and I think, 'Man, that reminds me of this.' And I play forms, like a landscape or something. Or like a figure moving. I've never thought about the academics of playing, the notes. Or the math of music. I never thought about that. Which, in the back of my head, kept telling me, 'You're *inadequate* to this situation.' I'd see guys writing, and saying, 'This melody doesn't go with this diminished here, why don't you play A?' and then they'll write the chord change F-sharp over A, or whatever. I never knew what the hell they were talking about. I was just waiting for them to play the chord so I could hear it and play what I wanted.

"This year will be about it for music. This is more important. For personal gratification. For being master of my own universe. I don't have to deal with anybody when I paint. I don't have to deal with anybody's petty emotions, never have to play up to them. Which I never did very much anyway. This way I can totally eliminate all that. It's like a perfect way to live."

I said, "There's a difference between music and literature compared to painting and sculpture. Painting and sculpture exist in space, music and literature exist in time. It takes you this long or that long to listen to a song or read a story. But a painting or a sculpture is simply there. It may take you a certain amount of time to perceive it and digest it, but that's your problem. But in music there's a constant flow-by."

John said, "When I paint—this is odd—it's work work work. People come by, and I get them involved with it. So I constantly have this dialogue. A woman came by last week, and we were arguing about something about how she makes salsa, so I got the paint and did it the way she saw it. Her eyes kind of lit up and she said, 'You're a performer even when you paint.' I said, 'I never thought about it.' The vibes coming from an audience when you're playing make you reach for that ultimate moment of magic, which we all do—or should. When that moment happens, and you're not thinking about it any more, you don't have to think about it, it's right and you know that it's right, the ambience in the room is perfect, the audience is perfect, their response is making you reach for things you normally wouldn't, because you're on that level . . . you try for that moment, and sometimes it comes out perfect. That's what keeps you performing that 85 percent of the time when it ain't happening, right? That one moment can make you say, 'Oh yeah, I know what that's like, I'm going to try for that again.' But painting, I can work on it at my own pace, my own rhythm, there's no hurry. It's not something that's here and then gone—that one note, it's not right, but it's gone. In painting you don't have to deal with that. I can try something and say, 'That's not exactly what I wanted,' and walk away and come back next day and say, '*That*'s what I wanted.' Music's not like that.

"And there's always the matter of playing up to other people, which is a role I had myself in for twenty-five years—playing in a sideman situation. And I'm not a company boy. Like, when a piano player calls out a tune, *How High the Moon*, and at that time I think, 'I don't want to play this tune.' But the piano player goes into *How High the Moon*, and I play *How High the Moon*, and since I'm there playing, I'm going to try to make this guy sound like the best piano player in the world. That's always been my attitude as a sideman: make the guy out front sound as great as he possibly can. Maybe that's why I work all the time. Rhythm is my thing. I like grooves. But many times, playing with people—Oscar, or Ahmad, or Count Basie's band—I'll be saying to myself, 'I don't like this tune,' but I'll always try to make it sound fantastic. Later for how I feel. But

I've done that, man, for twenty-five years, and now I want to get into the world where I'm master of my own thing, without having nobody else over me *or* under me."

I said, "So many musicians write well, so many are interested in photography and painting. Bill Evans used to doodle constantly with a pen, and the things he did were quite interesting."

"Yeah, I know," John said. "I've got some of Bill's things. We were hanging out one night, in a restaurant. He was talking and doodling, making things, and I said, 'I *want* them.' He says, 'Oh, I'll do you another one.' I've got them here in the house somewhere."

"Tony Bennett paints," I said. "So does Peggy Lee. I think the fascination with one form of art carries over into all the others. George Gershwin was a good painter. There's a wonderful portrait he did of Jerome Kern that I saw on the wall of Harold Arlen's apartment in New York. George Wettling was an artist of professional stature."

John said, "At Bradley's restaurant, in New York, on the walls of the office, there are a lot of Jimmy Rowles' caricatures, with little captions on them. They're little classics. Just a couple of lines. He's fantastic at that."

John fell silent for a moment, as if reflecting on that future time when he would no longer pick up the bass.

"I owned my first bass when I was twenty-two years old," he said. "I played first on a high school bass that was just a piece of lumber. One bass I played was made out of aluminum. Not much fun, if you really want to play.

"You should hear my bass now. I just had a new fingerboard put on it. Now I want to play! I'm really working on it. I told my wife, 'I think I messed up. I should have never started messing around with that bass.' It sounds really good now. The bottom end. I can hold a note forever on the bottom end! I've got a record date coming up with George Cables, and I can't wait!

"The instrument is totally unexplored. For one thing, jazz players haven't got that real clean arco playing down."

"They're often fuzzy and out of tune," I said.

"Yeah, they are. Arco tells on you, real fast, as opposed to pizzicato. That will probably evolve. And then that chord thing that Eddie Gomez and those guys got into, there's a lot more that could be done with that. And there's also false harmonics, that make the bass sound in the higher register, like a cello. They're all things I've done. But to *improvise* doing that—no one's ever played a solo with the bow in false harmonics. It would be incredible. And it's possible."

"And you say you're going to walk away from it?" I said. "We'll see! Are you going to go back to Nigeria?"

"You bet."

The man's name is Augustine Alibi, pronounced All-ee-bee. He is the son of a tribal chieftain, a warm and friendly man who speaks elegant English—"the King's English," as John put it. He is the police commissioner of Ibadon, one of Nigeria's largest cities. Some years ago, he attended a seminar on law enforcement at Pitt University in Pittsburgh. Through her position in the district attorney's office, John's sister Freddia met him, and married him.

Five years ago, John went on a concert tour of Nigeria with Pearl Bailey and Louie Bellson, partly in order to visit his sister. Much of the slave trade to America originated in Nigeria. The Portuguese began it. Then it was taken up by the British, though not for long. They outlawed slavery in 1807 and began a legitimate Nigerian trade in palm oil and other products. They also stationed a naval squadron off the Nigerian coast to intercept and interrupt the slave trade of other nations. These actions left Britain in good odor with the Nigerians, and they are part of the historical reason why Nigeria in 1960 became an independent state within the British Commonwealth. Nonetheless, for a time there was a brisk slave trade in Nigeria, the coastal tribes selling off captives, taken in internecine warfare, to white slavers in the markets of Lagos. Though John may know little about his grandparents, and nothing at all of their lineage, it's entirely possible that his people came from Nigeria, which touches the sea in that elbow of the West African coast.

Enjoying the company of his sister and his Nigerian in-laws, he made other friends as well. He told one of them that he was particularly interested in the country's tradition of ebony carving. In the city of Benin, his friend took him to the large work hut of a famous wood-carver. There were two or three generations of apprentices at work. Near the front of the hut, which was twenty-five or thirty feet wide, young boys were cleaning up the detritus of the work. Farther into the hut, somewhat older boys were sharpening and repairing the carving tools. Still farther in, young men were making carvings and taking their work to the master for finishing or approval.

The old man, with white hair, was seated at the back of the room. He did not rise. John's friend told him in Ibo, "We have a visitor from America. He has come to see your work."

The old man looked at John and said something. John's friend translated: "He says, 'Welcome home.'"

John began to come apart emotionally. The master carver smiled. "He reached up and patted me on the back," John said. "I stayed all day and watched him work. I learned a hell of a lot." His voice was becoming frayed as he recalled the incident.

He didn't sound so tough to me.

9

THE POET:
BILL EVANS

I T   I S   A   C O M M O N P L A C E   of psychology that people remember
very precisely the circumstances in which they learned of certain
historic events—for Americans, the death of John F. Kennedy, in
China the death of Mao Tse-tung. A great many musicians and
other music lovers can recall with comparable vividness their discovery of Bill Evans.

In 1963, in Auckland, New Zealand, a fifteen-year-old boy,
hearing piano music emanating from a shop, entered, listened to
his first Bill Evans record, and burst into tears. This event changed
the course of Alan Broadbent's life. He went on to become one of
the finest jazz pianists in a generation of players influenced by
Evans. And more than twenty years later, he recalled that moment
of discovery as if it had been a week ago.

I recall my own discovery of Evans with similar clarity. It
occurred in the early summer of 1959, shortly after I joined *Down
Beat*. In the office, I noticed among a stack of records awaiting
assignment for review a gold-covered Riverside album titled *Everybody Digs Bill Evans*, bearing the signed endorsements of Miles
Davis, Cannonball Adderley, Ahmad Jamal, and others of like stature. I took the album home and, sometime after dinner, probably
about nine o'clock, put it on the phonograph. At 4 a.m. I was still
listening, though by now I had it memorized.

I remember my amazement not so much at the brilliance of the playing—itself cause enough for wonder—as at the emotional content of the music. Until then I had assumed, albeit unconsciously, that I alone had the feelings therein expressed. His playing spoke to me in an intensely personal way. And as the years have gone by, I have discovered that he had the same effect on many people. Martin Williams, in his annotation to the complete set of Bill's Riverside recordings, reissued by the Fantasy label in 1984, refers to Bill's as "some of the most private and emotionally naked music I have ever heard."

Music is the art that expresses the inexpressible, the language beyond language that communicates what words can never convey, summoning shades of emotion for which we have no words. The Eskimo language is said to contain sixteen or so words for snow, since the people speaking it have need for such refined expression of the conditions they encounter. Our vocabulary for the nuances of emotion is inadequate, though we can somewhat compensate for this by creating compound words such as happy-sad, wistful-joyous, surprised-pleased, and the like. But music can go beyond that. It doesn't and of course can't name these subtle nameless emotions. It can evoke them.

And no one had ever evoked emotions that I feel the way Bill Evans did. Since he has had this effect on so many other people, many of whom are fanatic in their admiration of his work, musicians and laymen alike, one faces the inescapable conclusion that Bill Evans was "saying" something in his music of prodigious pertinence to our era and the people doomed to live in it.

Within a day or two of hearing *Everybody Digs*, I wrote Bill a fan letter. I recall saying that the album sounded like love letters written to the world from some prison of the heart. It struck me even then that to anyone of the sensitivity so manifest in the music, life must be extraordinarily painful—which turned out to be all too true.

I decided to put Bill on the cover of *Down Beat*, and assigned the New York writer Don Nelson, who knew him, to write the accompanying article. I myself wanted to know more about this young man from Plainfield, New Jersey. Bill always gave credit to this exposure for helping to loft his recording career, but I think he exaggerated the value of that article, and the many others that I wrote about him afterwards. His career would have crested inevitably because of that peculiar power he had to move people. To this day, people are extraordinarily possessive about him, so many of his admirers seeming to believe that he or she alone perceives and appreciates his music. This possessiveness is an odd phenomenon, without any precedent that I know.

Oscar Peterson had raised the level of playing the piano in jazz to the proficiency long the norm in classical music. One musician made this apt observation: "It was said in their own time that Liszt conquered the piano, Chopin seduced it. Oscar is our Liszt and Bill is our Chopin." The poetry of Bill's playing compels the comparison to Chopin, whose music, incidentally, Bill played exquisitely. The pattern of chords in eighth notes in *Young and Foolish* on *Everybody Digs*, for example, recalls the Chopin E-minor Prelude. Bill certainly knew the literature. I once saw him, in Warren Bernhardt's apartment, sitting with his head down over the keyboard of Warren's Steinway, in that characteristic posture, sight-reading Rachmaninoff preludes at tempo. Oscar Peterson brought jazz piano to the bravura level of the great Romantic pianists. Bill, influenced by Oscar in his early days, brought to bear coloristic devices and voicings and shadings from post-Romantic composers, including Debussy, Ravel, Poulenc, Scriabin, and maybe Alban Berg. After listening to a test pressing of *Conversations with Myself* that I had sent him, Glenn Gould phoned to say of Bill, "He's the Scriabin of jazz." I had no idea whether Bill was even that familiar with Scriabin, but sure enough, he turned out to be a Scriabin buff, and gave me a soft and enormously enlightening dissertation on that Russian, whose mysticism seemingly appealed to a like element in Bill's own half-Russian half-Welsh soul.

I quoted that remark of Gould's in print, only to have my friend the noted classical music critic Robert Offergeld take issue with it. "More to the point," Bob said, "he was the Bill Evans of jazz. He could produce a broader range of tonal color in thirty-two measures than Glenn Gould did in his whole career."

Bill managed to blend in his playing sophisticated methods with a trusting youthful emotionality, almost like the music of Grieg. I was discussing Grieg with Bill once, specifically the lovely *Holberg Suite*. "I went through a phase of pretending I didn't like Grieg," I said.

"So did I," Bill said.

And, anticipating his answer, I said, "I know what happened to me, but what happened to you?"

"The intellectuals got to me," he said.

The mood of the *Everybody Digs* album is one of springtime lilac poignancy. It is the second Riverside album. *New Jazz Conceptions*, which preceded it, is brittle by comparison. Bill had electrified the profession before that with solos on *All About Rosie*, a tune in a record by Tony Scott, and *Billie the Kid* by his composer friend George Russell.

Something happened in the two years between *New Jazz Conceptions* (September 1956) and *Everybody Digs* (December 1958): Bill found his way into the heart of his own lyricism. After that Bill formed a standing trio, with bassist Scott LaFaro and drummer Paul Motian, with which group Orrin Keepnews produced a series of Riverside albums that constitute one of the most significant bodies of work in the history of jazz.

Bill wanted it to be a three-way colloquy, rather than pianist-accompanied-by-rhythm-section. And it was. LaFaro, still in his early twenties, had developed bass playing to a new level of facility. He had a gorgeous tone and unflagging melodicism. Motian, Armenian by background, had since childhood been steeped in a music of complex time figures and was able to feed his companions patterns of polyrhythm that delighted them both.

Pianists waited for their albums to come out almost the way people gather at street-corners in New York on Saturday night to get the Sunday *Times*: *Portrait in Jazz*, *Explorations*, and the last two, *Waltz for Debby* and *Sunday at the Village Vanguard*, derived from afternoon and evening sessions recorded live on June 25, 1961. These albums alone (which are best heard in the compact-disk reissues from Fantasy, which have superb sound), if Bill had never recorded anything else, would have secured his position in jazz. Indeed, his solo on Johnny Carisis's tune *Israel*, a soaring flight of breath-taking melodic invention, which is in the *Explorations* album, would almost have done that. There is a deep spirituality in those Riverside albums, the more astounding when you realize that Bill was at that time sinking into his heroin addiction, to Scott LaFaro's helpless dismay. If you look at the album covers in sequence, you find Bill's face getting thinner.

In the photo taken for the interior cover of *Undercurrent*, the duet album he made with Jim Hall for the UA label a couple of years later, you can see a tell-tale Bandaid on Bill's right wrist.

Warren Bernhardt said of Bill in 1963, "Everything he plays seems to be the distillation of the music. In *How Deep Is the Ocean*, he never states the original melody. Yet his performance is the quintessence of it. On *My Foolish Heart*, he plays nothing but the melody, but you still receive that essence of the thing.

"Pianistically, he's beautiful. He never seems to be hung up in doing anything he wants to do, either technically or harmonically. When he's confronted with a choice in improvisation, he doesn't have to wonder which voicing of a chord is best. He *knows*. A given voicing will have different effects in different registers, especially when you use semitones as much as he does. So he constantly shifts voicings, depending on the register. And he is technically capable of executing his thought immediately. It's as if the line between his brain and his fingers were absolutely direct."

"It's reached the point," Bill said, "where I'm seldom conscious of the physical effort of playing. I simply think, and there's no conscious transmission to the fingers."

Bill had his clichés, as every jazz musician does. But they were very much his. Many pianists have adopted them, and still more have tried. He was far and away the most influential jazz pianist after Bud Powell. And he used his various configurations in interesting combinations. There were, however, times when he seemed stuck in them. Had I not known of what he was capable, I would doubtless have found these performances marvelous. But his work at such times bored me, a fact I always tried to conceal from him, although he probably knew. Perhaps he too was bored by it.

There was something special in *Everybody Digs* that had been lost. And he seemed to want to combine both qualities.

Bill was one of those elegantly co-ordinated people. His posture and his bespectacled mien made him seem almost fragile, but stripped, he was, at least in his thirties, strong and lean, with well-delineated musculature. He had played football in college, he was a superb driver with fine reflexes (who, like Glenn Gould, had a taste for snappy cars), he was a golfer of professional stature, and he was, by all testimony, a demon pool shark.

When he was young, he looked like some sort of sequestered and impractical scholastic. There is a heartbreaking photo of him on the cover of the famous Village Vanguard recordings, made for Riverside in the early summer of 1961. Whether that photo was taken before or after the grim fiery death of Scott LaFaro in an automobile accident ten days after the sessions, I do not know. But there is something terribly vulnerable and sad in Bill's young, gentle, ingenuous face. I knew Scott LaFaro only slightly, through Bill, and I didn't like him. He seemed to me smug and self-congratulatory. But he was a brilliant bass player, as influential on his instrument as Bill was on his, and Bill always said LaFaro was not at all like that when you got past the surface, which I never did. The shock of LaFaro's death stayed with Bill for years, and he felt vaguely guilty about it. This is not speculation. He told me so. He felt that because of his heroin habit he had made insufficient use of the time he and Scott had had together. LaFaro was always trying to talk him into quitting. After LaFaro's death, Bill was like a man with a lost love, always looking to find its replacement. He found not so much a replacement of LaFaro as an alternative in the virtuosic Eddie Gomez, who was with him longer than any other bassist.

In any event, to look into that face, with its square short small-town-America 1950s haircut, is terribly revealing, particularly when you contrast it with Bill's later photos. He looked like the young WASP in those days, which he never was—he was a Celtic Slav—but in the later years, when he had grown a beard and left his hair long in some sort of final symbolic departure from Plainfield, New Jersey, he looked more and more Russian, which his mother was. She used to read his Russian fan mail to him, and answer it. Russian jazz fans, I am told, think of him as their own.

Bill was politically liberal and passionately anti-racist. His speech was low level, but he was highly literate and articulate. He was expert on the novels of Thomas Hardy, and he was fascinated with words and letters and their patterns. The title *Re: Person I Knew*, one of his best-known compositions, is an anagram on the name of Orrin Keepnews, who produced for Riverside all Bill's early albums and was one of his first champions. Another of Bill's titles, *N.Y.C.'s No Lark*, is an anagram on the name of Sonny Clark, who Bill said was one of his influences, along with Nat Cole and Oscar Peterson and Bud Powell.

Bill's knowledge of the entire range of jazz piano was phenomenal. Benny Golson says that when he first heard Bill—they were both in their teens—he played like, of all people, Milt Buckner. One night late at the Village Vanguard in New York, when there was almost no audience, Bill played about ten minutes of "primitive" blues. "I can really play that," he said afterwards with a sly kind of little-boy grin. And he could.

He had a big technique. I doubt if anyone in the history of jazz piano had more. Yet he never, never showed off those chops for the mere display of them. He kept technique in total subservience to expression. But he assuredly had it.

One of the greatest glories of his playing was his tone. Trilingual people will often be found to speak their third language with the accent of the second. I suspect this phenomenon may carry over into music. Oscar Peterson learned to play trumpet almost as soon as he learned piano, which may in part explain his brilliant projecting sound. Bill was a fine flutist, although he rarely if ever played the instrument in the later years.

The level of his dynamics was often kept low, like his speech. He was a soft player. But within that range, his playing was full of subtle dynamic shadings and constantly shifting colors. Some physicists have argued that a pianist cannot have a personal and individual "tone" because of the nature of the instrument, which consists of a bunch of felt hammers hitting strings. So much for theory. It is all in how the hammers are made to strike the strings, as well of course as the more obvious effects of pedaling, of which Bill was a master.

Bill's was a comparatively flat-fingered approach, as opposed to the vertical hammer-stroke attack with which so many German piano teachers tensed up the hands and ruined the playing of generations of American children. Bill used to argue with me that his playing was not all that flat-fingered, but I sat low by the keyboard on many occasions and watched, and it certainly looked that way to me. On one such occasion, I kidded him about his rocking a finger on a key on a long note at the end of a phrase. After all, the hammer has already left the string: one has no further physical contact with the sound. "Don't you know the piano has no vibrato?" I said.

"Yes," Bill responded, "but trying for it affects what comes before it in the phrase." That is more than a little mystical, but he was right. Dizzy Gillespie and Lalo Schifrin were once in Erroll Garner's room at the Chateau Marmont in Los Angeles. Erroll was putting golfballs into a cup against the wall. Dizzy asked if he might try it, took Erroll's putter, and sank one ball after another, to the amazement of Erroll and Lalo, who asked if he had played a lot of golf. He said he had never done it before. How, then, was he doing it? "I just imagine," Dizzy said, "that I'm the ball and I want to be in the cup." He with a golfball and Bill with a vibrato influencing events in time already past were, deliberately or no, practicing something akin to Zen archery.

Bill did not always have that sound, or more precisely that astonishing palette of colors. Some time before he recorded *Everybody Digs*, he took a year off and went into comparative reclusion to rebuild his tone, with which he was dissatisfied. I doubt that he consciously sought to be flute-like, but some ideal derived from playing that other instrument surely was in his conception. Whatever the process, the result of that year was the golden sound that in recent years has often been emulated though never equaled.

And that year was typical of him.

He made absolutely no claims for himself. Orrin Keepnews had a hard time talking him into making his first album as a leader, *New Jazz Conceptions*, in late 1956, when Bill was twenty-eight. It is, incidentally, a remarkable album even now, a highly imaginative excursion through bebop, in which we hear strong hints of the Bill Evans that he would within two years become. When Orrin gathered those testimonials from Miles Davis and the rest for the cover of *Everybody Digs*, Bill said, "Why didn't you get one from my mother?" But what he was—an emergent genius—was apparent to every musician with ears. Credit for the earliest discovery goes to Mundell Lowe, who heard him in New Orleans when Bill was still an undergraduate at Southeastern Louisiana College. (He was graduated as an honor student with two degrees, Bachelor of Music with a piano major, and Bachelor of Music Education.) Mundell hired him for summer jobs during that period.

Bill always disliked formal practice and evaded it in childhood. He would play through a huge pile of second-hand sheet music his mother had bought. It contained sentimental turn-of-the-century songs, marches, and classical music. Because of that experience, Bill was an uncanny sight reader.

He retained his cavalier attitude to practice even at Southeastern Louisiana. His teachers found his attitude frustrating and infuriating. He would turn up at classes unable to play the scales and arpeggios assigned him but able to execute flawlessly any composition that contained them. "They couldn't flunk me," he said in what for him was an intemperate burst of immodesty, "because I played the instrument so well." And now that same college houses the Bill Evans Archives.

"It's just that I've played such a *quantity* of piano," he said. "Three hours a day in childhood, about six hours a day in college, and at least six hours now. With that, I could afford to develop slowly. Everything I've learned, I've learned with feeling being the generating force.

"I've never approached the piano as a thing in itself but as a gateway to music. I knew what I wanted to play. But I relaxed with it, knowing I would be able to eventually."

Whereas many jazz musicians build solos in sections of four, eight, or sixteen bars, Bill seemed able to think in units as large as or larger than the full thirty-two-bar chorus. He would obliterate the chorus unit, building an entire solo into a seamless whole. To be sure, there was not as much form as one would find in classical music.

"Obviously," Bill said, "you can't find in jazz the perfection of craft that is possible in contemplative music. Yet, oddly enough, this very lack of perfection can result in good jazz. For example, in classical music, a mistake is a mistake. But in jazz, a mistake can be—in fact, must be—justified by what follows it. If you were improvising a speech and started a sentence in a way you hadn't intended, you would have to carry it out so that it would make sense. It is the same in spontaneous music.

"In good contemplative composition, the creator tries to *recapture* those qualities—the trouble is that there are a lot of so-called composers who compose primarily by putting together tones in a logical structure they have set up. But spontaneous material can be worked over and developed, according to the limits of the person's craft. And the result will in some way be in touch with the universal language of understanding in music."

"If," I asked, "through travel in a time machine, you could hear Beethoven or Chopin improvising, would you call it jazz?"

"Jazz is not a what," Bill said, "it is a how. If it were a what, it would be static, never growing. The how is that the music comes from the moment, it is spontaneous, it exists at the time it is created. And anyone who makes music according to this method conveys to me an element that makes his music jazz."

Bill said once, "I had to work harder at music than most cats, because you see, man, I don't have very much talent."

The remark so astonished me that some ten years later, I challenged him on it.

"But it's true," he said. "Everybody talks about my harmonic conception. I worked very hard at that because I didn't have very good ears."

"Maybe working at it is the talent," I said. Like working on the reconstruction of his tone for a year. The bassist Ray Brown remarked once, "They," meaning, I suppose, jazz fans and some critics, "think we just roll out of bed and play the D major scale." The implication was that major musicians, major artists of all kinds, work very hard at their craft. Perhaps that is what makes the difference, as Bill intimated. He once told me that when he and the late Don Elliott, a friend during their adolescence in New Jersey, were in high school, they knew several young musicians they thought were more talented than they. But those young players to whom it had come so easily all dropped out of music, while Don and Bill remained in the profession to join the ranks of its serious practitioners—perhaps because they had the deeper fascination with its mysteries.

I do not for a moment pretend objectivity about the life and work of Bill Evans. I was much too involved in it, at several levels. It went far beyond that first *Down Beat* cover. One of the most important relationships of his life was with Helen Keane, tall and blonde and Nordic, who became first his manager and later his record producer as well. I introduced them in 1962. The three of us profoundly affected each other's lives. Like many men, I am reticent to discuss personal relationships, but Helen talked about ours in an interview with Linda Dahl for the book *Stormy Weather*, a collection of essays about women in jazz, so it's no secret.

She told Dahl, "Along the way I met . . . Gene Lees. He had just left his editorship at *Down Beat*. After he came to New York, we fell in love and we were together for years. Right away he said, 'I want you to hear Bill Evans . . . You should be his manager.'"

In that summer of 1962 I found Bill's life and career in hideous disarray. Due to an error of the American Federation of Musicians, he had validated contracts with two managers, one of whom was the late Joe Glaser, president of Associated Booking Corporation and Louis Armstrong's personal manager. Glaser was a harsh and rather crude man with known underworld associations. He and his company, which made capital of Armstrong's show-boating, were indifferent to an artist of Bill's sensitivity, if indeed anyone in that office was capable of perceiving it. And Bill was in the worst phase of his narcotics habit, borrowing money wherever he could.

He played a gig at the Hickory House on 52nd Street. His bass-ist on that job was Hal Gaylor, an excellent player from Montreal who had been with Chico Hamilton and Tony Bennett. Hal, about six feet tall, had very large and sinewy hands, full of the strength that years of playing the bass impart.

Bill was late for the job one night.

"I knew where he was," Hal recalled in 1987. "He was down at this guy's apartment in the Village, getting his stuff. I knew where he was because I used to pick him up there. And I used to cop there myself." Hal was at that time an occasional heroin user. Later he became firmly addicted, then kicked his habit and now works as a drug counselor in Monroe County, New York. "I went down there, and the guy had just got in his shipment. And he was toying with Bill, playing games with him. I could see that Bill was sick, and I just wigged. I banged the table, the stuff flew up in the air, and I grabbed this guy. I scared him—scared myself, too. The guy's wife was screaming, it was a bad scene, and Bill was just sit-ting there, sick. I told the guy, 'You fix him up, right *now*! Or I'm going to blow all this stuff away!' So the guy gave Bill his bag, and we left. Bill did it up right in the car."

One day Bill came out of the office of Riverside Records in mid-town Manhattan, having just borrowed some money from Orrin Keepnews. He got into a taxi to head for his connection. Another well-known musician, also an addict, opened the taxi door, grabbed the money out of Bill's hand, and ran off.

I was only too aware of the sordid conditions of Bill's life—of the pushers, including one named Bebop who came to Bill's apart-ment one day while I was there, and of the loan sharks threatening to break his hands if he did not immediately repay the money he'd borrowed for his habit.

I felt that Helen Keane was one of the most conscientious and capable talent managers in the business. At that time she was Mark Murphy's manager. She had been substantially instrumental in launching the careers of Marlon Brando and Harry Belafonte. I took her to see Bill at the Village Vanguard.

"Oh no," she said, after she'd heard about sixteen bars, "oh no, not this one. This is the one that could break my heart." How prophetic that remark turned out to be. Nonetheless, when we went back uptown and sat in a back booth in Jim and Andy's and talked about Bill, she agreed to manage him, assuming that he was willing to have her do so, which I knew he was.

But there was the problem of his contracts with the two other managers. Bill got copies of the contracts for me. I telephoned the late Herman Kenin, then president of the American Federation of Musicians, with whom I was on cordial terms. I had done some favors for the union and, as they say in New York, he owed me. I asked him to have lunch with me. Toward the end of the lunch I showed him the two contracts, bearing union validations.

"There's no doubt about it," Herman said. "The union made a mistake. Which contract do you want cancelled?"

"Both of them," I said, and Herman Kenin annulled the contracts, opening the way for Helen Keane to become Bill's manager.

Bill followed a daily routine at that time. He would go into a telephone booth—the phone in his apartment on West 104th Street was usually disconnected—and leaf through his address book, calling one friend after another. One day Bob Brookmeyer lost his patience and told him angrily, "How come you only call me when you want to borrow money?"

Bill phoned me late one afternoon. I was going through a tough time of it myself. He asked if I could lend him ten dollars. Remembering Brookmeyer, I too lost my temper and said, "God damn it, I don't even have enough money to eat tonight!" and hung up on him.

Perhaps an hour later the phone rang again. I heard that low-key voice. "Gene? This's Bill. I got enough money for both of us. Let's go and eat."

During this period, Bill's wife, Ellaine, of whom I was extremely fond, made a valiant attempt to get them both off dope. In an amazing display of strength, she quit using, and composed a pledge that she tried to get Bill to sign—a promise that he too would quit. One severe winter night, probably in January or February of 1962, I went up to their apartment. The three of us had planned to go to a movie, but it was obvious that Bill had no intention of going anywhere. Ellaine, fiercely angry, insisted that I take her anyway. Bill urged us to go. We went to some movie house on 42nd Street, which had not then been taken over by the porn industry, although it was seedy enough. Afterwards, when we came out of the theater, it was cruelly cold. We didn't have enough money for a taxi. We stood waiting for a subway train in the station under Rockefeller Center. Ellaine was shivering. I opened my rain coat and put it around her and held her in my arms. She was so fragile from the dope; she seemed birdlike. We waited and waited, and at last got a train heading north. I dropped her off at their apartment and walked home in the cold.

All of us who cared about Bill were desperate about his condition. I became part of a conspiracy against him. Some of us reasoned—naively—that if he couldn't get money from his friends, he'd have to quit heroin. So Orrin Keepnews, Creed Taylor, Helen, and a few more of us tried to cut off his money sources. It didn't work. He'd just go to the loan sharks, who would then threaten to break his hands.

Ironically, at this very time, his career, under Helen's management, was beginning to take off. Riverside Records was going out of business. Helen negotiated a contract with Creed Taylor and Verve Records. And Bill began to get money from Creed. One day Helen went to Creed's office to discuss getting Bill yet another advance. She called me. She and Creed wanted me to take a message to Bill: Creed said that he would pay Bill's rent, pay his electric, telephone, and grocery bills, and would even pay for hospitalization if Bill would submit to it, but he wouldn't advance him one more penny in cash.

"Why me?" I said indignantly. "Why is it always me who has to take him the news?"

"Because you live near him," she said. "And he's waiting for an answer."

So again I went up to Bill's apartment. The electricity had been turned off. He had run an extension cord from a light fixture on the wall of the hallway up to and under his door. To this line a lamp was attached, the only one working in the apartment. We went out to a hamburger joint on Broadway, just above the point where West End Avenue intersects it. I gave Bill the news.

He was furious. "You people don't understand!" he said. "I'm kind of attached to shit."

"Bill," I said, "that may qualify as the understatement of the year."

"No, I mean it," he said. "You *don't* understand. It's like death and transfiguration. Every day you wake in pain like death, and then you go out and score, and that is transfiguration. Each day becomes all of life in microcosm."

This capacity of Bill's to be clear about and articulate the nature of his drug habit always mystified me. If he was the ultimate denial of the myth of the jazz musician as a folk artist, he also refuted every popular image of the drug addict. He told me some years later that he did not in his heart really regret his years of the drug experience, for he had learned something even from that: an understanding of and tolerance for his father, who was an alcoholic.

There was a moment, however, when I caught a glimpse of what heroin did for this extraordinarily intelligent and sensitive man. I tore a meniscus in my right knee and was told by doctors that it would have to be removed. The surgery was performed in Roosevelt Hospital. Evidently somebody didn't do something right, because the pain afterwards was terrible. The doctor ordered shots of some kind to relieve it. Bill came to see me. As we talked, the pain returned, gradually growing more severe. Finally I rang for the nurse, who gave me yet another shot. And I began to nod, in a way I had seen addicts do on many occasions. The warmth of the drug spread through my body and the pain dissolved in it, like sugar in tea. I would follow for a while what Bill, sitting at the bedside, was saying, then lose track of it, then return to it. Through a window I could see a steady rain. Somehow I didn't mind its melancholy. And the pain was gone, not only the pain in the knee but that of life itself. I felt reconciled to everything. Looking at Bill, I felt that I truly understood him. I fell asleep after a while, and when I awoke Bill was gone.

The next day I asked a nurse, "What is this drug that you're giving me?" I had noticed that I was vaguely looking forward to the pain in order to get the shot.

"Morphine," she said.

"What? Forget it!" I was terrified of the opium drugs, not only because of Bill but because of other friends such as John Coltrane, who'd been through the hell of quitting. "From here on," I told her, "I'll get by on aspirins."

It was about this time that the late pianist and teacher John Mehegan told Bill that some of his students knew of Bill's condition and were tempted to emulate him. Bill told John to turn on a tape recorder. He dictated an eloquent dissertation against drug use. It's no doubt lost by now. I do remember that he stated firmly that his style was well formed before he ever began using dope.

Orrin Keepnews said once that when So-and-So—he named a famous musician—came around to borrow dope money, it was easy to turn him down because he was an evil son of a bitch. But Bill broke your heart, Orrin said, because of the sweetness of his nature, and his immense moral decency. He would sit there in the outer office at Riverside, waiting patiently, until Orrin would advance him some more money.

One day—probably when Helen first negotiated the contract with Creed Taylor and Verve—Bill received a large advance, something like ten thousand dollars. He came by my apartment in a taxi and asked me to go with him on some errands. We went from one apartment building to another. I would hold the taxi while he went up and paid debts to friends. Then he would come down and consult the file cards he was carrying and order the taxi driver on to the next stop. He'd kept careful track of every penny he owed! He went through about six thousand dollars that afternoon, and at the end of it handed me two hundred dollars.

"What's that for?" I said.

"I hocked your record player, didn't I? And some of your records too."

A few years after this, I mentioned the experience to the late Zoot Sims, himself one of the many jazz musicians of that generation who had broken the heroin habit.

"Yeah," Zoot said. "I remember that time. I was playing at the Golden Circle in Stockholm. Bill walked in and handed me six hundred dollars. I didn't know how much I'd lent him, but he knew to the penny."

It was during that winter of 1962-63 that Bill got an idea for an overdubbed album in which he would play three pianos. Overdubbing was by now a widely used technique. It had been pioneered by Les Paul and Mary Ford, then used as a commercial gimmick by many singers, Patti Page among them. But it had rarely been used to serious artistic purpose. Neither Creed Taylor nor Helen nor I had any idea what Bill had in mind, but we took it on faith that he knew what he was doing. In January and February of 1963, the album was made in a series of remarkable sessions that made us all intensely aware of the clarity of Bill's musical thinking.

The album was recorded with the tape running at thirty inches per second. The industry standard was fifteen i.p.s., but the higher speed would more accurately capture Bill's tone. The album was made at Webster Hall, and the engineer was Ray Hall. Bill was playing Glenn Gould's Steinway.

Ray would tape Bill's first track. Bill was particularly fussy about the first one. He said that if that wasn't right, the other two couldn't be. Then, listening in headphones to what he had played before, he would add the second track, and finally a third.

The four of us in the control booth—Ray, Creed, Helen, and I—were constantly open-mouthed at what was going on. On the second track, Bill would play some strangely appropriate echo of something he'd done on the first. Or there would be some flawless pause in which all three pianists were perfectly together; or some deft run fitted effortlessly into a space left for it. I began to think of Bill as three Bills: Bill Left Channel, Bill Right, and Bill Center.

Bill Left would lay down the first track, stating the melody and launching into an improvisation for a couple of choruses, after which he would move into an accompanist's role, playing a background over which Bill Center would later play *his* solo. His mind obviously was working in three dimensions of time simultaneously, because each Bill was anticipating and responding to what the other two were doing. Bill Left was hearing in his head what Bill Center and Bill Right *were going to play* a half hour or so from now, while Bill Center and Bill Right were in constant communication with a Bill Left who had vanished into the past a half hour or an hour before. The sessions took on a feeling of science-fiction eeriness.

In the acclaim for his tone and his lyricism, it is easy to overlook Bill's time. By this point in his life, it had become extremely subtle. But it was *there*. Bill made several basic tracks on Alex North's *Love Theme from "Spartacus."* Bill had seen the film with Scott LaFaro, liked the theme, began performing it, and added it to the jazz repertoire. He somewhat altered the release of the tune. After he'd made about six passes at it, Creed Taylor pushed the log sheet along the console to Helen, silently pointing to the times he had marked. Though there were retards and pauses in the music, the time on the first take was, say, five minutes and four seconds. The rest of the takes were 5:06, 5:04, 5:05, 5:06—never a variation of more than a second or two. The final take was 5:05.

Warren Bernhardt had said that Bill always played the essence of a melody. But on *"Spartacus,"* he was playing more than the essence of a love theme, he was playing the essence of love itself, the essence of all tenderness. You love a woman with this feeling, or the autumn or a sunrise or a child.

When the album was finished, I found that repeated playing of that track yielded up constantly new beauties. But there was a mysteriously exquisite something, some sense of unfolding discovery, for the four of us who were in the control booth that day that would haunt my memory for years.

Empty Coke bottles stood all about Bill's feet. Bill had that taste for sugar that goes with heroin addiction. He ran out of dope and began to go into withdrawal. He was sweating. We all knew what he was suffering. I couldn't get the image of the final crucifixion in the movie out of my mind. Creed asked Bill if he wanted to call the session off. "No," Bill said. "Let's finish it." And he went on.

He played a lovely rippling figure at the opening, one that turned up again at the end, transformed into some spiritual quintessence. There is a cheerful and jaunty, almost martial, quality to the recording at one point, which makes the memory of the session all the more poignant. When Bill had completed the first two tracks, Creed and Helen and I all thought that he shouldn't do a third—that another one would only clutter what he had already done. We were wrong.

As the end of the track neared, the "third" Bill took the opening figure and extended it into a long, fantastic, flowing line that he wove in and out and around and through what the other two pianists were playing, never colliding with these two previous selves. That final line seemed like a magical firefly hurrying through a forest at night, never striking the trees, leaving behind a line of golden sparks that slowly fell to earth, illuminating everything around it. I think Helen and Creed were close to tears when he completed that track. I know I was.

Bill accomplished another prodigy at that period of his life. Putting a needle into his right arm, he hit a nerve. The arm went numb, becoming all but useless. Bill was contracted for a week's engagement at the Village Vanguard, and he needed the money. So he went to the job on the first night and played with his left hand only. His pedaling was always very skilled. That night he played accompanying chords below middle C with his left hand, depressing the center pedal, which sustains only lower notes, then jumped the hand up the keyboard to execute his fluent running lines. With one's eyes shut, it was hardly possible to tell there was anything amiss in his playing. This went on during the whole engagement. Word of it spread through the jazz community, and pianists flocked to the Vanguard from all over the city to watch this amazing event.

Then Bill told us he was going to leave New York for a while. He said he was going to kick his habit. He said he couldn't do it in these familiar haunts, where the stuff was so available. He thought he would have to get away from his usual life, at least for a while, if he were to succeed. He thought that the best place to do this would be at his mother's home in Florida. He and Ellaine gave up their apartment, she went home to her parents, Bill gave us his mother's telephone number and left.

After a while the musicians began to be aware of his absence, and a rumor went around in Jim and Andy's that he was dead. When I entered the place one afternoon, several of them asked me with alarm if it were true. I went directly to the phone booth and called the number in Florida. Bill answered. I remember the almost audible sigh of relief that went through the place when I stuck my head out of the booth and said, "Any of you guys want to talk to Bill Evans?"

Bill came back from Florida free, for the present, of his habit, and lived with me for a little while in the basement apartment I had on West End Avenue at 71st Street—right around the corner from Erroll Garner. Bill was nominated for a Grammy award for *Conversations with Myself.* Just before the banquet, he broke a front tooth. "How d'you like that? It's the first time in years I've had a reason to smile, and I have to go and do that."

Turn Out the Stars dates from that period. One night, while Bill was playing a gig somewhere, I was looking for a movie on late-night television, and came across a listing for a film called *Turn Off the Moon.* I didn't know then and don't know now what it was about. But the title stuck. Bill had been after me to write some songs with him—*Waltz for Debby* already bore my lyric. He wanted titles, or complete lyrics, to set to music. But I preferred to work the other way around, putting words to music. When he came home, I said, "I've got a title for you. *Turn Out the Stars*." He wrote the melody in the next day or two, and I then completed a lyric which, later, I found almost unbearably dark. *Yesterday I Heard the Rain* also dates from that period. It has music by the Mexican composer Armando Manzanero and my lyrics; Bill got in the habit of playing it, and recorded it in the Tokyo concert album.

That little apartment in the basement of a brownstone on West End Avenue, with a sofa and rumpsprung bottlegreen armchairs, a rented spinet piano and worn carpet, seemed hidden and safe. It was a kind of haven for both of us. Its kitchen and living room gave onto a small cement courtyard from which, if you looked up, you could see a rectangle of sky. Warren Bernhardt used to come by, and Gary McFarland, and Antonio Carlos Jobim. Bill used to wake me up mornings and give me impromptu harmony lessons. "I think of all harmony," he said one such morning, "as an expansion from and return to the tonic."

It was years before the value of that struck me.

"Why does a flat ninth work with a dominant chord?" I asked.

"It has to do with counterpoint more than harmony," he said. "It's the ninth of the dominant moving through the flat ninth to become the fifth of the tonic."

The day of the Grammy awards dinner arrived. Just starting to put his life back together, Bill had very little money, and nothing appropriate to wear. As it happened, I was storing a closetful of clothes for Woody Herman, one of the dapper dressers in the business. There was a particularly well-made blue blazer which, to Bill's surprise and mine, fit him perfectly. So he donned it. Just before we were to leave, I turned somehow and spilled a drink in his lap. Fortunately there was another pair of slacks that fit him. We picked up Helen and went to the banquet. And I managed to repeat the trick: I turned and spilled another drink in his lap. He laughed and said, "Man, are you trying to tell me something?" At that moment, they called his name. Bill picked up his Grammy for *Conversations* in soaking pants and Woody Herman's blazer.

Bill had never met Woody Herman, one of his early idols, and I arranged for the three of us to have lunch a few days later. Bill turned up wearing, to my horror, that blazer. "Do you like the jacket?" Bill said, after the formality of introduction.

"It looks faintly familiar," Woody said.

Bill flung it open with a matadorial gesture to show its brilliant lining. "How do you like the monogram?" he said. It was of course WH. "It stands," Bill said, "for William Heavens." And Woody laughed. Fortunately.

That evening we went to hear the band. Woody tried to introduce a tune only to be interrupted by some drunk blearily shouting, "Play *Woodpeckers' Ball*." Woody tried to talk him down but the drunk persisted, "Play *Woodpeckers' Ball*."

Finally Woody said, "All right, for Charlie Pecker over there, we're going to play *Woodpeckers' Ball*."

"Man," said Bill, who was quite shy, "that takes real hostility. If I tried that, some cat would come up on the bandstand and punch me in the mouth."

Bill had remarked to me at some point that, despite the obvious differences in their playing, he and Oscar Peterson played alike in that their work was pianistic. The influence of Earl Hines had become widespread, resulting in the phenomenon of so-called one-handed pianists, that is to say pianists playing "horn lines" in the right hand accompanied by laconic chords in the left. It was an approach to piano that reached a zenith in bebop, but for all the inventiveness of some of the players, it was an approach that eschewed much of what the instrument was capable of.

Precisely because it is not inherently an ensemble instrument, Gerry Mulligan had good reason to leave it out of his quartet— and precedent for doing so in the marching bands of New Orleans. Played to its full potential, the piano overwhelms everything around it, and so, in jazz, it must in a context of horns be played with exceptional restraint. The perfect orchestral jazz pianist was Count Basie, who understood this and actually restricted a considerable technique.

If the piano is to be what it inherently is, it must be taken away from the horns, allowed to do its solo turn, like a great magician or juggler. It is not by its nature an ensemble actor but a spell-binding story-teller. It is Homeric. Because jazz is a music whose tradition is so heavily rooted in horns, the instrument is therefore very much misunderstood, which fact results in those strange comments that Oscar Peterson plays "too much," the logical extension of which is that Bach writes too much. Art Tatum so thoroughly understood the nature of the problem that he preferred to play without rhythm section. If, however, a pianist wants to partake of that special joy of making music with a rhythm section, the logical context is the trio, a format elected by Nat Cole in those too-few years before his success as a singer overshadowed his brilliance as a pianist.

Oscar had changed the nature of jazz piano, Bill was changing it further, and perceptive listeners noticed that if Oscar had once influenced Bill, Bill was now influencing Oscar, at least in ballads.

I was asked to write an essay on Oscar Peterson for *Holiday* magazine in New York. I was musing on what Bill had said about the similarity in their playing. I realized that there were also similarities in personality, including a profound stubbornness. When Oscar made up his mind to something, he was absolutely intractable. And Bill was the same.

I noted that Oscar was born August 15, which made him a Leo. On a whim I phoned Bill, who was then living in Riverdale, and said, "What's your birthdate?"

"August 16," he said. "Why?"

"You're going to laugh," I said, and told him.

But he didn't laugh. He said, "I used to think there was nothing to it, but over the years I've noticed with my groups that the signs have often worked out. Leos do seem to be stubborn. You know," he said, naming a certain bassist whom he had fired, "he's a Leo. And he was always trying to run the group. I told him, 'Look, if you want to lead a trio, form your own.' But it didn't do any good, and I let him go." He paused a second, then said, "I'd never have a Leo in my trio."

I laughed out loud, partly at the sound of it and partly because he had in that generalization illustrated the very quality we were discussing. On the one hand, I cannot imagine Bill rejecting a man solely for his sun sign. On the other hand, as far as I know, Bill was ever afterwards the only Leo in that trio.

Bill's fortunes continued to rise. He and Ellaine moved into an apartment in Riverdale, and his life took on some of the elements of what is called normalcy.

Creed Taylor left Verve to form his own CTI label. Helen said to me, "Who's going to produce Bill now?"

"You are," I said. And she did, from then until the end, making some of Bill's finest albums.

The rest of the 1960s were good years, very productive years, for Bill, for me, for Helen. I became involved in the fledgling Montreux Jazz Festival in 1967. The next year I arranged for Bill to play it. I had already been there three weeks when Helen and Bill arrived with the rest of his trio, which at that time included Eddie Gomez on bass and Jack deJohnette on drums.

Bill, Helen, and I went to the Chateau de Chillon, just off the Montreux lakeshore, made famous by Lord Byron in the poem so many of us were forced to memorize in our school days. I took a photo of the castle; it became the cover of the album Helen produced from the concert Bill played that night. The three of us prowled the dungeon where Bonivard had been imprisoned, chained to a pillar for four years. We puttered through ancient chambers and examined a secret passage or two and a few beds wherein many a noble affair was doubtless consummated.

I was bitching about the music business.

Bill said, "Well, man, you and I have something most people don't—freedom. And you have more than I do, because you don't have to play a gig every night."

Bill played Montreux several times after that—and Rio de Janeiro and Tokyo and Paris.

The Verve period was followed by a brief one at Columbia Records, neither the most successful nor the most creative time of

Bill's life. Clive Davis, president of Columbia, tried to get him to make a rock album. Needless to say, the suggestion got nowhere. Then followed the long association with Fantasy, which is documented in an eleven-album package reissued by Fantasy in 1988.

I did not see Bill often in those years. I had moved to Toronto. Bill would occasionally play there. I realized that he was becoming a legend.

On arriving for a week at the Town Tavern, he called and said he needed a dentist: he had a toothache. I knew, from the Toronto musicians, of a dentist who was not only good at his work but was an accomplished pianist as well. I called him. His nurse said he was busy with a patient.

About six that evening, the dentist called me. He said that he had just finished a busy work day and asked the nurse if there had been any calls. She said someone had called on behalf of a Mr. Bill Evans, who needed a dentist.

"What did you tell him?" he said in alarm.

"I said you were too busy today to see anyone else," she told him.

"What?" he said. "Do you realize you turned down God?"

He packed a kit of tools, met Bill at the Town Tavern, and fixed the ailing tooth in the kitchen.

Bill had pianist friends in cities all over the world. When he was in Toronto, he would spend a lot of time with Doug Riley, a superb pianist who was strongly influenced by him. Doug's little boy heard Doug talk so much to his wife, also a musician, about Bill that when Bill was visiting them, he looked up adoringly and said, "What's your first name, Billevans?"

I followed Bill's Fantasy albums as they came out, marveling as always at the grace and intelligence of the playing. One track of one of them shattered me. This was Bronislau Kaper's tune *Hi Lili Hi Lo*, which Bill recorded with Eddie Gomez in the duo album titled *Intuition*. The song bore a dedication on the album cover: "for Ellaine." The tune is happy-sad in character; in Bill's treatment, it had a profound melancholy. I realized I hadn't spoken to Bill in many months and phoned him in New York. I told him how much I liked the album, we talked for a while, and then I said, "Give my love to Ellaine." There was a crushing silence on the line. Then Bill said, "Didn't anyone tell you? Elaine took her own life."

I blurted, helplessly, "How?"

"She threw herself under a subway train."

Instantly I thought of that ghastly cold night in the subway with her. That she should have died there was a thought I found almost unendurable. I can hardly listen to that performance of *Hi Lili Hi Lo*, her favorite song. And I can only guess what Helen went through at the time: Bill was out of town, and she had to identify the body.

Bill went back on heroin for a while, then got into a methadone treatment program in 1970. For the next ten years or so, he was free of it. He remarried. I met his second wife, Nenette, once or twice, but I never really knew her. Friends described a very troubled marriage. They had a son, whom Bill gave the very Welsh name Evan Evans. Bill moved out and took an apartment in Fort Lee, New Jersey.

After I moved to California in 1974, Bill and I remained in loose touch by telephone, and once I heard him at Howard Rumsey's Concerts by the Sea at Redondo Beach. Philly Joe Jones was the drummer with him at the time, and in the dressing room they were telling funny stories about their junky days.

Around 1980, I began to hear on the musicians' grapevine that Bill was back on dope, but not heroin. He was shooting cocaine. He came to Los Angeles for an engagement. One of the musicians went to hear him, then urged me to go to see him the following night. "How is he playing?" I said.

"Brilliantly."

"How does he look?"

"Awful."

"I don't want to see him," I said. "I can't go through that again." Hal Gaylor told me some time later, "Cocaine is far worse than heroin, because you have to do it again a couple of hours later. It's deadly."

Joe LaBarbera, the drummer, was with Bill at the end. Bill was taken with severe stomach pains in his apartment in Fort Lee. Joe drove him to the hospital. "The funny thing is," Joe said several years later, "that he was in control of the situation even then. I didn't know where the hospital was, and he was directing me."

Joe took him to Mount Sinai Hospital and checked him in. Bill died there.

If I can remember vividly my discovery of Bill's playing, I can similarly remember the moment when I learned of his death. I went home to Canada to see my mother, who was dying of cancer. I walked into her house in Kingston, Ontario, and looked down a hall toward the kitchen, where she stood in a pale blue bathrobe. She seemed so frail and old. I had hardly had time to embrace her when the telephone rang. It was the Canadian Broadcasting Corporation in Toronto. How they even knew I was there, I don't know. But they told me of Bill's death and asked me to do a network interview about him. I agreed. I managed to suspend all feeling about his death: I had to contend with my mother's pending departure.

A few days later in Toronto, I did the interview. The engineer played Tony Bennett's record of *Waltz for Debby*, the version he made with Bill—Tony has recorded it three times. I thought of the cities I had been in with Bill: Los Angeles, Toronto, Chicago, Paris, Montreux, New York. I remembered writing the *Waltz for Debby* lyric in Helen's living room. (Jobim always calls it *The Debby Waltz*.) It hit me that Bill was really gone, and I think this awareness was getting into my voice. It was at this point that the lady producer of the show asked possibly the most tactless question I have ever had in an interview. She said, "Can you tell us any funny stories about him?" I didn't know whether to laugh or cry. Or maybe it was a clever question, a good one, to pull me back from the brink. I talked about Woody's blazer.

After I finished the interview, the one person I wanted to be with was Oscar Peterson. As I drove out to his house in Mississauga, I remembered an evening in New York when Bill and I went to hear him. I had suggested that they make a two-piano album together, and they were both interested in the idea, which, for various contractual and logistical reasons, never happened. When we entered the club, Oscar brought whatever he was playing to an early close and then played, beautifully, *Waltz for Debby*. Bill said, "I don't thing I'll ever play it again." He did, of course.

Oscar too had heard the news of Bill's death, and the banter and insult in which we usually indulge were suspended that day. He knew what I was feeling.

Two or three years later, I was having dinner with Oscar's former wife Sandy, with whom he had remained friends. "I think," I said, "Oscar was much more affected by Bill's death than he would admit to me that day."

"You better believe it," she said.

Oscar almost always plays *Waltz for Debby* in his concerts now.

After Oscar and I had talked of all manner of other things that afternoon, we at last got around to discussing Bill, including his drug habit.

"Maybe," Oscar said gently, "he found what he was looking for."

In 1984, growing curious about the actual status of various pianists with other pianists, I did a survey of the sixty-odd well-known pianists who subscribed to the *Jazzletter*. The forty-seven respondents included pianists such as Alan Broadbent, Dave Brubeck, Kenny Drew, Dave Frishberg, Dizzy Gillespie, Roger Kellaway, Junior Mance, Nat Pierce, and Billy Taylor. I asked them to name, in no particular order, five pianists in three categories: those they considered the "best," those they thought the most influential, and their personal favorites. The results were startling.

As best, Art Tatum garnered 36 votes, Bill Evans 33, and Oscar Peterson 27. As most influential, Tatum 32, Bill 30, Bud Powell 24. Among personal favorites, Bill won: Bill 25, Tatum 22, Oscar 19.

While this was by no means a "scientific" survey, it gave some idea of the respect in which he was held by pianists. I think if you surveyed musicians on all instruments, the results would be similar.

And yet not everybody gets it. A friend of mine wrote to ask, "What is the source and meaning of the rarified (important, influential, virtually deified) position occupied by Bill Evans in the world of jazz—in both the large world of listeners and critics as well as in the community of jazz musicians? I've listened to Evans' music, both his performances and his compositions, for fifteen or twenty years, and he has moved me frequently. But no more than many other pianists, none of whom achieved the influence or reputation associated with a cult. [While] I can well understand why Thelonious Monk became a seminal and vastly influential figure in jazz, I can't quite comprehend Evans' comparable status."

My friend says elsewhere in his letter that Oscar Peterson "has greater range and technical facility." Not so. If you're talking about sheer speed, go back and listen to the runs Bill plays on the *"Spartacus"* track of *Conversations with Myself.* He's as fast as Oscar, fully as facile. But he doesn't use his speed in the same way that Oscar does. And the flow of tones from one chord to another is part of "technique." That night we went to hear Oscar, I asked Bill why Oscar didn't use some of the voicings Bill had brought into jazz. Bill said, "It wouldn't be appropriate to what he does." Both of them were blessed with a sense of the fitting. And in time of course Oscar did embrace certain things that Bill had brought into jazz.

These comparisons—which are one of the curses of the jazz world—are wasteful. In jazz, more than any form of music I know, you are listening to individual expression. You may listen to a Frenchman for what his philosophy of life contributes to your own; to an American Indian or an Australian aborigine or a Swede for the insight he offers. But you are not going to get the same thing from all of them, nor should one want to. Therefore to compare them on some sort of competitive scale is foolish, and meaningless. You accept them for what they are. Jazz fans, perhaps encouraged by all the polls that have plagued the art, too often ask who's "best"—and excoriate one pianist or trumpet player for lacking what another one has. It is like derogating Lester Young for not having Ben Webster's tone. *My favorite pianist is better than your favorite pianist, my favorite tenor player is better than your favorite tenor player.*

Bill was strikingly individual. Anyone who knew his work well could turn on a car radio, catch a jazz piano track, and know he was hearing Bill within two bars, because of his use of chord scales, his tone, his attack, and his rhythmic sense. His rhythmic placements were unique—much emulated but never successfully captured by anyone else. His sense of the balance of chords and of the linear motions within them was wonderful. He introduced into jazz certain voicings, and a use of inversions, that captivated and then captured a generation of pianists to the point that some among them have consciously sought ways out of the trap of sounding like him. He changed the tone character of jazz piano. Tone was a negligible element in previous jazz playing. For all his brilliance, Bud Powell had a painful tone. Nat Cole began the change, producing crystalline sound, Oscar Peterson took it further, and Bill brought into jazz the kind of tone appropriate to Debussy and Ravel and modern harmonic function and obvious in the classical world in the playing of Walter Gieseking and Emil Gillels. Everyone else picked it up from Bill. Bill's tone, or variations of it, spread all over the world. Jazz pianists everywhere touched the keyboard differently after Bill came along. Finally, there is his control of dynamics. In any given thirty-two bars of a Bill Evans solo, there are infinite gradations of intensity, dozens, maybe even scores of levels of loudness, all contributing not to technical dazzle but to the intense feeling in his work. I have gathered that not everyone's ear detects this.

His imagination was enormous. Though he had, as I say, his personal vocabulary, his clichés if you like, his bag of tricks, just like everyone in jazz, which is not as totally improvised a music as some of its champions pretend, he was genuinely one of the most imaginative, inventive, and adventurous improvisers the art has known.

Maybe Martin Williams said it best: "The need to know what he was doing, intellectually and theoretically, was one pole of the dichotomy of the remarkable combination of careful deliberateness and intuitive spontaneity, of logic and sensitivity, of mind and heart, that was Bill Evans the musician."

When Modigliani died, the prices of his paintings shot up overnight and now are astronomical. In a delicious example of funereal opportunism, his home town of Livorno, Italy, which ignored him when he was alive, began in the early 1980s dredging its canal in search of sculptures he deep-sixed there one night in 1914 in disgust with this aspect of his own work.

That an artist's work rises in "value" with his death is inevitable, but the record industry is outstanding in the exploitation of necrophilia, as witness the cases of Janis Joplin, John Lennon, and Elvis Presley. Nor has jazz been free of this kind of avarice.

If it is true that an artist has a right to be judged by his best work, it is only just that in most instances the recordings a jazz musician has rejected be left in obscurity. He clearly did not want to be represented by them. To issue flawed or interrupted takes to milk a few more dollars out of the departed is despicable.

No such unfortunate story attached to the two albums that Helen derived from tapes of two concerts played in Paris November 26, 1979, by Bill's last trio. They are not only not inferior Evans. They are, to me at least, the best and highest examples of his art to be found on record.

What those albums, recorded less than ten months before his death, prove beyond question is that he had begun to evolve and grow again, which is unusual in artists in any field. Artists tend to find their methods early and remain faithful to them, which sometimes leads in actors to the kind of mannered and self-satirizing performance so sadly typified by John Barrymore at the end. It is rare to see sudden growth in older jazz musicians, as in the case of Dizzy Gillespie after he changed his embouchure in his late sixties. Bill, on the clear evidence of those Paris albums, was in his most fertile period when he died.

Bassist Marc Johnson and drummer Joe LaBarbera, who were with him at the end and in these Paris recordings, were beautifully sympathetic to Bill. Characteristically, he gave them much credit for what had happened in his playing, suggesting a direct relationship between this final trio and the one with LaFaro and drummer Paul Motian.

The two Paris albums consist almost entirely of material he had recorded before, which gave me a chance to compare his early and late work. The first, Elektra Musician 60164-1, comprises *I Do It for Your Love; Quiet Now*, a Denny Zeitlin composition of which Bill was particularly fond; *Noelle's Theme; My Romance; I Love You Porgy; Up with the Lark* (a Kern tune; Bill had a flair for reviving forgotten gems); *All Mine*; and *Beautiful Love*. The second, Elektra Musician 60311-1-E, contains *Re: Person I Knew; Gary's Theme*, a Gary McFarland tune; three of his own tunes, *Letter to Evan*; *34 Skiddoo; Laurie*; and the Miles Davis tune *Nardis*.

My Romance was in that first Riverside LP, *New Jazz Conceptions*, made when he was so young and uncertain of his worth and uncomfortable with the praise that was being poured on him. He truly believed he didn't deserve it, as he said to me once in a long letter I lost in a fire in Toronto, which is all the more unfortunate in that it was one of the most remarkable examples of self-analysis by an artist I have ever encountered. He was explaining why he had become a heroin addict. He said that the acclaim he was receiving by the time he was with the Miles Davis group—February to November of 1958—made him acutely uneasy. He didn't feel he deserved it. I remember the next line of that letter verbatim: "If people wouldn't believe I was a bum, I was determined to prove it."

That early *My Romance* is two choruses long, ballad tempo, without intro. He simply plays the tune, twice, solo, with minimal variation. But already there is that enormous control of the instrument, and those intelligent voice leadings. To go from that version to the one in Paris twenty-two years later, is fascinating, and somewhat disturbing. The later version opens with a long intro that has only the most abstract relationship to the tune. Bill moves through a series of chords that float ambiguously (to my ear at least) between A-flat and E-flat, then goes into the tune itself, in C, up-tempo, with rhythm section. It is like a sudden sunburst, so bright, and the audience applauds. C, incidentally, is the key of the early Riverside version. Bill was very fussy about keys. When he was taking on a new tune, he would try it out in all the keys—and such was his influence on other pianists that Warren Bernhardt learned Bill's *My Bells* with Bill's voicings in all twelve keys, as a discipline. In any case, *My Romance* stayed in C for all those years, but the last version is profoundly different, a distillation of years of musical wisdom, quite abstract, exploding with energy and life.

But the most striking thing to me about the Paris albums is that Bill seems to have struck the perfect balance between his intuitive lyricism and deliberative intelligence, to have resolved the dichotomy of which Martin Williams perceptively wrote. Without any loss of the worldly wisdom he had accumulated, his work at last is filled again with that indefinable something that he and others recognized as the essence of the *Everybody Digs* album.

It is said that all men go in search of their youth. The Paris albums suggest that in the end, Bill found his.

Not long after Bill died, Phil Woods went into a fury when he read a critic's comment that Bill didn't swing. "Swing" is a tricky verb as applied to music. What swings for one person may not swing for another, since the process involves a good deal of the subjective. It is impossible to state as an objective "fact" that something "doesn't" swing. What Bill did not do was swing obviously. If you want to hear Bill swing obviously, go back to the first Riverside album. The influence of Bud Powell was, it seems to me, not yet internalized, and Bill goes bopping happily away, backed by Teddy Kotick and Paul Motian, banging out the time in a way that only the deaf could miss. But like Turner making the implicit assumption that you don't need obvious waves and horizon and clouds to know what the sea looks like and giving you only his heightened perception of them, Bill often in his later years didn't hit you over the head with the time. He assumed you knew where it was.

He once explained to me how he felt about it, and I do not know whether he ever told anyone else. He drew an analogy to shadow lettering in which the letters seem raised and you see not the letters themselves but the shadows they apparently cast. That's how Bill played time, or more precisely played with it.

Finally, there is an ineffable quality in Bill's playing that I am more and more inclined to see as mysticism, whether Russian or something even more Oriental. Bill had extraordinary powers of concentration. He told me once that you should be able to focus your mind on a single tone for as much as five minutes. That would have been an uncanny feat, possible to yoga adepts but few others in this world. Yet that is how Bill thought, and his total involvement with the tone or the chord or the scale happening *now* was very deep indeed. All this is beyond my powers to describe, as for that matter all music is beyond my powers to describe. But I hear it, and I am moved by it. And I can't say or do anything to help or instruct those whose neurological organization and life conditioning do not predispose them to its perception. I would tell them that a certain famous arranger told me he went through a long period of being unable to hear what the fuss was all about. And then one day Bill's work hit him.

I don't think music is accessible through explanation, in any case, although explanation may deepen one's appreciation of it. It has to be discovered, and no musician's work more than Bill's. I discovered it, Alan Broadbent discovered it, countless others discovered it. And now Bill is being discovered by a new generation. I got a letter from a young man just out of graduate school. He named as his favorites the three pianists so admired by the pianists I polled—Tatum, Peterson, and Evans.

He said he listens to them in the dark.

Bill would like that.

10

THE TEACHER:
BILLY TAYLOR

BILLY TAYLOR walked across the lobby of the Westwood Marquee in Los Angeles with his friend, actor William Marshall. The Westwood Marquee is a luxury hotel catering to those who need tax write-offs and those on expense accounts. Billy was there on a tab from CBS, the Columbia Broadcasting System. The Westwood Marquee is one of those modern glass towers, which in the interior affects an older and reassuring decor, and it wasn't there back when Gerry Mulligan wrote *Westwood Walk*, nor were any of the tall apartment and office buildings that have made a traffic impasse of a once quiet corner of Los Angeles near the campus of UCLA.

A man stopped them, shook Billy's hand, and told him how much he appreciated his segments on jazz, seen monthly or so, on the excellent CBS *Sunday Morning* show with Charles Kuralt. The man apparently did not recognize Bill Marshall, whose list of television and movie credits is long.

Billy smiled as he recalled the incident a day or two later, this evidence of the power of television to make one's face famous. Would that its power were used to the full enhancement of the culture it so inexorably affects, rather than irresponsibly debasing it. But that's, as Walter Cronkite used to remind us, the way it is. Mr. Marshall's feelings at the incident have not been recorded, and in any event he passes immediately out of our tale, having appeared like Rosenkrantz and Guildenstern just long enough to

176

deliver a message, in this case to point up what recurrent appearances on TV can do for a jazz musician, one of a breed who live lives of total obscurity to that larger public that likes the likes of Madonna. CBS has changed that for Billy, and Billy is using the power the network has given him sensibly and well for the cause of jazz.

Billy Taylor was born July 24, 1921, in Greenville, North Carolina, his father a dentist and his mother a schoolteacher. Except on television, whereon one has the advantages of makeup and skilled lighting, I had not seen him much in recent years, since he remains a denizen of New York City, though of that leafy part of it, somewhat above the crush of Manhattan, known as Riverdale. I had every reason to expect that by now, when he was sixty-six years old, time had wrought its relentless handiwork on his hairline and the composure of his features, as it has on the serenity of Westwood Village, which is no longer referred to as a village. Just Westwood now. But Billy shares with bassist Bob Cranshaw (who was once a third of his trio) and singer Ruth Price some peculiar genetic good fortune that makes them seem to inhabit a Shangri-la of their own. They don't age, or at least not much and not fast, and Billy looked all of forty-five. His hair remains thick, well forward on his forehead, and black. His skin is a medium orange-brown, remarkably unlined, and clear. He is tall, erect, and if not quite slim at least not thick-waisted. There is a slightly Oriental cast to his features, as if he too partakes of that Cherokee lineage that so many black Americans can claim as part of their heritage. He is habitually dapper, and this day he was wearing a khaki safari jacket. He always did have a teacherly mien, and, looking at you through his dark-rimmed glasses, he still did. And teaching is one of the things Dr. Taylor, who attained a combined master's and doctoral degree in education from the University of Massachusetts in 1975, does best. It was for his prodigious energies as a teacher that Stan Kenton, shortly before his death in 1980, commented that Billy was the most important figure in jazz today.

Billy's playing has the crystalline tone of a perfectly aimed touch that marks the work of jazz pianists with extensive "legit" training.

And like Bill Evans, who studied flute and violin in his youth, and Oscar Peterson, who played trumpet, Billy first played a linear instrument, saxophone, before settling into piano. This experience probably contributes in all three men to the quality of their legato playing. From the age of thirteen, when Billy undertook further and more dedicated "classical" studies, the piano was his instrument. Yet it was as a sociology major that he enrolled at Virginia State College. It is less likely that this is the reason for the breadth of his viewpoint than that these tendencies of character caused him to take the subject in the first place. In any event a teacher convinced him music was his true calling, and after graduating with a bachelor of science degree, he undertook—on the recommendation of Teddy Wilson—piano studies in New York City with Richard McClanahan.

Billy's credentials since that time have accumulated like peanut hulls on the flattened grass of a county fair. He has honorary degrees from six universities, including humanities degrees from Fairfield University and Clark College, and honorary doctorates from Berklee College of Music and Virginia State. Virginia State is his father's alma mater. (His father took his pre-med degree there, his dentistry degree at Howard.) Billy is a Duke Ellington Fellow at Yale. He still plays nightclubs, but more and more he is doing seminars and clinics at universities. The number of universities at which he has lectured is enormous. He founded and still runs the Jazzmobile in New York City.

"The Jazzmobile is a very important part of what I do," he said. "Education and media are two areas that we need to do something special about. So in the Jazzmobile, which is now twenty-five years old, we give free concerts on the streets of New York. All the jazz players have played on the Jazzmobile. But we also have a workshop, which is run by Jimmy Owens, and has twenty-six instructors, who share their on-the-bandstand experience with people who aspire to do what they do. People like Jimmy Heath are on the staff. We try to engage people in the active participation in performing jazz, understanding it, relating to it, and using it for whatever purpose they think is suitable."

What is all this educational activity doing to his own playing—a style he himself sees as rooted in Art Tatum, Fats Waller, Debussy, Ravel, Bach, Ben Webster, and Eddie South? How much time does he have left to perform?

"I'm playing more than I ever played. I do four or five school concerts a month. For example, this coming week I'm going to Savannah State College. We'll spend a full day doing workshops and clinics. Normally I'll do a clinic, and workshop, culminated by a concert. We do four or five of these a month. I do sixteen or seventeen appearances with symphony orchestras a season, and that's plenty of playing. I've got one of the best trios I've had in years. I've got Victor Gaskin, who's worked with me for many years, and I've got Bobby Thomas, who used to be my drummer on the Frost show."

Before Charles Kuralt and *Sunday Morning*, Billy was musical director of the David Frost talk show. There was much chat in the trade at the time about his being the first black musical director of a major TV series, which says something about the state of America then. It says something about the state of America now that he is still the only one ever to have held such a post.

"That," Billy said, "was the most visibility that I have ever had on a regular basis. It was a daily show, and David started every show with, 'O.K., Billy,' the camera would cut to me, and the show began."

A maid was making up Billy's room at the time, so we sat in the bar just off the lobby.

Billy achieved his present eminence slowly and quietly but clearly as the consequence of a passionate drive. He has all the credentials to be so visible a spokesman for jazz. He is richly articulate in a sort of halting manner, hesitating in a way that is at odds with the way he plays. There is usually a relation between the way jazz musicians speak and play: Jack Teagarden in a lazy laconic drawl, Bill Evans with low-level but definite dynamics, Miles Davis in raspy short bits paced by articulate spaces, Bob Brookmeyer in an eloquent ironic mumble, Ben Webster in a great low boom,

Gerry Mulligan with a kind of cheery chuckling sadness. Billy is one of the exceptions, and there are uhs and ahs in his speech that are quite absent from his fluid playing.

What makes him effective is a kind of psychological sure-footedness, possibly the consequence of his training in sociology, although as I suggest, it may be the bent in his temperament that led him to the study in the first place. The processes of intimidation are widespread in our society, in all societies, and the Irish, who were abused in New York when they arrived, later abused the Italians, leading to a kind of self-effacing quality common in people of that city and that heritage. I once heard Tony Bennett talking intelligently about Picasso, and suddenly a veil seemed to cross his face, and he said, "But who am I to be talking about Picasso?" and he ended the dissertation, cheating me of keen insights. Julius LaRosa, another New York Italian—he was born not far from Tony—for a long time had a similar quality, which we have as a private joke come to call the Picasso syndrome.

But no group of Americans has been as viciously intimidated as blacks, and the evidence of this is everywhere to be seen in jazz. I remember vividly the occasion when a nightclub publicist brought Blue Mitchell, whom I admired and was anxious to meet, to my office at *Down Beat* in Chicago. To my keen distress, not to say horror, he seemed uncomfortable in this atmosphere, and I moved quickly to put him at his ease, after which Blue and I became rather good friends. Only a few months ago, I was talking to Curtis Fuller about an insight he gave me during that period— the perception that in music you sacrifice tone for speed. I've since come to see this as axiomatic, but Curtis was the first to make me aware of it. When I reminded Curtis of this, he reminded me in turn that I took him to lunch that day. It is significant. I remembered the insight; Curtis remembered the lunch. That tells you something about being black in America, the more revealing for being a tiny detail of daily living, rather than some great matter of criminal injustice. Or again: in New York in the early 1960s, I wrote some songs with Floyd Williams, a gifted composer who had been Lionel Hampton's drummer. I managed to get us a publishing contract. As we rose in the elevator to the publisher's office, Floyd did a mock Mantan Moreland number, something he could do to hilarious effect. He said, "We're on our way up to see the white man boss! Am I gonna got screwed by the white man boss?"

I laughed and said, "Listen, baby, the white man boss will screw me as fast as he will screw you." But I sensed that Floyd was kidding on the square, that there was real apprehension there. (Floyd later took his doctorate in black cultural studies and now teaches music at Allegheny College in Pennsylvania.)

The black experience in America seems to produce in men two extremes of conditioned personality, with broad variants within them. One seethes with hatred, open and flagrant hostility and contempt toward whites, as manifest in Wynton Marsalis, who during his interview with Billy on *Sunday Morning* talked of the way "we" play jazz and the way "they" play jazz, citing as his example of the white jazz player Herb Alpert, of all people! Who has never claimed to be a jazz musician, has never made a jazz album in his life. The other extreme manifestation of the experience is the kind of pre-defeated personality I think I saw in Blue Mitchell, who was a man of great inherent sweetness. Wilhelm Reich spoke of the shrinking biopathy. If it exists, Blue would seem to have been the classic example of it, and he died of cancer. To someone shy, as I think Blue was, the pain of being black in a white world must be incommunicable.

Contrary to legend, the black American population was not universally docile and intimidated during its earlier history. There were other uprisings besides that of Nat Turner, although the brutal suppression of that one—horrifyingly described in the William Styron novel—makes it perhaps the most dramatic. Nonetheless, the numbers of these rebels were insufficient against the vast controlling force, the people who had the education, who could read and write, who owned the guns and controlled the armies. It is all too easy to sit back now and call Louis Armstrong an Uncle Tom. But the black man of anger, and Armstrong evidently concealed an enormous anger, often had no choice but to grit his teeth in what looked like a smile, and ingratiate himself against his own wishes with white people some of whose money it was his intention to get.

Billy Taylor is one of a generation of black men who had begun to reject this solution to the problem, to stand up—as Dizzy Gillespie did—with a man's pride and make his way in the world and make his music along that way. A revolution was dawning in the 1940s, and Billy came in on it. What is exceptional about him is his equanimity. As far as I can see, he has always had it. He does not of course come from poverty but from the educated middle class. Whatever the reason, a stable home led by an educated father, a temperament that led him to sociology and an awareness of the world beyond music, the solid "classical" training (although that was more common among black pianists than myth now has it), the awareness of European and other cultures as well as American culture, or just something in the congenital temperament, Billy has always walked securely in both worlds, black and white, with an awareness of injustice probably deeper than that of most blacks because of the sociologist's knowledge of history, yet without a self-corroding rage. It is a remarkable achievement, and Billy Taylor is a remarkable man. He has the sunny disposition of the fulfilled teacher.

Billy shares my reservations about the historical image of the emergence of jazz. Those happy singin' an' dancin' folk who ignorantly invented this music out of thin air and inspiration. The inventors of jazz were often extremely well-trained musicians who may, of course, have found it politic to conceal this fact from the white customers for it. "The noble savage," Billy said sardonically.

"I think the housekeeper must be finished by now," he said, and we took the elevator up to his room.

She had finished. The room was fresh and clean and modern. A pale yellow bedspread was pulled as tight as the blanket on an army cot. Billy took a soft chair by a round table near the window, whose gauzy curtains filtered the relentless California sunlight. Occasional toots of car horns from the streets below penetrated his comments. Two packed soft-leather black travel bags, evidence of a quick hit-and-run trip, lay in a corner, poised for departure. It was just after noon. Billy had been in California to shoot a feature on Horace Silver for *Sunday Morning*.

The portrait of Horace would become, after editing, something like the hundredth such study Billy has done on the show since he became its correspondent in jazz, and in turn the jazz community's delegate to television, a medium that has not been hospitable to it. On camera, curiously, the uhs and ahs drop out of Billy's speech, and he is a clear and articulate interviewer, at ease with the medium and the subject matter.

His portraits have not been universally flattering: the camera is a dispassionate machine, and sometimes it has captured the darker elements in the personalities Billy has examined. In the editing these have been allowed to show through. On the whole, though, his portraits have been affectionate and admiring, reflecting his love of the subjects and their music.

"I was particularly pleased with the one I did recently on Dave Brubeck," he said. "Dave isn't always comfortable in interviews, and he doesn't always come across. But it was just two piano players, old friends, talking, and he was at ease.

"You know," he said, and the racism in jazz lay at the heart of his remark, "you'll hear guys say, 'Dave Brubeck doesn't swing.' He swings, believe me. On my radio show, I'd play Dave Brubeck tracks and not identify him and guys would say to me later, 'Who was that?' and I'd say, 'Dave Brubeck?' and they'd say, 'That was Dave Brubeck?'"

I told Billy the story Cannonball Adderley told me: that he had played some records for his group by a pianist he said he was thinking of hiring, and, after his colleagues had committed themselves to enthusiastic approval, sprang it on them that the pianist was white. And English. And incidentally Jewish. Victor Feldman.

Billy chuckled.

Billy has done *Sunday Morning* portraits of Peggy Lee, Ella Fitzgerald, Joe Williams, Carmen McRae, Sarah Vaughan, Benny Carter, Gerry Mulligan, Maynard Ferguson, and many more. These studies have not been limited to performers. A particularly interesting piece portrayed Max Gordon, the founder and still owner of the apparently indestructible Village Vanguard, the Greenwich Village cellar nightclub that has been providing a bandstand for jazzmen since the 1930s. He has done pieces on disk jockey Jonathan Schwartz and pioneer jazz record producer John Hammond.

How did Billy's association with the show come about? "They did a profile of me. The person who wanted it done was Robert Northshield, the show's producer. Shad Northshield is in my opinion a genius. He created *Sunday Morning*. He thought of those nature segments at the end of the show. He is just a marvelously creative producer. It was his view, and Kuralt concurred, that this should be a magazine show that gave equal emphasis in whatever it did. If you're doing something on jazz, you don't give that any less time and production values than you would an exhibition at the Metropolitan Museum of Art. When Valdimir Horowitz went to Russia, we took our heavyweight people and did a major study of this world-class artist who was returning to his native country. So that's the kind of thing Northshield did. He did this piece on me. Peter Levinson—" Peter Levinson is a publicist, probably the best known in the jazz field. "Peter told him, 'You really should use Billy on some of these things. You don't have anybody doing jazz at the moment.' He knew Shad is a jazz fan. Shad asked me and I of course said yes, and I've been doing it ever since."

Kuralt too, Billy said, is a jazz fan, and in the folksy manner in which he conceals a superb journalistic mind, he will play the uninformed straight man in his questions, allowing Billy to give him the inside on a story. Kuralt takes the role of the lay listener. He casts himself as the audience.

Billy spoke with warmth about his associates in the show, including Bob Shattuck, who got an Emmy for editing the piece they did on Quincy Jones. "Brett Alexander, who produces the segments, is a knowledgeable writer, who knows a lot about sports, a lot about jazz, a lot about popular music. He used to write for the *New York Post* and a lot of magazines. As a non-musician, he'd keep me from being too technical or too inside. He'd say, 'Well, hey, they won't know what you're talking about if you say Bird, why don't you just say Charlie Parker?' Things like that."

"Alas, they still won't know what you're talking about," I said.

Billy laughed. "A classic example of the kind of overall production values Shad Northshield would give me is the piece I did on Count Basie. When we finished the piece, Shad looked at it and said, 'Well, all the information is here, but when Basie played the piano, there was a lot of space in it. We don't have enough space in this piece.' So he made it longer, spread it out a little, made it flow, changed the whole pacing. You don't get that from producers! That's hard to come by, man!"

A significant thing about the Taylor portraits on *Sunday Morning* is that he is not preaching to the converted. One of the undiscussed tragedies of the contemporary American culture is its ghettoization—jazz radio for the jazz fans, rock radio for the rock fans, and even subdivisions of it for the fans of those subdivisions, country radio for the country fans, and classical music for the classical fans. But Billy's work at CBS goes to millions of people who are not necessarily even music lovers, much less jazz fans, and, yes, he confirmed, "It's very satisfying to me when somebody comes up and shakes my hand and says they enjoyed a piece on So-and-So, and they'd never thought about it before, but now they were interested and they were going to listen."

Billy is optimistic—it is hard to imagine him ever being pessimistic—about a resurgence of jazz that he sees happening. One of his recent *Sunday Morning* pieces had been on exactly that.

"Do you really think there's a resurgence? Or are we just succumbing to a fit of wishful thinking?"

"Oh, yes," he said. "There are a lot of things which have come into being in the twenty or twenty-five years of jazz instruction, when you have all the mistakes that have been made by all of us trying to teach jazz—whether you're talking Berklee, North Texas State, Jamie Abersol, me, Jazzmobile. We've learned from the experience. In the process of doing it, we have created a large body of people who are knowledgeable about the music. There are holes in their knowledge. But they know what the music sounds

like, they know what's good about it. Many of the people have
gone to jazz camps, have studied privately, and they have added
to this ever increasing group who understand what the music is
about. This, compared to rock groups and rock fans, is a small
group. But compared to the former jazz audience, it's a growing
group. You've got this, and the availability of jazz—or whatever
passes for jazz—on radio, with two hundred and some National
Public Radio stations playing whatever they call jazz all over the
country. You've got the jazz festivals presenting whatever they call
jazz all over the world. You've got the books, such as the fake
books, that have been put together. All these things have contributed to a large body of players and listeners who are not satisfied
with New Age music, or whatever is being given to them. They
want something more. They don't necessarily know what it is, but
they are a part of the people who look at the *Sunday Morning* show,
who listen to National Public Radio, who are buying up the reissues of the cutouts of the things they've heard about either in a
jazz class or wherever else they heard it. Or they read a news piece
and say, 'Oh, Billy Taylor said he was in Russia and found out
about this guy who plays tenor. Let me check him out.' So it's not
only in this country, where things are slower to be changed, it's
going on in Russia, in South America, in Singapore. This year I've
been to Hawaii, South America, Russia, Australia, and Hong
Kong. That's just this year. Prior to that, the jazz festival in
Singapore . . .''

"There's a jazz festival in Singapore?"

"Absolutely. There's more and more of them everywhere. The
Modern Jazz Quartet, Betty Carter, Jimmy Owens, Jimmy Heath,
Roland Hanna, and myself were part of a newly established festival
in South America. There's a lot of growth, and it's healthy."

"Do you see jazz becoming then a world language? It started as
a New Orleans language but now seems to be becoming—with the
Japanese players and the European players—an international
language."

"Yes, although it seems to be necessary for them to make some
sort of contact with America to develop fully. In Russia, I met Igor
Butman, who is a tenor player about nineteen now studying at

Berklee. Paquito de Rivera is from Cuba, and Adam Makowicz from Poland. Each one of them said essentially the same thing. I want to come to America because I've done about as much as I can here. Paquito was with one of the world's greatest fusion bands, Irakere. One of the damnedest bands I ever heard in my life. They were playing really good music, any way you want to cut it. But he said, 'Hey, I want to get here and play with these great American players, so I can grow as a musician.' And he has. This guy is a totally different musician now than when I first heard him in Irakere. Adam Makowicz had all the facility in the world, he could get over that piano. But now that he's been here and played with Marc Johnson and other good players, he's really swinging. He's speaking the jazz language without accent. The emotion in his playing has expanded, you can hear the depth. And the same thing is going to happen to this young Igor Butman, because he has the basic talent.

"So the music is an international music. It comes from the black experience, but one of the strengths of that experience is that it can be appropriated by people who don't belong to that ethnic group. All of my career, because I am black, it has been assumed that I think only blacks can play jazz. And I don't think that. When I had the band on the David Frost show, it was a mixed band not because I had any axe to grind but because I just picked the guys who could best do that job for my needs in that show. Yet, as a black man, I resent the fact that a lot of guys who are not black don't have the same view. I see a lot of white bands that would be better served if they were racially mixed, because it would be a better blend for what they are doing.

"That's not an axe I want to grind. My whole thing is that the music itself has grown. Whether you're talking about Phil Woods or Zoot Sims or Bill Evans or any number of people who come immediately to mind, they epitomize the best in jazz creativity and playing. That takes nothing away from other guys I admire—Art Tatum or Charlie Parker—you're talking apples and oranges. Each one brings to the music his own experience and ability. One guy does it one way, another guy does it his way."

"How do you explain a kid growing up in Canada or England

or Sweden, getting turned on by people like Basie? What does the black experience mean to a white kid like me in Canada, or another kid in England like Victor Feldman, and why?"

"It means that the music Basie was playing and Ellington was playing and many other black musicians were playing had such truth and spoke with such clarity that the message came through to people who were not of that ethnic group. That's the strength of the music. The Mississippi blues can do that if you listen to it properly. Any kind of truthful experience in aesthetics can reach you if you're open to be reached. Some people close themselves off and won't for a variety of reasons allow specific kinds of things to touch them—gospel music, for example. And yet what we used to think of as purely of the black church, gospel music, as done now by André Crouch and James Cleveland and Shirley Caesar and many others, you look out there now in the audience and many of the people who are responding are not black. They're getting the message. I did a piece on gospel music on the *Sunday Morning* show, we ended in a Catholic church, St. Augustine church in Washington, D.C., with as mixed an audience as you are ever going to find—white, young, old, black, middle-aged, fat, skinny. They were responding in a Catholic church, they were responding to the strength and truth of the music."

"That leads to the thought," I said, "that if this were not so, Leontyne Price and Martina Arroya would not be able to sing opera."

"Absolutely," Billy said. "Absolutely."

"I've heard people put down the *Porgy and Bess* score," I said. "Then I saw Todd Duncan, who originated the role of Porgy on Broadway, in an interview. I guess there weren't many black opera singers in those days. Todd Duncan said that it is nonsense, putting that score down, this is opera, it's a broad emotional dramatic experience. He really defended that score. We can say, I guess, that if George Gershwin as a white composer cannot use the black experience as a subject for an opera, then you had better cross the grave and tell Verdi he can't write an opera set in Egypt, and Puccini that he can't compose music about a Japanese girl in love with an American. *Madama Butterfly* is Puccini's perception and emotional projection of an American and Japanese experience based on an American play, and it even has meaning to Americans, who go to see it at the Met in Italian. And it has meaning to Martina Arroya and Leontyne Price, or they couldn't sing Italian music. And apparently *Madama Butterfly* is meaningful even to many Japanese."

"Summertime," Billy said, "is not only a lovely aria, it's a blues. Gershwin was a very perceptive and astute student of the things he was writing about. You don't have to be black to like soul food."

"Yeah," I said, "it seems to me that if we are all restricted to the artistic materials of our ethnic origins, our art becomes very narrow indeed."

"Absolutely," Billy said.

"Now," I said, "we still have the question of what we mean by jazz. If memory serves, you were the first one to call it, at least as part of the definition, America's classical music."

"Yes I was. There are different kinds of classical music. There's a Chinese classical music, there's an Indian classical music. These are different from European classical music. In Indian classical music, which is based on an oral tradition, there is improvisation.

"Just to rule jazz out as a classical music, because it is a tradition transmitted orally from one person to another, is not good enough. I defined the music simply because the Louis Armstrong and/or Fats Waller definition, 'If you have to ask, you'll never know,' was never very satisfactory to me. There are people who are honestly asking, who want to know. I could appreciate that those two musicians and others don't suffer fools gladly. But there is an answer.

"To me, jazz is a way of playing which is defined by a repertory. And that repertory codifies the vocabulary that has been developed over the years. The simple way of defining it is to say that jazz is a way of playing, and it's a repertory. But when you define the way of playing, it has something which has developed from master to pupil—certain kinesthetic principles and certain aesthetic principles that have by trial and error been accepted. And so there is a definite language which starts with early ragtime and has been expanded right up until today, inclusive of ethnic input, musical input, inclusive of many other things. And all of these things have validity and they are found to whatever degree the individual wants to use them in his work. In my book *Jazz Piano* I took styles and examined them. I didn't take artists, to say that Louis Armstrong did this and then he handed the baton to Roy Eldridge who handed the baton to Dizzy, who did this . . . That's too easy. That leaves out all the other great people—Buck Clayton, Bunny Berigan, Red Allen, Bix Beiderbecke—so many musicians who in their own way added to the vocabulary and added to the repertory.

"When you think of it from that point of view, it's impossible for me to say—as much as I loved him—that in his most productive and influential period Art Tatum was the only guy. How could I leave out Teddy Wilson? How could I leave out Hank Jones? How could I leave out Milt Buckner? How could I leave out a whole bunch of other people who were operating on a different wave length at the time Art Tatum was doing his most creative work in putting together his version of what the jazz vocabulary was about? One can take Bill Evans and say, He took this aspect of jazz and did this with it. It's possible to take one guy and say, he did so much! And there's all these guys who imitate him. But that leaves out a whole bunch of other guys who were doing things that are ultimately going to be as important to the overall vocabulary as whatever this great giant did.

"So. It's a way of playing, and it's a repertory of pieces which defines that way of playing. And I really am delighted that that simple definition is one that can be used by people. I'm not talking about raised ninths and contrapuntal playing and this scale or that scale and all that. If you want to study music, fine. But to me, some things can be defined in such a way that it's useful in moving from this plane of knowledge to a higher level of knowledge. And that's all a definition is—a tool. And we have needed one that's helpful to the layman."

"You haven't used the word 'improvisation' once in the definition."

"No, and that's deliberate. I think too much emphasis is placed on the spontaneous creativity that we call improvisation. Louis Armstrong played things which were set solos. Art Tatum too did things which were set solos. I've heard him do it. You can't say that it wasn't jazz and that it wasn't swinging. And I heard Louis Armstrong play . . ." He sang a Louis Armstrong lick. "I've heard him do that a million times, and those quarter notes swung every time.

"If the New York Philharmonic plays *Sophisticated Lady*, they're playing jazz. They may be playing it badly, but they're playing jazz."

"Now," I said, "there's an opposite side of the coin. Bill Evans made a recording of *Danny Boy*, which is an Irish tune. He plays two choruses of melody, he doesn't play a thing that isn't the original theme. He plays it his way, of course, with his chord voicings. Do you call that jazz?"

"Absolutely."

"You know, Bill strongly emphasized the element of improvisation in his definition of jazz, as does Dave Brubeck."

"I'm not de-emphasizing the improvisational aspects of it in my overall definition. The reason I stay away from it in my limited version of the definition is that it is too easy for either a dyed-in-the-wool jazz fan or a non-jazz fan to get confused and say, 'O.K., if what this guy is playing is not new, absolutely different, it is not jazz.' That's the reason with students, I stay away from it. Whenever I make a statement like this, I don't talk about improvisation.

"For instance, the way that Dizzy Gillespie created some of his songs, like *Groovin' High*, where he took the basic harmony of *Whispering*, changed the harmony, changed the rhythm, and added another melody. That's a tradition, and it didn't start with bebop. Guys were doing that back in the '20s; ragtime players were doing that. But that was one device that led to one kind of improvisation, regardless of style. There are a lot of devices that have to do with improvisation that are looked on as *defining* what the music is, and that's wrong. The device of reharmonizing. The device of rhythmatizing something. Or making something a Latin rhythm. They may enhance somebody's idea of the way to present a given type of material. But the devices are just devices, they are not the essence of the music.''

"What about ballads? You love ballads.''

"Bill Evans and I used to laugh about this thing. He was my neighbor in Riverdale for some time, you know. When I was house pianist in Birdland, Bird would play *Koko* or something like that, and then when Bird gave me a piano solo, I'd play *Laura*. I'd play ballads every chance I got, because that was the way I really expressed myself. And guys put me down for it, they said, 'Man, that's cocktail music, that's not jazz.' And I used to tell Bill, 'You come along a few years later and play the same gorgeous things I enjoyed playing, and people said, 'That's great art!' I said, 'You're standing on my shoulders,' and he'd laugh and say, 'Well you have to stand on somebody's.' Bill's creativity in that context was undeniable. He was one of my favorite artists.

"You know, I gave Bill his first major television show. In 1958, I was musical director of a show called *The Subject Is Jazz* on National Educational Television, which was the predecessor to PBS. We were working out of studio 8-H in New York, and I was told by the producers at the end of the thirteen weeks that we needed to make a prediction: where is jazz going? I said, 'There's a young man who's just recorded a piece written by a friend of mine. I'm not good at predicting, but I really believe that this is one of the directions that jazz is going. George Russell has just written this piece called *Billy the Kid* and the soloist is Bill Evans.' And they said, 'Who?' I brought the record in and played it, and I said, 'We don't have sufficient time to rehearse a work of this difficulty so why don't we bring in the guys who did the record?' We'll keep our band on, and bring them, and blow the whole budget. It's the last show anyway.' They went for it. So we brought the band in, and for some reason the drummer on the record date couldn't make the TV date. So Ed Thigpen, who was my drummer, read the son of a bitch at sight. I mean, *sight read* that son of a bitch. And he played the hell out of it. He's one of the damnedest musicians on earth."

We looked at our watches. It was almost one o'clock, time for Billy to leave for the airport and New York. We descended to the street, gave two attendants the tickets for our cars. They disappeared into the maw of the hotel garage.

"Tell me about your kids," I said. "How old are they? What are they doing?"

"Casey is thirty-five now. He lives here in California. He works with the Herman Miller furniture company, which makes what they call office environments. He's in charge of their west-coast installations. My daughter Kim's a lawyer in Washington, D.C. She is thirty. She graduated top of her class at Yale. She's kind of the family brain. She went to Washington and had everything going for her: she's a black *woman*, so she was immediately snapped up."

"A few years ago she'd have been dead on both counts."

"Right! But that's changed. They got two for one. She was hired immediately by a very prestigious firm in D. C. at a salary that just blew my mind. So she worked long enough to get a house and a car, quit, and now she's working for the public defender. Teddi, my wife, was a model when I married her, but she decided she wanted to be a mother, and she gave up all of that and she's been as good a mother as you could possibly ask for."

"Is that why you look so young?"

"In the last few years I've been able to concentrate on things which are very exciting to me. Everything that I do—radio, television, playing the piano, writing music—those are things that I enjoy doing. The combination of that and being married to the same lady for forty-six years. She's to be congratulated on that, it's her doing."

Billy's car came up first, a rented Cadillac the shiny blue-gray shade of a dolphin. He grinned. "One of the perks of the job." We shook hands, and he got in and drove off on his way to Los Angeles Airport. I got into my car and followed him through the carbon monoxide of Westwood.

Westwood Walk indeed.

11

THE MIRROR:
ART FARMER

IN FEBRUARY OF 1963, Addison Farmer, the bassist, suffered a
cerebral aneurism. Quincy Jones, who survived one, later asked his
doctors if there was anything he might have done to prevent it.
Yes, he was told. You could have chosen other parents. The insult
results from a congenital weakness in an artery wall that is unde-
tectable unless a physician is specifically looking for it. A few
months after Quincy's emergency operation, the surgeon who
saved his life himself died of this condition, which occurs when the
artery balloons out until it finally blows. People rarely survive cerebral aneurisms.

Addison and Arthur Farmer shared even closer genetic traits
than most brothers. They came into this world together in Council
Bluffs, Iowa, on August 21, 1928. Art was the elder by one hour.
They were fraternal, not identical, twins, but nonetheless they so
closely resembled each other that their friends, Benny Golson
among them, on first knowing them had trouble telling them
apart. I met them in the summer of 1960. Addison was a little
taller, and in time you observed that his hairline was a bit different
from Art's, his cheekbones were a little more pronounced. But at
first you did not note these distinctions. That summer I asked Art,
"How do you tell *yourselves* apart?" Without so much as a trace of
a smile, he replied, "When I get up in the morning, I pick up the
bass, and if I can't play it, I must be Art." His wit is always like
that, quick and clever and very dry.

They were both very good-looking, tall, clean-cut, with full mustaches, erect posture, and good shoulders. There was a slight Oriental cast to their features, and I sometimes wondered if they had some Indian background. I never got around to asking about it until the late summer of 1986, a good twenty-six years after I met them. There is a look in many Americans, both "black" and "white," that you begin to notice after a certain number of years, particularly if you live in the West. The actor Burt Reynolds, who is part Cherokee, has it: it's around the eyes. Stanley Dance thinks the Indian presence and influence in jazz are a great untold part of the music's history. Duke Ellington, he points out, was part Indian on his mother's side, and Johnny Hodges, he noted, looked like a Mexican Indian. It is, alas, Stanley says, a factor in the music's development that is probably lost forever, since it is too late to interview the people who knew about it, and no one was much concerned fifty years ago with compiling genealogies of black men and red men in America.

Art looked startled when I asked him about this possible ancestry. "Yeah," he replied, his eyebrows a little raised, as if no one had ever posed this question. "Blackfoot, on my mother's side."

"John Lewis is from New Mexico," I said, "and he has that kind of handsome Indian look about him. Bobby Scott is part Seminole. Jo Williams says he's part Seminole. Dave Brubeck probably has Indian background. His father said the family was part Indian, but his mother denied it. I suppose it was uncool in her day. Dave looks as if he could be. I tell him he looks more and more like a Buffalo nickel as he gets older. Frank Trumbauer was part Indian."

"It's been left out of the books," Art said. "Not to diminish the black contribution, but the Indian part of it has been overlooked. There was a great mixture of the Indian and black in America. So many guys."

"Mingus certainly looked Indian. Helen Humes, Harry Edison, Gene Ramey."

"Jay McShann, Aaron Bell," Art said.

"Carl Fischer, the pianist, who wrote *We'll Be Together Again* with Frankie Laine, he was pure Indian. He wrote that gorgeous suite, *Reflections of an Indian Boy*, that Victor Young orchestrated after Fischer died."

"There was another pure Indian, Big Chief Russell Moore," Art said. "Trombonist. He was from Pima County, Arizona. He used to play with Louis Armstrong. He used to play on the side of his mouth."

"I've seen people do that and I could never understand how they did it."

"It's a habit they develop. It's a bad method. Jack Teagarden was Indian, I think."

"No," I said. "Not Jack, surprisingly enough, although it's widely thought so. Jack wasn't Indian. I checked that with his brother Charlie and then, more recently, with his sister, Norma, who's still playing piano in San Francisco. Charlie said that the family was German and Irish, going 'way back. But Jack sure had a sort of Indian look."

Somewhat later, I was talking to Benny Golson. For all the years of their friendship and professional association, Benny did not know of Art's Indian background. "And do you know who else has Indian in them?" Benny said. "Me. You can see it in family photos. My mother's people had that straight black Indian hair. But I never mention it, because I got so sick of black guys going around talking about their Indian heritage. When Oscar Pettiford would get drunk, he'd start saying, 'I'm an Indian!'"

When Benny described Art as "always kind of stoic," I said, "Sure, that's the Indian in him."

"You know," Benny said, "I think you're right. People misunderstand Art initially. One of two things happens. They walk away. Or, when they stay, they become very close to him. He's not a surface person. If you ask him a straight question, you're going to get a straight answer, no flattery. There is a great directness in his playing—not that he is recondite in other ways. He listens, and he remembers. He remembers names and faces. And he keeps his friendships."

"I've noticed," I said, "that in conversation, he listens intently to what someone else is saying, without interruption. And then when he says something, he expresses it in full paragraphs. And he never loses track of his point. He plays his horn that way, too."

"Art is a thinker," Benny said. "He just doesn't do things for the sake of doing them. He always has a reason in his playing."

In 1845 Alexandre Dumas published his novel *The Corsican Brothers*, a tale about twins attached at birth and surgically parted. The movie version of the story with Douglas Fairbanks, Jr., was tricked out with all sorts of plot complications, Hollywood derring-do, and a love interest quite absent from the book. What Dumas dramatized was the old wives' belief that there is some sort of profound and mystical emotional attachment between twins. Research in recent years on twins separated at birth and brought up apart strongly suggests that there is more than superstition to this notion. Such twins have often proved to have similar interests and hobbies and careers, and have been stricken by the same ailments. In one case, separated twin brothers took up careers in law enforcement, married women with the same name, and vacationed at the same beach in Florida, without ever crossing trails.

There have been many examples of brothers in the jazz and dance-band worlds—Tommy and Jimmy Dorsey, Hank, Elvin, and Thad Jones; Tootie, Jimmy, and Percy Heath; Les and Larry Elgart; Guy, Carmen, and Liebert Lombardo; Ray and Zoot Sims; Oscar and Chuck Peterson; Bart and Erik Van Lier among them. The only instance I know of twins, and certainly at the higher level of the profession, is that of Addison and Arthur Stewart Farmer.

Art and Addison grew up in Phoenix, Arizona, where their mother had moved with her parents after her divorce from the twins' father, James Arthur Farmer. He subsequently died in an Omaha steel mill explosion, and the boys never really knew him. The family, which included Art's sister Mauvolene, made the move to Arizona to alleviate his grandmother's asthma. Phoenix at that time was comparatively free of pollens, a condition that has changed with residential buildup and the attendant installation of gardens. His grandfather was a minister in the African Methodist Episcopal Church, and the family lived in its parsonage. Among

Art's various relatives there were many doctors and lawyers, a good number of whom were amateur musicians. His mother played piano and sang in the church. Arthur very early started playing piano and violin, and in high school played sousaphone in a marching band for a year, then took up the cornet.

Arizona was highly segregated, so Arthur was unable to find a proper teacher of the instrument "on our side of the tracks," as he put it. He taught himself to play his horn, as Bix Beiderbecke had done before him, and, like Bix, he played wrong. This would within a few years play hell with his chops.

There was nothing of interest for the boys in Phoenix, and they began to do some California dreaming. They had persuaded their mother to let them go there for vacation when, in the summer of 1944, the Zoot Suit Riots, as they became known to journalism and then history, occurred in Los Angeles. She withdrew permission for the trip, and they did not go until the summer of 1945, when World War II was coming to a close. The boys were four years old when the family moved to Phoenix, sixteen when they left.

"There was so much going on in L.A. we just couldn't go back to Phoenix," Art recalled. "We stayed there. Our mother said, 'Okay, long as you graduate from high school.' That first summer, Addison and I and another kid from Phoenix had a short-lived job in a cold-storage warehouse, stacking up cartons of fruits and vegetables. We got fired for having fights with the spuds, throwing them at each other. That fall Addison and I just enrolled in high school, as if we were living there with our parents. The school never found out. We were in a very good position. We were able to duck school and write our own excuses. We'd say, 'Please excuse my son, because he had to do such-and-such.' We were hanging out every night until two and three and four o'clock. And then we had to be in school at 8:30 the next day. The hardest thing, I remember, was that my first class was gym, and I didn't feel like that.

"Addison and I got some gigs. He made more gigs than I did. I worked with Horace Henderson and Floyd Ray. A lot of guys were still in the service. We lived in rented rooms. At one point we lived in a hotel on Central Avenue, but rented rooms were cheaper. There were a lot of them then. When we couldn't pay, we'd move on. Charlie Parker spent some nights with us. We had a room with twin beds and a couch. That's when we got to know him.

"He had a bad reputation about money, but not with us. If he said to Addison, 'Lend me ten dollars, I'll pay you back tomorrow,' he'd always pay it back. Freddie Redd will tell you the same thing. Freddie said Bird would slip him some money and say, 'Don't tell anybody where you got it.' You talk to Dizzy or to Red Rodney, they'll tell you good things about Charlie Parker.

"He and I used to go to movies along Central Avenue when they were half over. We'd ask the people to let us in, because we had no money.

"Then I got a job with the Johnny Otis band. They were going back east, leaving a month before the school year finished. It was my last year, and I wanted to get that diploma. So I went to the principal and I explained to him what my situation was. I said, 'This is my chance to get started. But I'd still like to get my diploma.' So he said, 'All right. Your work has been good, and you have it coming.' I said, 'Will you put that in writing, please, and leave it in the safe?' And he did. I went back there maybe ten years later, and he wasn't there any longer, but that letter was, and I got it."

"You went to Jefferson High School, right? And you were in that band led by Samuel Browne?" Thomas Jefferson High was a school with a good reputation, and the band led by Browne has taken on some proportions of legend, because of the distinguished musicians it turned out.

"Yeah. It was what is now called a stage band, but at that time it was just a dance band. We used to go around and play at other high schools. It was a very good experience. There were people in the band writing, and we played a lot of stocks. *A Train, Bijou*, things like that."

"Dexter Gordon came out of that high school," I said. "Ed Thigpen, Frank Morgan."

"Cecil McNeeley—now known as Big Jay McNeeley. At that time he was called Bebop McNeeley, because everything he played he was doubling up. Thigpen was there at the same time I was. He was a couple of grades under me."

"Was that a mixed school at that time?"

"It was mostly black by then, but there were some Orientals and Mexicans and Caucasians."

"Vi Redd lived near there, and she said it was a pretty nice neighborhood."

"It was."

"So you went out with Johnny Otis."

"Yeah, I went east with Otis. We went to Chicago and worked at Earl Hines' place called the El Grotto. We worked there about ten weeks. That was my introduction to the east. Chicago isn't east, but it was east to me. Working ten weeks in a place like that was a great experience.

"After El Grotto in Chicago, we went to New York and played the Apollo Theater, and I was given my notice. This was the end of the war, and all the experienced musicians were coming home. Johnny said, 'Well, no hard feelings, man, but when I hired you, I hired you to do a job. And you can't do it.' Because I'd really messed my lip up, playing with pressure, I had a big hole in it. I finished my time with the band in Detroit, and went back to New York and hung around for a few days, and somebody introduced me to Freddy Webster. I explained to him what my problem was. He said, 'Well you should go down town and see a guy named Maurice Grupp, a trumpet teacher.' So I went down and talked to him, and had a lesson. He asked me what I intended to do, and I said, 'Well, I have no money and no job, and I either go back to L. A. or back to Phoenix.' He said, 'Well, I think you shouldn't go any place like that until you get yourself in better shape. Why don't you stay here and take some lessons? You don't have to play music to survive, you can do some other kind of work.'

"Which is what I did. I started working as a janitor at the Alhambra Theatre on 125th Street at Seventh Avenue, then at Radio City Music Hall, for about twenty bucks a week. They would close about eleven, and I would be there about twelve cleaning up, and I did that for over a year. And during that time, I might have made two gigs. I would go downtown and go to 52nd Street first, one time I even sat in with Dizzy's band. And then I would go around the corner and do my gig. But sometimes I would get too involved with what was going on on the street, and I got late to the gig. I went there one time and the boss met me at the door and said, 'You're fired,' and I said, 'Okay,' and I just went right across the street to the RCA building, and went to work that same night. There was a lot of turnover in that kind of work, because the pay was low. I'm very glad I did it, that I was there, and that I studied like that. I had a good teacher, and I heard a lot of good music. I was better off there than being back in L.A. or a lot of other places. Man, when I look back over the years that I've been playing, and what I went through right then, and think of so many guys who are no longer playing at all, that were at that time in much better shape than I was, who had the gigs and were able to play the horn.

"My brother was working with Jay McShann. He stayed west when I went east with Johnny Otis. McShann was on the road. Benny Bailey was with McShann. Then Benny got a job with Dizzy's big band, so that left a chair open with McShann's band, and my brother told him about me, and the next thing they sent me a telegram, saying I should join them. I was going to join them in some town down south, but I got there a day late, so I sent a telegram to my teacher in New York, and he sent me some money. He was a very nice guy. And I finally joined up with McShann, and we worked our way back to Los Angeles. And that was about the end of the band. I made my first record with McShann.

"I was in Kansas City recently, I played a concert there, and I met the three original trumpet players of the original McShann band when Charlie Parker was in the band. One guy, Buddy Anderson, was the guy who introduced Bird and Dizzy. There's a hotel there now called the Plaza International, on Twelfth Street. It's very jazz oriented. The ballroom is called the Count Basie Ballroom, they have a Yardbird Suite, and the Mary Lou Williams

Room, the Jay McShann Room, and on the sidewalk outside they have stars, like on Sunset Boulevard. I remember playing there with McShann. The way things have changed. We played on Twelfth Street, we played in some jazz club, opposite Joe Venuti. We played a set, and when Joe played a set we had to go down in the cellar. The management didn't want us up there with white people."

"You know, Jesus," I said, "these things still shock me to death. It stupefies me."

"The thing about it," Art said, "was that we were glad to have the job. We'd just go down there and play tonk or hearts or some simple card game, and when the time came, we'd go back up and play. Charlie Parker came to town and he wanted to come in there, and they wouldn't even let him in."

Back in Los Angeles, out of the McShann band, Art played gigs with Teddy Edwards, Hampton Hawes, Gerald Wilson, Dexter Gordon, and Wardell Gray—whenever, that is, they could use him. "But it wasn't," he said, "really enough to take care of the rent, so I was working at Los Angeles County General Hospital as an X-ray clerk. There were sessions going on. Frank Morgan and I used to go to them, and run into guys like Mulligan, Getz, Chet Baker, whoever was in town. One Sunday afternoon I went to a session, Lionel Hampton's band was in town, and I ran into Quincy Jones and Buster Cooper and a couple of other guys from the band. A couple of days later I got a call from Quincy or somebody to say that there might be an open chair in the band soon, and would I be interested. So I went around for, I guess you could call it, an audition. But all it was was Hamp saying," and Art went into a perfect imitation of Hampton's voice, "'Come on, Gates, let's play some *All God's Children Got Rhythm*.' If you could play that, you got the gig. When I joined, Benny Bailey was in the band, and we had six trumpets. Benny left a couple of weeks later. I took over his solos. That situation existed for about ten months until Brownie came in. Clifford took the place of a trumpet player named Eddie Mullins, we called him Moon Mullins, a very good ballad arranger who left to go with Duke. Clifford was just in the band a few weeks before we went to Europe.

"In Los Angeles Wardell recorded one of my tunes for Prestige. It was untitled. The master went back to New York. Ira Gitler heard it and called it *Farmer's Market*, and he decided to call me Art Farmer. Until then no one had ever called me anything but Arthur. When I went east with Lionel, I went over to the Prestige office and introduced myself to Bob Weinstock. He said, 'Glad to meet you. Maybe you'd want to make some recordings for us.' The summer we went to Europe, I made the first recording for Prestige. Quincy was playing the piano. Gigi Gryce, James Cleveland, and Monk Montgomery were in the group. The drummer was Sonny Johnson from Indianapolis.

"Weinstock knew we were going to Sweden. He made arrangements through Claus Dahlgren to record in Sweden with Lars Gullin, Bengt Hallberg, and all those guys. We knew Lionel would raise hell, so we didn't tell him anything, we sneaked out the back door of the hotel, and made the recording. We went directly to the concert hall the next night, and one of the flunkies said, 'Hey, Lionel wants to see you guys right away.' So we went to his dressing room, and he said, 'What happened to you guys last night?' So I told him, 'Gates, you shoulda been with us, we ran into some of the baddest chicks, man, we partied, we had a nice time.' He said, 'Oh yeah?' We went on to Paris. George Wallington had come into the band, and he didn't know what a character Lionel was. He told Hampton we had recorded, and Lionel called a meeting, and he was going to fire the whole band, but he couldn't because the band was so successful. We did the whole tour over, without going back to the States. The album came out as Art Farmer and Clifford Brown, or maybe the other way around, and the Swedish All Stars, a ten-inch LP. After the tour, we all left the band, Quincy and Gigi Gryce and Cleve. I would never say anything against Hamp, though. He gave me a gig. And if he hadn't, I don't know how I'd ever have gotten out of Los Angeles.

"After the tour I stayed in New York and started to freelance. Gigi and I had a quintet. We recorded three or four records for

Prestige. I worked with whoever called me. I worked about a year with Horace Silver. Lester Young had a contract to work so many weeks a year at Birdland. I would make all those. That was a great experience. He walked sideways, sort of shuffled over sideways, like in the army. He walks over to me, he says, 'Hey, Prez, there's a little bitch sitting over there shootin' me down. She don't know that all I want to do when I get through with this gig is go home and get my sandwich and go to bed.' He was okay the two years I worked with him. When he died, in '58, I was with Mulligan.

"I'd been working with Horace. On some session, I ran into Dave Bailey, who was playing drums with Gerry. Bob Brookmeyer had left, and Chet Baker came back to the group, but that didn't work out, and Mulligan was looking for a trumpet player. So I left Horace and went with Mulligan. Henry Grimes was the bass player, but shortly afterwards Bill Crow took his place. We really had some nice times. We made one record on Columbia called *What Is There to Say*. It was a good record, but it didn't really show what that group could get into. I really learned a lot with Gerry. But it was strange, at first, to work with no piano after working with Horace, who was such a dominant pianist.

"I'd been studying with George Russell, and one night when I got through with my solo, Gerry came over and said, 'Those things you're playing on that solo, they're interfering with my background.'" Art laughed.

"Oh! That's wonderful," I said. "Oh! But you gotta know Gerry to appreciate it!"

"Gerry is a great guy," Art said. "We used to get into arguments, and it wouldn't mean a thing the next day."

"That's one of his wonderful qualities," I said. "You know, I've never seen anyone who grew as much as Gerry has."

"He really has. Gerry is a *nice* guy."

"What happened after Gerry?"

"We toured in Europe, and after we got back he wanted to start his concert band. I didn't want to play in a big band again. During the time I was with Gerry, Benny Golson and I and Bill Evans had won the *Down Beat* critics poll, and Monte Kay, who was in charge of jazz at UA, had the idea of recording an album by the poll winners. Bill and I had a very nice relationship. We recorded the album, with Addison on bass and on the drums Dave Bailey. Once the record was made, Monte decided to put it out in my name under the title *Modern Art.*

"I got the idea to call Benny to work with me. He had been working with Art Blakey. And Benny called me to come to work with him. So we decided to become partners. Benny said that rather than just have another quintet, it would be nice to have another horn. Benny had worked on an extended gig with Curtis Fuller for eight months one time. So that's how it started. The name for the group came from Curtis, who really has a talent with words. He came up with the idea of calling it the Jazztet."

Benny Golson was born five months after Arthur and Addison Farmer, on January 25, 1929, in Philadelphia. James Lincoln Collier's point that jazz was not a black music played only for black audiences but a black music played to a large extent for white audiences turns out on close scrutiny to have much validity. Blacks were barred from many of the nightclubs where the music was heard, as Art notes in his recollection of Kansas City. Many black parents despised jazz and forbade their children to listen to it, those of Billie Holiday and Fats Waller among them. Nor did the black intellectual establishment champion jazz. In their anxiety to emulate, and enable their students to rise in, a white world, black universities all too often ignored black cultural history, jazz particularly. Benny majored in clarinet at Howard University. Such was the official contempt for jazz that he hardly dared admit that he owned a saxophone, and he practiced the instrument in the laundry room so that no one would hear him.

"I guess," I said to Art, "it was when you and Benny brought the Jazztet to Chicago that I first knew you guys, and I did that cover story on you for *Down Beat.* It was such a promising group. Gigi Gryce and Benny wrote such lovely things for it; it was such an intelligent integration of writing and blowing, and of course you had Curtis. What happened to that group?"

"The Jazztet started about the same time Ornette Coleman and Don Cherry came to New York," Art said. "In fact we opened at the Five Spot opposite each other. We were kind of shoved aside. We didn't get the attention that we would have liked. And we were struggling and scuffling, and we got gigs, but we never really got a solid start. McCoy Tyner left to go with 'Trane, and Curtis Fuller left, and we started having personnel problems, getting this guy and that guy. The idea of the group at the beginning was to have these two guys, McCoy and Curtis. We were able to get good piano players, but to find someone to play like Curtis was impossible. We got to the point where we were rehearsing *Killer Joe* all the time. At that time, when you had a group, you had a group, and the ambition was to work every week. It wasn't like now, when you play a few weeks and then go about your business. We just got to the place where it was a rut. I wanted to play more. Benny was getting much into the writing, jingles and all kinds of stuff. I'd heard Jim Hall with Sonny Rollins. I made a record with a big band for Mercury, and Jim was on the record. I asked him would he be interested in doing some gigs with me. We had that quartet for a year."

"That must have been about the time I moved to New York," I said. "You told me to meet you at Jim and Andy's. You introduced me to to the place. Just recently I talked to somebody who said they'd run into you at the airport in New York, and you were looking very bleak and forlorn, and he thought you were on the way to a gig or something, and you said you were taking Addison home."

"To Phoenix," Art said.

"That was such a shock to me. I can't conceive of what it must have been to you."

"Yeah. He'd been by my apartment that afternoon. I had been working at the Half Note. He went home. I took a nap. His wife was on the phone, said he was very sick. I jumped in the car and drove up there. He lived on 95th Street. I lived down on 20th Street. You were by that place. And he said, 'I have a terrible headache. I slipped in the bathtub, and I hit my head.' He had had an accident a couple of weeks earlier. He borrowed my car and he hit his head on the windshield, but he seemed all right. He'd told me at one time recently, 'Sometimes, you know, I get so wrapped up in what I'm doing, practicing this or going to this gig, I forget to eat, and I get a terrible headache. And then I eat and it's okay.' I didn't pay it no mind. So he said he had this headache, and I said, 'Okay, we should get you to the hospital.' We called the ambulance, and I went to work. And I called up from the gig to Knickerbocker Hospital in upper Manhattan, and the woman said they had packed him in ice to bring down his fever. I rushed up there, and I asked Lois, his wife, 'How is he?'

"Lois said, 'He just died.'

"I spoke to the doctor, a lady, and she said his heart had stopped about three times, and they had always been able to get it going, but this time it didn't happen."

Whatever John F. Kennedy was or was not, he embodied an optimism that had always been a strong characteristic of America and Americans. He was not only the youngest president in American history, he was the handsomest, and with his attractive wife and beautiful children, he seemed like a man with a stake in the future. He got the Russians to remove their missiles from Cuba and opened a dialogue with Nikita Khrushchev that boded well for humanity's survival.

Popular music both reflects and affects the emotional state of a nation. In the second year of Kennedy's presidency, popular music, led by Dizzy Gillespie, Bob Brookmeyer, Charlie Byrd, and a few others, imported from Brazil a musical style faddishly known as *bossa nova* and integrated it into jazz. It was gorgeous stuff, rhythmically subtle, harmonically sophisticated, melodically sensuous, and incomparably romantic. It swept the United States, and then the world. Jazz seemed to be in excellent condition, with all the major labels and a proliferating number of smaller ones dedicated to it. Stan Getz, Jimmy Smith, Erroll Garner, Herbie Mann, Cal Tjader, Dave Brubeck, and others had hit record albums.

Nine months after Addison Farmer died, John F. Kennedy was assassinated. So, immediately after him, was his alleged assassin, and then his assassin's assassin died in jail of what some people think was an induced cancer, both deaths hermetically sealing the main actors from any further inquiry. In the next few years, his brother, Robert Kennedy, was assassinated, and so too were Malcolm X. and Martin Luther King. All of these deaths, official Washington tried to persuade the public, were unrelated to each other, the discontinuous acts of individual madmen. Whether they were or they weren't, what *seemed* to be so was that anyone who appeared able and likely to lead America and the world toward a better life would not be allowed to live. There *seemed* to be a "they" who would dash any hopes one allowed to arise.

In the trauma that followed Kennedy's death, guitars began to snarl with distortion, voices began to shriek and scream, psychedelic lighting in discothèques assaulted the nervous system, and rock-and-roll singers commenced an advertising campaign for drug use that created the atmosphere for the United States, which comprises 5 percent of the world's population, to consume 60 percent of the world's illegal psychotropic substances. There were ugly riots in Chicago during the Democratic convention of 1968. A young man who at fifteen promised to be a superb jazz flutist told me five years later that you couldn't expect his generation to wait for gratification in music or anything else when most of its members didn't expect to live to be thirty.

It is small wonder that the hopes of black Americans started to flicker out after the death of Jack Kennedy. Riots began, and jazz fell on hard times as a popular music of unprecedented ugliness reflected and reinforced the mood of the young while the napalm splashed and splattered in Vietnam. Whether jazz was or was not a popular music—and some of its best practitioners have insisted that it is—it had no choice now but to be an art music; it certainly was no longer a part of the pop-music mainstream. Quite a number of American jazz musicians, most of them black but some of them white, left the land of their birth, and the music's, in the decade following Kennedy's, and incidentally Addison Farmer's, death. Ben Webster moved to Europe and sent us all a card at Jim and Andy's saying, "I ain't had so much fun since I been cullid." Dexter Gordon left; Don Byas had been gone for some time. Sahib Shihab, Richard Boone, Ernie Wilkins, and Kenny Drew moved to Copenhagen, and in time Thad Jones and Ed Thigpen did too.

Arthur Taylor, Phil Woods, and Michael Zwerin took residence in Paris, where Kenny Clarke was already living. Red Mitchell moved to Stockholm, Jiggs Whigham to London, Al Porcino to Munich, Benny Bailey and Idrees Suleiman to Germany, Jimmy Woode to Switzerland, Johnny Griffin to Holland.

"You remember how it was over here in the '60s," Art said. "I was in a real rut in New York, working in Slug's in New York, and places like it in Philly, working in the ghetto. There were riots in the street, and the cities going up in flames.

"One night I went down to the Half Note, where Donald Bird was playing. After he got through, he drove me home to 20th Street. The riot was going on in Newark that night. We were sitting in front of the building, just sitting there talking, last words. And here comes a cop's car. The cops shine the lights in our eyes. You remember, down in that neighborhood, there were lots of factories."

"Yeah," I said, "I remember the look of streetlamps on those red-brick cobblestone streets."

"Well," the cop said, 'What are you all doing down here?'

"I said, 'I live here.'

"He said, 'What are you doing sitting in the car?'

"I said, 'We're just sitting here talking. Can't I do that?'

"Donald said, 'Cool it, man, cool it, cool it.'

"So shortly after that, why, I decided I might as well try it on the other side."

In 1965 he was invited to Vienna to act as a judge in a jazz contest sponsored by a bank. The contest lasted three weeks, during which he met local musicians who told him they were forming a radio jazz band—a common phenomenon in European countries—and invited him to join it. Since his services would be required for only ten days a month during nine months of the year, the offer was very tempting and he accepted it. Twice married and twice divorced, Art was a single man at the time. He met Mechtilde Lawgger, who worked for the bank sponsoring the jazz contest, and married her.

He has lived in Vienna ever since, though he travels much of the time, about half of it in America. His career is cresting, both as a soloist and as part of the Jazztet, which has risen phoenix-like from its own ashes, twenty-six years after its birth. Benny Golson, who had worked so hard to get into film and television music, was now weary of it, and looking around for other things to do. One of the shows he scored was *The Six Million Dollar Man*, which had been Oliver Nelson's gig until his death. Benny would sit writing all day in his workroom, feeling a slave to another medium. And anyway, things were going wrong for film composers, with the nasal squeal and whoof-whoof-whoof of synthesizers replacing real music in scores. Art said it took Benny two years to get his chops back on saxophone; Benny says, "More than that. It was like coming back from a stroke." And, wonder of wonders, Curtis Fuller, so important a part of the Jazztet at the start of it, was interested in re-forming the group.

I heard them in September 1986 at the Monterey Festival. In the chill of the outdoor stage, faced by a noisy and unruly audience that George Shearing, farther down that evening, upbraided, they were not particularly impressive. But later, on an indoor stage, in the "nightclub," as they call it, that has become part of the festival, they played superbly. Curtis Fuller long ago taught me a simple clear musical principle: "You sacrifice tone for speed," he said. "That's right," Art said, when I quoted this to him. "You have to lighten up a little to get speed." "It's true," Benny Golson said, "although the exception to that rule seems to be Curtis himself. And Art." The group had changed. It was hotter, harder, more adventurous, and Golson himself—for all he protested that his playing still isn't up to what it was—was a much more exploratory and daring player than he used to be. Benny's playing always projected his cultivated and gentle nature, and it still did, but it was much gutsier now.

Art Farmer illustrates a principle that has been stated of literature but can apply equally to music: the greatest style is no style at all. There are no identifiable mannerisms in his playing. All that distinguishes it is its brilliance, and its lyrical warmth. He still remembers an incident that occurred during his youth in Los

Angeles. He and Addison and friends were walking one night on Central Avenue from one jazz club to another, to catch the action. They were stopped and questioned twice by cops. The third time this happened, Art said, in that quiet sarcasm that is his nearest approach to overt rage, "Hey, which way are you guys walking? Do you mind if we walk with you, and then your other cops won't bother us?" The secret of Art's playing, I think, lies in his cultural heritage, the stoicism that probably is the legacy of his Blackfoot ancestry leashing the anger of the man told by Donald Bird that night to cool it, cool it.

The quiet and clear intelligence that controls his actions also controls the tones coming out of his horn—only fluegelhorn now, the instrument he finds much more congenial and natural to him than trumpet. And those tones rise from a well of emotion ranging from deep love to dark anger. It is as if Arthur Farmer is always trying to control his feelings and failing to do so, to the immense enrichment of this era's music.

"In my opinion," Benny Golson said, "Art Farmer is the foremost instrumental interpreter of the ballad. When he plays such, it's as though one is privy to a love triangle—a man, his horn, and the song at hand. Writing ballads is one of my favorite pastimes and somehow I intuitively write them with Art in mind. There is no greater fulfillment or reward than hearing him play them.

"But I must say that since he plays a ballad so superlatively well, one might tend to overlook him as a complete trumpet (and fluegelhorn) player. This is a rather bad mistake. At any tempo he's able to evince a certain pervasive melodism. And he can particularly fulfill the requirements of a swift tempo *without* sacrificing sound, fullness and tone, quality, for speed—no small thing. Were one to competitively jump onto the bandstand with him, that person would probably get skinned quite badly.

"Another thing about him. Art Farmer, like Art Blakey, is didactic without ever being aware of it.

"Finally, there's a side of Art's talent that has been overlooked, even by Art himself to some degree. He has great merit as a composer. All of his tunes are unique in that the structures, particu-

larly nowadays, are completely unexpected. They challenge pre-
dictability. His choice of chords is odd, different, because they
gallantly defy convention and conventional resolutions. They just
might resolve anywhere, and yet, when linked with his melodies,
they sound quite logical—and haunting, to say the least. At the
moment, this source of creativity has not been fully tapped, which
indicates we can expect more interesting and exciting things, as
there are obviously more things yet to be extracted from his volu-
minous creative closet—things screaming to get out."

"I'll tell you something else," I said. "I think he's happier than
I've ever seen him."

"You're right. Art has really come out in the last year. He cracks
jokes on the mike, and it's all the funnier coming from him. Have
you noticed that his voice on the telephone is a little higher now?"

Art treasures his time at home in Vienna with his wife, although,
he said that if the election to the presidency of Kurt Waldheim had
occurred when he first went there, he would never have settled in
Austria—and he doesn't hesitate to tell Austrians that. By now his
son by his first wife, Renee, was thirty-two, and his boy in Austria,
who speaks English with an accent, was fifteen. Art said he looks
more like Addison than like himself, although that is a distinction
he alone could make.

"Losing Addison," he said, "was like getting my hand chopped
off suddenly.

"There was a deeper attachment that you don't even think
about. We were so close that certain things we didn't have to say.
There were a lot of disagreements, too. You can have the most
disagreements with the person you're closest to because they know
exactly what you're thinking. Basically, though, we agreed on
things.

"The funny thing is that, subconsciously, Addison is still alive to
me. I still have dreams about him. In the dreams we're doing this,
doing that, talking, arguing, going some place, playing, practicing,
rehearsing, traveling.

"The little things of life."

12

THE LAST DAYS
OF JUNIOR'S

THOUGH JIM AND ANDY'S was the favorite tavern of jazz musicians in New York in the 1960s, there were three more in which they habitually congregated—Joe Harbor's Spotlight, Charlie's, and Junior's. Sometimes late at night Gerry Mulligan and I would end up on the East Side in Elaine's, which attracted writers and socialites, because that was Paul Desmond's lair and he'd lure us there. But generally Gerry and I were habitue's of those four musicians' bars, and mostly Jim and Andy's at that.

Jim and Andy's died when Jim Koulouvaris died, Joe Harbor's when Joe Harbor died. Charlie was already gone. But Henry Solomon, who owned Junior's, outlived it. The place was effectually murdered by elements of the New York Police Department. Mulligan and I are among the few persons who know the story.

Joe Harbor's was on Broadway near 53rd Street. It was, Gerry remembers, patronized largely by studio and network-radio players. If you walked south and headed west on 52nd Street, you passed Junior's on your right and, four or five doors farther along, Charlie's. Proceeding still farther you encountered the Roseland Ballroom, though it was the second Roseland, not the earlier one where Louis Armstrong and Fletcher Henderson and Bix Beiderbecke made history.

Charlie's, Mulligan remarked, was home to everybody: studio and club-date and Broadway pit-band musicians, jazz musicians,

musicians from the Latin bands. Junior's, Charlie's, and Roseland were on the same side of the block as the Alvin Hotel, that faded storied refuge of faded storied road musicians. Across the street was the Alvin Theater, and across from Junior's was Gallagher's restaurant, owned by Henry Solomon's brother Jack.

I knew about Charlie's and Junior's before I ever laid eyes on them. I was introduced to them, as it were, in 1959, through Ed Sherman's *Out of My Head* column in *Down Beat*, written under the pseudonym George Crater, a play on the name of the long-vanished Judge Crater.

Eddie was a denizen of Junior's and Charlie's, and references to them were always turning up in his column. He would stage imaginary contests between the two places, with improbable prizes, one of which was often an eight-by-ten autographed glossy photo of Tony Graye. Eddie said he was a less than impressive tenor player who was constantly importuning the masters to let him sit in. Eddie said that Tony Graye was author of the line, "Bird said I was unbelievable." I accused Eddie of inventing Tony Graye, along with the other more obviously fictional musicians who peopled his column, such as Zoot Finster, Prez Glick, Zig Priff, and Miles Cosnat. Eddie insisted he really did exist, and one day I received proof of it: Eddie sent me an autographed eight-by-ten glossy photo of Tony Graye.

"Oh, he existed all right," Bill Crow says. "He was a regular in Junior's and Charlie's, handing out those autographed photos even to musicians. He was good looking, and had all the paraphernalia of a bandleader except the talent. I once worked a gig with him in the Bronx. It was unforgettable. I remember coming into Junior's one night and seeing Phil Woods sitting at the front table near the window, staring at one of those autographed photos of Tony Graye, shaking his head and saying, 'I guess I'll never make it, I don't have any eight-by-ten glossy photos.'

"Do you remember Al Thompson, the saxophone player? He died recently. He was an old road rat. He was a regular at both Jim and Andy's and Junior's. He used to sit at the bar calling out the changes of the tunes on the juke box. He was also a baseball nut. One night Gene Quill came into Junior's, half loaded I guess. I seem to remember there were three steps down as you entered. Gene stumbled and came sliding into the place, and Al Thompson yelled, 'Safe!'"

Among Eddie Sherman's many ingenious felicities was his co-invention of the wind-up dolls. His conspirator, he said, was Bob Brookmeyer. One of the first was the Stan Kenton wind-up doll: you wound it up, put it on the table, and it raised its arms. Then there was the Gerry Mulligan wind-up doll (and it could only have been invented by Brookmeyer): you wound it up, put it on the table, and it called room service. The Miles Davis doll turned its back, the Thelonious Monk doll disappeared, and the Charlie Mingus doll punched you out.

The wind-up dolls were soon taken up by writers in other magazines and used in other contexts and applied to other professions, but they were invented one night by Eddie Sherman and Bob Brookmeyer, and they were invented in Junior's.

ˋ Mulligan figured in one of Eddie's earliest columns, that of September 17, 1959. He wrote: "Why doesn't Gerry Mulligan marry Judy Holliday and get it over with? And then record an album titled *The Bells Are Swinging*." That bit of humor was to have a strange and sad aftermath.

Eventually I encountered Eddie Sherman face to face. I called him before a trip to New York, and he met me—where else?—at Junior's. He was a delicate, fragile young man in his late twenties, a feather of a figure a wind could carry off. He wore a dark suit and white shirt and slim tie, in the Miles Davis mode of that period, and he was serious of mood and manner, as those who are professionally funny so often are. It was obvious in Junior's that Eddie was as popular with the musicians as his column. By then Orrin Keepnews at Riverside was preparing to record him, an album with Eddie in the personna of George Crater. This and his *Down Beat* column launched him as a comedy writer. He became one of the writers on the TV show *That Was the Week That Was*. The show folded, but Eddie was on his way. I was quite proud of my protégé.

If my primary loyalty in those days was to Jim and Andy's, I raised my share of glasses in Junior's and Charlie's, and now and then a few at Joe Harbor's Spotlight. Taverns are fine and comfortable places, neutral grounds on which we meet and overcome fears with a little chemical assistance, the only drug, really, to which civilization for all its ancient knowledge of psychotropics has extended even a conditional approval. In restrained and decent use alcohol produces a mood of reconciliation, which leads to laughter and philosophic musings. This was particularly true in Jim and Andy's, Junior's, and Charlie's. Joe Harbor's struck me as a more raucous place. I liked the others better.

Yet Charlie's at first made me uncomfortable. The owner was not the maker of the establishment's mood; I never even met Charlie. The bartender set its tone. And the bartender was Gene Williams, whom I had first heard of in high school when he was one of the two singers—the other was Fran Warren—with the Claude Thornhill band at a time when Mulligan, Lee Konitz, Mickey Folus, Barry Galbraith, and Billy Exener were among its players, and Gil Evans, whom Thornhill had met in the Skinnay Ennis band, was its chief arranger. Such people seemed like gods to me then, and to encounter Gene Williams behind the bar at Charlie's filled me with unease. I didn't know how to behave. Was it proper, when he served me a drink, to tip him? I soon got over this discomfiture, however, with Gene's help. One night he told me how he felt about things.

The big band era was over, he said, and that was that. He hadn't hit it big, like Frank Sinatra or Dick Haymes, hadn't had a hot record to launch him as a single, but those were the breaks. He had no intention of traveling the country to sing in dives and dumps and toilets for lousy money and nothing to show for it at the end of the year. To hell with it. He liked working here, he made good money, and he liked seeing all his friends from the band days, to hang out and talk and laugh with them. He was happily married and content with his life. Gene Williams struck me as one of the sanest men I'd ever met. He was tough and calm and realistic, and I came to admire him.

If you were a patron of Charlie's, you'll remember that the place was long and narrow. The bar, of dark wood, was on the east wall—to your right as you entered. It curved out from the wall, ran straight back for maybe twenty feet, then curved in again to meet the wall near the rear. I was sitting one night on a stool near the curve at the back of the place when an altercation broke out.

The antagonists were two outsiders, shaggy street people loaded on who knows what: this was in the early days of acid, and there was a lot of it around, but maybe they were just juiced. One of them pulled a switch-blade knife.

I was talking with Gene Quill, who sat next to me, and Gene Williams, who was leaning on the bar between us, sharing in the shmooz. At that moment somebody yelled, "Hey, Gene!" And of course all three of us looked toward the voice. Gene Williams headed swiftly along the duck boards behind the bar. The shaggy made a lunge for his companion. One of the musicians swung at his arm, chopping it downward. The blade, which had a mother of pearl handle, fell from his hand and clattered along the floor, sliding to a stop almost at my feet. I grabbed it and flipped it up over the bar. Gene Williams saw it coming and, as it hit the floor, snatched it up and threw it into an ice bucket. It was weird, as if this co-ordination had been choreographed: Tinker to Evers to Chance. The bladesman didn't know what had happened.

Puzzled, and stoned, he looked at his empty hand and at the floor and said, pitifully, "What happened to m'blade?" He looked at Gene imploringly. "What happened to my blade?" he repeated. Quill and I started to laugh.

"I don't know what you're talking about," Gene Williams said, "but I want you to get outa here."

"Not till I find my blade," the shaggy said, looking around the floor. "My girlfriend gave me that knife."

"I didn't see any knife. Any of you guys see a knife?" Gene said as the other two Genes, Quill and I, kept laughing. "Now, get outa here, before I call the cops and have them help you hunt for your knife." Still the man wouldn't leave.

Gene saw a police cruiser in the crowded street. He hailed it.

Two cops came in. The bladesman complained that his knife had disappeared. Even the cops started to laugh, and told him to clear out. The man left with his companion, their animus ended in the mystery of the vanished knife.

Gene Williams told us later that they came back about one in the morning, still looking for the blade. By then Gene had had a friend take the knife, wrapped in a napkin, out to the street and drop it down a sewer. Still lamenting his lost knife, the man said he was going to lodge a complaint with the police. You just do that, Gene said, you just go ahead and file a complaint.

That winter, 1962, the Brazilians arrived. I had met Antonio Carlos Jobim in Rio de Janeiro earlier that year, probably in June, which is winter there. I had first heard his songs in Chicago, introduced to them by Dizzy Gillespie and Lalo Schifrin, then Dizzy's pianist. In the course of the State Department tour of all the South American countries with the Paul Winter Sextet, I made it a point to look him up in Rio. I went out to his house in Ipanema one rainy night. João Gilberto was sitting on his sofa with a guitar, singing *So Danco Samba*. Jobim and I went out to the kitchen. He spoke little English, and I spoke little Portuguese, though I could triangulate its meaning from French and Spanish. But his ancestors were French, and he spoke the language a little, and so at first we talked French. He poured me a Scotch as we stood by the refrigerator. "I'm crazy," he said, "but he," nodding toward João Gilberto, "is crazier."

I told him he reminded me of a friend of mine back home. Jobim was thirty-five then. "Who?" he said.

"Someone named Gerry Mulligan."

"Ah, but we *know* Gerry Mulligan," he said, and told me—as did João Gilberto later—how profoundly Mulligan had influenced the development of what became known as bossa nova. Gerry was the primary American influence in the development of that music, and I have that on the authority of most of its principals. Jobim said he liked very much the contained controlled sound of what American critics were calling the cool school, often inaccurately ascribed to a Miles Davis authorship.

Brazilian music publishers and record companies had long been exploiting a tacky commercial version of the samba. Serious younger musicians like Jobim and João Gilberto and Sergio Mendes and others rebelled against this. "The authentic Negro samba is very primitive," Jobim told me. "They use maybe ten percussion instruments and the music is very hot and wonderful. But bossa nova is cool and contained. It tells the story, trying to be simple and serious and lyrical. João and I felt that Brazilian music until now had been too much a storm on the sea, and we wanted to calm it down for the recording studio. You could call bossa nova a clean, washed samba, without loss of the momentum. We don't want to lose important things. We have the problem of how to write and not lose the swing."

They wanted to achieve a controlled acoustical balance in recording, rather than have the engineer determine the mix. It was one of Mulligan's ideals, and these Brazilian musicians had heard it across all the thousands of miles and implemented its aesthetics in their own music. But of course it had all come originally from Claude Thornhill and Gil Evans.

I told Jobim that I had studied the lyrics to his songs in recent weeks and had had them explained to me. I said I'd like to try to translate them. "Do you think it can be done?" he said.

"Yes, I do."

I wrote the lyrics to *Desafinado*, an allegory about how the conventional samba musicians had deplored the bossa nova movement with its tinges of jazz and impressionist harmonies, in a taxi one day later that week. The second chord is a joke, a put-on of old-style commercial samba musicians. In F, which is the original key, the second chord is G 7 b5, and the melody falls on the D-flat. It was right out of bebop, and it sent conventional Brazilian musicians up the wall. It was critically important to retain the tongue-in-cheek quality of the lyric, and I think I did, staying very close to the original meaning. I gave the English version to Jobim just before we left Rio. *Corcovado* became *Quiet Nights of Quiet Stars* on a bus as Paul Winter and the group and I headed for Bello Horizonte. I mailed the lyrics back to Jobim.

Word of the new music was reaching North America, partly

because of the film *Black Orpheus*, whose score contained music by both Luiz Bonfa and Jobim. Guitarist Charlie Byrd had toured Latin America some months before, bringing back the three albums Jobim had made with João Gilberto. From one of these he transcribed *Desafinado* (pronounced day-ZOF-ee-naw-doo), somehow getting one of the chords wrong. Byrd recorded a Verve album with Stan Getz called *Jazz Samba*, and one of its tracks, *Desafinado*, became a hit, launching the bossa nova fad in North America and around the world. Bob Brookmeyer had also heard the new music and begun playing it. Bossa nova, then, came to North America through jazz. But the pop-music people jumped on what looked like a hot fad, bringing out such trivia as *Blame It on the Bossa Nova*.

Sidney Frey of Audio Fidelity Records had gained control of the publishing of a lot of the bossa nova material. At that very time, Huntington Hartford's stumbling *Show* magazine—mismanaged until it died—was devoting an issue to Latin America and looking for a promotion stunt. The magazine linked up with Frey. They hired Carnegie Hall for the evening of November 21, 1962, and began advertising what they called with bumptious press-agentry "The First Annual Bossa Nova Festival." It was also the last. The Brazilian government had a vested interest in this burst of attention to their country, and Varig, the Brazilian airline, got into the act. Many of the best Brazilian musicians were flown in for the concert, including Sergio Mendes, Jobim, and the guitarist Bola Sete, a nickname that means Seven Ball, as well as guitarist Baden Powell.

Backstage at Carnegie, I introduced Jobim to Mulligan. Then the concert got under way.

It was a disaster, a fiasco, a trashy flashy commercial exploitation job. Sidney Frey was recording everything, and there were microphones everywhere. But most of them led to recording mixing boards, not to the sound system, and the audience could hardly hear the music. Afterwards the press in Rio racked Jobim, Gilberto, and their colleagues for failing to make a better showing for the motherland. The *New Yorker* headlined a flippant review

"Bossa Nova Go Home." It was cruelly unfair. The Brazilian musicians were the victims, not the villains.

And all these Brazilians were left to their own resources in New York, like beached dolphins. Mulligan and I took some of them in tow, particularly Jobim, whom we introduced to Junior's, Charlie's, Jim and Andy's, and maybe even Joe Harbor's. One of the television networks wanted to do a feature on Jobim. It was shot in Gerry's penthouse apartment, which was on the West Side near Central Park, and a block or two south of the Dakota, where Judy Holliday lived. Between takes, Jobim and I and Gerry would walk out on the terrace and look at the lowering winter sky. I waved a hand to take in the skyline. "São Paulo," I said. For that's what it looked like. "Yes," Jobim said, "São Paulo."

White birds were soaring near us, emitting sharp anguished cries. "What do you call those?" Jobim asked.

"Sea gulls," I said.

"Sea gulls," he said, repeating it in a manner that would become familiar: he was assimilating the language. "Sea gulls. Yes, we have those at home." No one ever sounded more homesick. We went indoors and the interview continued.

Most of the Brazilians lived in a small hotel on West 43rd Street. Nearby was a Brazilian restaurant where they could get the dishes they liked and missed, although Jobim rapidly acquired a liking for the cuisine of Horn and Hardart's, which mystified me. "It's good honest food," he would say in defense of this peculiar taste.

Lalo Schifrin gave a party for the Brazilians around Christmas time in his apartment in Queens. The weather had turned bitter cold, and the Brazilians had no clothes to cope with it. Poor Baden Powell, how he suffered. He went to the party with his guitar wrapped in a hotel blanket, to keep it warm. He played duets that night with Jimmy Raney.

Probably the first time I ever saw Gerry Mulligan was during the time he and Gene Williams were with the Thornhill band, but the first time I *remember* seeing him was at the Newport Festival of 1960, when he unveiled his concert jazz band. It was pouring rain that night. I was back in the band tent when they went on. Voice of America was videotaping the show. I slipped into the control room, which was at the front of the stage. The stage was at chest height, and, under the roof of that improvised control booth, I had the perfect vantage point. I could see not only what was happening on stage but the TV monitors showing what the cameramen were picking up. The band began to play Bob Brookmeyer's chart on Django Reinhardt's *Manoir de mes rêves*, an exquisite thing. I watched a monitor as a camera panned across a sea of black umbrellas in the rain and then picked up a great puddle onstage in which was reflected the image of Gerry Mulligan, upside down, as he started his solo. The raindrops fell into this puddle, making the image tremble, like the music. The memory is indelible.

But I actually met Mulligan for the first time some weeks later when the band played the Sutherland Hotel in Chicago. No one in Chicago saw much of him, though. Judy Holliday was in the hospital in New York. She had been doing out of town tryouts in *Laurette*, a play about Laurette Taylor, when she lost her voice. Her doctor ordered her into hospital. The late Dorothy Kilgallen, that most vicious of gossip columnists, wrote of her that it was amazing what some actresses would do and say to get out of a show. Judy had a mastectomy. Later I asked her why she hadn't replied to Kilgallen, even sued her. She said she wouldn't dream of trading on public sympathy.

Mulligan during that period was finishing his show at the Sutherland in the small hours of the morning, catching a red-eye to New York to sit by her bedside, and flying back to Chicago for the night's performance. The only reason I knew this is that Brookmeyer told me.

It was during that first winter in New York, with Jobim, that I began to know Gerry well. "Why aren't you writing more?" I chided him. He had begun writing for bands when he was fifteen. It was as a writer that I had first become aware of him: Gene Krupa's *Disk Jockey Jump* is Gerry's composition. After that he wrote for Elliott Lawrence, then for the Claude Thornhill band when Gil Evans was its chief arranger. Gil and Gerry have always insisted that Thornhill has never been given his due as an influence in the development of jazz composition. Though Gil, and to a lesser extent Gerry, wrote for the band, they wrote what Thornhill wanted; and he knew what he wanted. The French horns he added to the instrumentation were part of the Thornhill sound, but he also sought a cool suspended feeling, perhaps rooted in the kind of floating chords that Debussy had explored to such effect.

In the late 1940s, there were gatherings of musicians in Gil's apartment in New York, and in 1949 he and Gerry had an idea for an experimental band. "We kicked the ideas around all that winter," Gerry remembered during one of our conversations in that winter of 1962. "We were looking for the smallest ensemble to give the writers the maximum possibilities. We got it down to six men and the rhythm section. You couldn't write for the sections because there were no sections." Such like-minded friends as John Lewis and Johnny Carisi also contributed to the writing. Miles Davis proved to be the most effective member of the group at arranging jobs and recordings, so they named him leader. The band played the Royal Roost and recorded for Capitol, inaugurating what became known as the era of cool jazz. Mulligan then led a series of groups, including the Tentet with which he recorded for Capitol, a quartet with Chet Baker, a quartet with Bob Brookmeyer, Bill Crow, and Gus Johnson, a quartet with Art Farmer, then the concert band. It was this influence that so affected the Brazilians, but behind Mulligan stood the figure of Gil Evans, and behind Gil, Claude Thornhill. Miles Davis and Gil continued their association in a series of masterpiece albums for Columbia.

"I don't know why I'm not writing more," Gerry admitted. "There are so many reasons that there's no one.

"My approach to the thing was always to simplify rather than complicate. I've concentrated on the small band lately, but I've used my arranging ability not in written orchestrations but in making spontaneous arrangements and un-writing things we worked out. The main point has been to be able to change our arrangements to suit our whim. This has been true of all the groups I've had.

"If I haven't written much for the big band, I've always tried to be clear about what I wanted the writing to be like. I made my taste the criterion in my approach to the band, and usually if I made myself explicit to the arrangers, they were happier, because they knew the restrictions within which they could work.

"But I wanted to keep freedom in it too—to permit the guys to improvise patterns, riffs, and the like, in ensemble behind the soloist. Bob Brookmeyer would wisecrack, 'We're having a rehearsal. Bring your erasers.'"

But I was not satisfied with Gerry's answer. I still wondered why one of the great writers in jazz history was not writing at all. And as much as I enjoyed his baritone playing, I was sorry that he wasn't spending time over the score paper. Generally, I have noticed a difference between the writers and the players in jazz. The writers are inherently more reclusive than the players. They are not the extraverts, and in time they tend to set aside the horn or the piano and retire to a room somewhere and put it on paper rather than facing the audience. Duke Ellington was the great exception. Gerry struck me as a man with both temperaments, and for the nonce the player in him was predominant. It was always said that Gerry was the great sitter-inner of all time: any time, any place, any style. But still, I wondered: I wondered if psychoanalysis had halted his writing, wondered indeed at the moral implications of the entire field of psychology, with its unceasing tinkering in areas its practitioners do not always understand. Few of them, for example, understand the effects of language on the psyche.

And Gerry was a complicated man, much more so than he is now. He had experimented with a career as an actor, playing a priest in the movie based on Jack Kerouack's novel *The Subterraneans*, and doing a comedy turn as an out-of-town square who dates Judy Holliday in *Bells Are Ringing*. It struck people on the periphery of jazz—not within the profession so much as along its edges—as strange, just as Artie Shaw's writing had done. It was by no means without precedent, and others would experiment with careers in both. Even then, Conrad Janis, who frequented Jim and Andy's and Junior's and Charlie's and Joe Harbor's, had careers as a sometime trombonist and as an actor. Long before this, Bud Freeman had almost become an actor. Musicians were forever being turned into comedians, Jerry Colonna, Sid Caesar (who had been in the Claude Thornhill band), Mel Brooks, and Milt Kamen—a French horn player—among them. Later on, Jack Sheldon would have his own TV series, *Run Buddy Run*. Nobody has combined the two as successfully as John Rubenstein, who has balanced successful careers as a film actor and film composer. And Dudley Moore is a composer and pianist whose degree is not in drama but in music.

Gerry said that winter that he'd got a lot out of his experience of acting. The whiff of mockery that had come his way because of it annoyed him. "It seems in this country," he said quite accurately, "you're expected to be a specialist. People get used to you in a certain role in life, and they don't like you to step out of it. It other countries, particularly the Latin countries, it doesn't surprise anyone when a man is an attorney and a jazz musician, or a playwright and a painter. People in this country seem to find it hard to understand that a man can have a deep and abiding interest in one art and a lesser, but still real, interest in another.

"Who knows what I'll eventually be able to do because of this broadening of experience? When, for example, we're doing something with the quartet on television, it helps to understand the production problems and the nature of the work of the people you're dealing with."

At that time he was working on a Broadway musical with lyrics by Judy Holliday, based on the Anita Loos play *Happy Birthday*, and set in a New York Irish bar. Someone told them it would never go on the boards, because the primary patrons of theater in New York were Jews. "Jews," they were told, "go to theater. The Irish go to bars." Whatever the reason, the musical, which has an excellent score and some brilliant lyrics by Judy, has never been produced.

One night when we were hanging out in some bar or another, I asked Gerry—knowing he was what they in that religion call a lapsed or fallen-away Catholic—if he felt Catholic. He said, "What do you mean?"

"Just what I said."

He mused for a minute. Then he said, "No, I don't feel Catholic. But I *do* feel Irish."

And it was at this point that we discovered we had arrived separately at a theory, two theories actually, about music in general and jazz in particular. One is that language has a powerful effect on the rhythmic character of a people's music; the other is that jazz players are strongly affected in style by their ethnic origins— the Italians reflecting that Puccini-like lyricism, the Irish sounding Irish, the Jews sounding Jewish, and so forth. There were, we noted, very few jazz players of truly English origin, as there was virtually no English influence on European classical music, and as indeed there were almost no Broadway composers of stature of English origin; and among Hollywood film composers, the only one from England was Lyn Murray. For that matter, most of the best jazz players of England on examination turned out to be Jewish, like Victor Feldman, or Scottish. I would tell Mulligan that his solos reminded me of *I Met Her in the Garden Where the Praties Grow*, and Gerry said that Judy Holliday would say of Zoot Sims, another Irishman, "There he goes, playing that Barry Fitzgerald tenor again," and she would imitate the ah-ha-ha-ha lilting fall of Fitzgerald's laughter, which, you will notice, in some of his old movies, is peculiarly like Zoot's joyous playing. There is no more melodic vocal tradition in all Europe than that of Ireland, in which is combined yearning lyricism and wry laughter. Listen to the music of Dave McKenna. Or Bill Finegan. Or Zoot. Or, come to that, Mulligan.

We talked about Hindemith that winter of '62. "When I was writing for Gene Krupa and other big bands," Gerry said, "I became involved with the naming of chords I was writing.

"And then I came across the Hindemith technical books, not all of which I had the equipment to understand.

"He was criticizing the formal theories of harmony. They make up rules of harmony that are so loaded with exceptions that the rules don't mean anything. Traditional harmony says that a fourth isn't a chord. And that's ridiculous. It is. Hindemith showed that going up the overtone series you cover everything. I was delighted to see this. I voiced chords in fourths—chords for which there was no name, but which implied the sound of some chord for which there was a name.

"A-D-G-C sounds like a C-chord, but it's not. A C-chord is E-G-C. Through that period, when I was reading the Hindemith books, I learned the lack of importance of naming chords."

Maybe that was an element in the appeal of the Brazilian music to both of us, the nature of the voicings. The guitar is tuned in fourths, and fourth-voicings are natural to it. There is an openness to its chords, an airy transparency. Certainly we both loved the harmonic character, and of course the sinuous melodic character, of the Jobim tunes. Jobim would write on the guitar. He was staying in that Brazilian hotel. Sometimes he would come over to my little basement apartment on West End Avenue and play my guitar, a smaller than normal one that I had bought from the man who made it in a narrow sloping cobbled street in La Paz, Bolivia. The steam heat of New York was slowly destroying it, drying it out; all the Brazilians used to worry about their guitars in New York. Jobim described mine as "a nice friendly little guitar," which it was. Eventually it came apart completely, but we wrote some songs on it. He would play the instrument and sing a line, sometimes saying, "Does this sound like something else to you?" We wrote *Dreamer* (*Vivo Sohando*) that way, and that winter also produced *Someone to Light Up My Life*. He liked to work in what he called "the deep way"—that is, face to face. And I detested it. The search for a lyric is so painful to me that I like to take the music away somewhere and work on it alone, always doubting that I will ever find anything adequate.

The conventional wisdom held that Jobim was strongly influenced by jazz and the French impressionists. I noticed that he was strongly influenced by the natural lay of chords on the guitar. He

was influenced indeed by all sorts of things, and Gerry noticed, as
I did, that the harmonic sequence in the early measures of Jobim's
O Insensatez bore a distinct resemblance to the Chopin E-minor
prelude. So Gerry, with Puckish humor, recorded the E-minor
prelude as a samba.

I was enamored not only of the music of the Brazilian songs but
by their lyrics as well. There was a quality of gentle melancholy
about them, a sort of lyrical fatalism, that led me to a conclusion.
I speculated that this was due to the long Moorish occupation of
the Iberian Peninsula, and the gradual absorption by the population of the Islamic doctrine of kismet—fate—and the requisite
submission to the will of Allah. The traditional song of Portugal
was known as *fado*, meaning fate, and it seemed to me that this
resignation had been transported intact to Brazil to find its way
into the samba song.

Jobim had sent some of the lyrics I had written in Rio up to New
York to those publishers who had links to his Brazilian publisher.
He had no idea that they were even less interested in art than their
Brazilian counterparts. *Corcovado* went to Leeds Music.

The lyric to the song in Portuguese has an interesting relationship to the chords. The melody starts and ends on what Jobim calls
a D 7 over an A bass, though most people are content to call it an
A minor sixth. The difference, however, is important, since the D
7 is a secondary dominant that demands a resolution. It propels
that tune. And so to end the melody there creates a suspended
feeling that forces the song to start over again. The song is thus
an endless circle. And Jobim—who wrote the Portuguese lyric—
rhymes it throughout, then breaks rhyme in the last lines. The
effect is impeccably appropriate to the music, and I retained it in
English, breaking rhyme exactly as Jobim had done. And I
retained that sense of resignation, the sweet despair of the original, so typical of the Brazilian song. Leeds apparently concluded
I didn't know about rhyming. They got Buddy Kaye to rewrite the
last half. He inserted a rhyme Jobim and I loathed ("my world was
dull each minute until I found you in it") and the rhymed happy
ending that American commercial "art" required. Jobim
demanded that they change it, but Jobim was nobody of impor-

tance, and neither was I, and Buddy Kaye after all had converted a Rachmaninoff theme into *Full Moon and Empty Arms*, an authorship that was mentioned on his business card.

Jobim and I decided to make a demo of the song, to show how it should go. We did it on our own. The singer was me, the guitarist was Jobim, and the pianist was Bill Evans. I lost the tape of that session some years later in a fire. And not until Jobim recorded with Frank Sinatra did we succeed in more or less replacing that altered version of the lyric with its pure original, though the altered version turns up even today, the world that's dull each minute sounding to Jobim and me like a mustache on the Mona Lisa.

The year turned over into 1963. As late as May, Jobim—and as far as I know most of the other Brazilian musicians—had not been paid for the Carnegie Hall concert of November, though they were presented with shiny plaques honoring their participation in the "First Annual Bossa Nova Festival." Jobim decided to go home, but he had to wait for the money from a Verve recording with Stan Getz to buy plane tickets for himself and his wife. One of the last things he said to me before going was, "In Brazil I met the sorcerer's apprentices. In New York I met the sorcerer."

In September I wrote an article in *Stereo Review* called "The Bossa Nova Bust," making note that Sidney Frey still had not paid the Brazilians for Carnegie Hall. Frey sued me and the magazine for libel. I challenged him to show canceled checks proving he'd paid the musicians. He couldn't. I asked the officers of local 802 of the American Federation of Musicians to show me the records on the concert. They were curiously dilatory. Finally *Stereo Review* said it wasn't worth the legal fees it would take to fight Frey, though their lawyers assured them we would win easily. They sopped him off with some free advertising and the suit was dropped without jeopardy. The record business was full of Sidney Freys. It hasn't changed.

And Judy Holliday was there through it all. She was Gerry's lady, and Ed Sherman wasn't the only one to wonder why they didn't marry. But she was a friend to so many of us—Bob Brookmeyer,

Alec Wilder, Willis Conover, myself. Everyone had heard the story: how, when Jean Arthur had purportedly fallen ill just before the out-of-town opening of Garson Kanin's *Born Yesterday*, the young Judy Holliday had memorized the script overnight and gone on and done the part flawlessly without rehearsal. It was the stuff of mythology.

Willis Conover offered me a deck of cards one day. "Shuffle them," he said. I did. He said, "Cut them." I did. "Now," he said, "leaving the deck face down, touch the backs of the cards and by feel separate them into the red and black suits." I did it—and separated them perfectly. I was astounded. Was this some sort of example of ESP, or a trick? It was a trick, Willis assured me, one he had learned from an inebriated professional magician in the army. The magician, sobering up later, made Willis pledge never to reveal its technique, and Willis had never done so. "Do you want to know how smart Judy is?" Willis said. "When I tried it on her, she'd gone only about ten cards down into the deck when she said, 'Oh, I see how it's done.'"

One thing that gives New York its edge is its intellectual density. Photos taken from Bedloe's Island or, my favorite view, the Staten Island ferry show that astonishing crowd of great edifices seemingly standing on the water itself, defying nature. Why don't they sink? They do not sink of course because they are footed in bedrock. When you live in that city, you know that within blocks of you there are dozens, maybe scores or more, of people who do the same work you do, have as much talent as you do, and are probably awake working while you are wasting time in sleep or conversation or making love. You are not actually wasting time, to be sure. The very people you are talking to are teaching you. I by now lived on West 86th Street near Central Park West. Five blocks down, at the corner of CPW and West 81st, in a building called the Beresford that overlooked both Central Park and the Museum of Natural History, lived Sheldon Harnick; in the same building were Steve Lawrence and Eydie Gorme, and Lee Falk, who wrote the comic strip *The Phantom*, one of those I'd grown up on. Farther down CPW, Harold Arlen lived.

A group of us, all friends, lived within walking distance of each other, among them Willis Conover at the corner of West 83rd and CPW, Mulligan on West 71st near CPW, and on West 72nd at CPW, in the Dakota, Judy Holliday. Boris Karloff also lived there. It is a strange and gorgeous old monstrosity, styled after a French chateau, though no chateau was ever built in such exaggerated proportions, so American in their excess. Jack Finney used it as the setting of his fantasy novel *Time and Again*, and *Rosemary's Baby* was filmed in it.

Willis was in Washington half the time, playing his records on his *Music USA* program for the Voice of America, sending Duke Ellington and Woody Herman and Gerry Mulligan and Oscar Peterson and Art Blakey and Dizzy Gillespie to peoples far beyond the waters, and almost single-handedly turning jazz into a world language. Most of the great jazz players from other countries, particularly those in the Soviet orbit, will tell you that they were inspired to learn this music by Willis Conover. When Willis would arrive in Warsaw, cheering mobs would surround him, but we could walk down CPW to Judy's apartment or Gerry's and nobody knew him, because his program was not heard in America—just in Sri Lanka and the USSR and Algeria and, for all I know, Tibet.

Mulligan too was away much of the time, with his quartet or the Gerry Mulligan Concert Band with Zoot and Brookmeyer and Clark Terry and Don Rader and Mel Lewis and Bill Crow. I stayed home and wrote. Judy stayed home, too, and alas did not do much in those years, although such was her musicality that she was learning to play flute.

I have no memory of meeting her for the first time, although it was almost certainly in one of those four musicians' bars, and probably Jim and Andy's. But I remember the last time I saw her vividly. It was in Birdland, at the bottom of the stairs, in front of the cloak room.

I think every man who knew her loved her in some suspended and unadmitted way. I think this was true of Willis Conover and Bob Brookmeyer, and I know it was true of Alec Wilder.

Long before I knew her, I had read of her purported brilliance and dismissed it as the invention of press agents. For once they were not exaggerating. Her mind was incredibly quick, and relished puns, as Paul Desmond's did. The huge living room of her apartment in the Dakota overlooked West 72nd. In it there were masses of ferns, of which she said one day, "With fronds like these, who needs anemones?" To be in the company of Judy and Mulligan and Desmond (who loved Tom Swifties and may have invented them) was, Gary McFarland said, "like being caught in the middle of an acrostic."

She was, Alec Wilder said simply, "a healer." Alas she could heal everyone but herself. There was such a goodness about her. Once I called her apartment, looking for Mulligan. She said he was on the road for a couple of weeks, and then she said, "What's wrong?"

"Nothing," I said.

"Yes there is."

"Just down, just a little depressed."

With that little soft chuckle you know if you have seen her movies, she said, "You sound like you need a little body warmth. Why don't you come on over?" I spent the evening there and had dinner with her. I think that was the night she told me the story of going to Columbia Pictures.

It was after the success of *Born Yesterday* on Broadway. For once the girl in the play got the part in the movie. She went on to make *Adam's Rib*, *Full of Life*, *The Solid Gold Cadillac*, *Pfft*, *Bells Are Ringing* with Dean Martin (and Mulligan in that minor role), and more, each characterization a perfect etching.

She was a pretty woman. She was rather sturdy of build, small-busted and a little thick-waisted; and she worried about her weight. She had those remarkable dimples in her cheeks when she smiled, and, as you can see in her films, she could light up a theatre or a living room. She had a closed, tight-jawed way of speaking, and like many New York City natives she was almost unable to say the letter r: it came out halfway to being w. It was a distinctive voice, and although I dislike the word (and she would have loathed it), it can only be described as cute.

I also dislike the word "vulnerable" as it is used to describe actors or characters in stories, and in any case, though it fits her, it is inadequate. She had a talent for melancholy, there was a darkness in her, she was a hurt person, for, as she once said to Willis Conover, "I spent my childhood pulling my mother's head out of a gas oven." Her ancestry was Russian Jewish, and her true surname was Tuvim, from which she derived Holliday.

She was very musical, and she sang well in an ingenuous and unaffected way, as you can hear from her few albums, including the stage and film versions of *Bells Are Ringing*. In April of 1961, Mulligan took her into the recording studio with what was essentially his Concert Band and recorded her, using charts by himself, Ralph Burns, Bill Finegan, and Brookmeyer, and recorded her for MGM Records. Four of the songs were pieces she'd written with Gerry, showing her considerable ability as a lyricist. But MGM never released the album.

She was a sort of distaff Jack Lemmon. She was a brilliant actress who had established her reputation in comedy. But she had not yet made the transition to the character roles for which she was, like Lemmon, so well equipped, and The System wanted to keep her in the kind of parts that had established her, the likable dizzy blonde.

Her last Broadway show was a musical called *Hot Spot*. It was a piece of trash, and it achieved an early and just demise. I hated it, and so did she.

Script after script kept coming to her, and the character she was requested to portray was almost always a variant on Billie Dawn, her role in *Born Yesterday*. She turned them down, one after another. She was restless, not working, and after a year or so I said, "Why don't you take something, just to be busy?"

"I did that," she said. "It was called *Hot Spot*—remember?"

I offered no further career advice.

But the lack of good parts kept grinding on her. And time was passing. She was forty-one now, no longer the ingenue, yet she had not yet gone through that professional metamorphosis into the great character roles she deserved and would have ennobled. One night I was in Jim and Andy's with her. I don't know where Gerry was; possibly he was working a gig and had asked me to pick her up and bring her there. Or possibly he'd left for one and asked me to take her home. Whatever the reason, he wasn't there. We were sitting at the bar, talking quietly, when a girl in her twenties who obviously was not a regular of the place—none of the habitués would have done this, and they all knew her anyway—said, gushingly, "Aren't you Judy Holliday?"

"Yes I am," she said, a little apprehensively.

"Wow!" the girl said. "Oh wow! You know, you're my mother's favorite actress!"

"Oh God," Judy said, "that's all I needed," and put her head down on her crossed arms on the bar. I couldn't tell if she was crying, but I put my arm across her shoulder. She was wearing a mink coat. I still remember the feel of the mink under my hand.

Her medical problem returned. She went in for tests. I got a call one evening from Mulligan. He was on the road somewhere—Chicago, Pittsburgh, I don't remember. He said that Judy was home alone and waiting for the results of the tests. He couldn't be there. Would I go over and keep her company for the evening? I called her, then went over to the Dakota. We watched television. She was sitting in bed, wearing a pink bed jacket, quilted as I recall. We talked about the tests, and after that said little. There was little to say. She just needed some body warmth. She'd given it to me one dark night. I went home around midnight.

It must have been a week or two later that I ran into her and Gerry at the bottom of the stairs at Birdland. They were leaving as I was arriving. I gave her a hug; she was wearing that mink coat. "How're you feeling, m'darlin'?" I said.

"Rotten," she said with that unforgettable chuckle, "but at least I know I'm not going to die!"

I had to go to Paris on a job. When I got back to New York, it was in the midst of one of its taxi strikes, and I had no way to get my luggage home from the East Side terminal. I stored the bags in a locker and took a subway to Jim and Andy's, where, I figured, I'd find one of the guys with a car. I came up out of the subway on Sixth Avenue and looked down at a pile of *New York Post*s. The headline read: Judy Holliday Dies.

I called Gerry immediately. He sounded like death on the phone. I was asked to come to the funeral. I sat up all night and listened to records, watched the hour of the service approach and then pass. Bob Brookmeyer told me later he had done the same thing. Her death just shattered us.

Willis Conover told me he was worried about Gerry, who had been under almost unendurable strain in these last weeks. Willis arranged that in secret compact either he or I or Joseph Heller, the novelist, would be with Gerry almost around the clock. Willis was with Gerry in Charlie's, talking to Gene Williams, when the juke box played her recording of *The Party's Over*.

Gerry put his head on his arms on the bar, as Judy had done that night in Jim and Andy's with me.

Dear Judy. Her death left a great emptiness in our lives, though no one's of course as much as Gerry's. He was drained, wasted, depleted afterwards. Perhaps her sudden absence was the reason we spent so much time together in that period. We went to the theatre a number of times. One of the shows we saw, I remember, was Stephen Sondheim's *Company*, whose score we enormously admired. I went back and saw it several more times.

Gerry proposed that we write a musical. I agreed immediately. We began to search for a subject, and one of us came up with Diamond Jim Brady. I thought he would make a marvelous subject, given his flamboyance and the New York period setting. And given that Irish whimsy Mulligan could so easily summon up in his music, he seemed to me the perfect composer for it. We began to research Brady's life, running around to libraries and digging out old magazines and books that contained references to the man and his circle of acquaintants. We spent a lot of time in that inestimable national resource, the New York Public Library on Fifth Avenue at 42nd Street. It was great fun. We learned that Brady had lived in a big house on West 86th Street, almost directly across from the brownstone in which I had an apartment. Brady's house had long since been replaced by an apartment building.

There is a scene in Judy's movie *Full of Life* in which Aldo Ray, as her husband, has a dream of a new kind of roller skate, with ball-bearings in place of wheels permitting one to slide in any direction. Eagerly he sets about developing his invention only to see his very idea portrayed in a photo on the cover of *Life* magazine: someone had beaten him to it. Something similar happened to Gerry and me.

We had assembled a lot of material on Brady and his world and begun to sketch our script—and I loved working with Gerry, who I discovered had, aside from the literacy with which I was already familiar, a strong sense of story and drama. Gerry remembers that we went to see Hal Prince about the idea. Prince told us that Jackie Gleason and Lucille Ball had just signed a contract to appear in a new musical based on the life of Diamond Jim Brady, with Ball as Lillian Russell.

We abandoned the project there and then. The years passed, and Gleason and Ball never made that musical, and the work Gerry and I did has long since disappeared. I think we'd have done a good show.

One of the shows we saw at that time was *A Thousand Clowns*. I vividly remember running west on West 48th Street to get there by curtain time: one of us had been late getting to Jim and Andy's. The show starred Jason Robards and Sandy Dennis. Gerry would spend the next several years of his life with Sandy, this gifted actress and delightful lady.

He was off on the road again, and then I went to Europe for a while. I returned and that very night got a phone call from Mulligan. His voice was against a background of laughter and conversation that told me he was in a bar somewhere. "G.L.," he said. "There's someone here who wants to talk to you."

"Gene Lees!" said this warm and enthusiastic voice. "I am back." The Brazilians pronounce the a very flat and they put an audible tilde over it when it follows a consonant, so that the word came out almost beeack. The sound of the letter l has almost dropped out of their language, as it has in part in French and in some English words such as palm and salmon. I would tease them that they were always going beeack to Brazeo. I knew that voice instantly. It was Jobim's. "Gerry and I are in Junior's, and you must come immediately and join us."

"I can't, Tom, I'm exhausted," I said. "I just got off a plane and I haven't had any sleep. Let's get together tomorrow."

"No, no, now!" he insisted. "It will not be the same if you're not here, you must come now!" Jobim can be very persuasive, and I found myself saying, "Okay, but just for two drinks. No more. Then I must get some sleep."

And I found myself in Junior's with the two of them. Jobim was laughing, he threw his arms around me—the Brazilians call it *um abraco*, and the action is as common as the handshake—and kissed me on the cheek, as the French and other Latin peoples are wont to do, and I could not but respond in kind. So I hugged him back, and he said to Gerry, "Here he is, the man who can make English sound like Portuguese," an exquisite example of Brazilian chauvinism. And the three of us laughed at things and I ordered a Scotch. Jobim and I were still drinking Scotch together. Gerry was drinking Courvoisier.

I finished that drink, and Jobim ordered another. As little as I had consumed, I could feel my weariness rising within me. I finished the drink and said, "Guys, I gotta go. I'm tired out."

"No, no, one more!" Jobim said. "Just one more."

"Jobim," I said, "if I have one more drink I'm gonna have a heart attack."

"No you're not," he said, and held up three fingers to the bartender, who made us drinks again.

And so I started on a third drink. Jobim was telling Gerry how the publishers had altered my English lyrics for *Desafinado* and *Corcovado* but how at last they were being restored to their original form. By now Jobim had several successful albums of his own in the United States, and he had the muscle to get his way.

There were two rooms in Junior's. One was the bar, and, through a square arch, the restaurant. There was a piano in the restaurant. "Let's show him," Jobim said, and we went into the restaurant, which was deserted at that hour, and Jobim sat down at the piano with a big grin and an affectation of concert-pianist pretentiousness and flourished his hands in the air, and made Gerry and me laugh. Then he began to play, and I sang my lyrics to *Quiet Nights* and *Desafinado*, and Gerry noticed that I had rhymed "stars" with "guitar," a plural with a singular. I called him a picky son of a bitch and said if that kind of rhyme was good enough for Shakespeare it was good enough for me, and we were laughing when Henry Solomon, the owner of Junior's, came in to us with alarm and said, "Gene, you've got to help me! There are two cops out there and they're going to close me down for serving a drunk."

"Who?" I said.

"You."

"What? Where are they?"

The fun was gone now, and I went back to the bar with Gerry and Jobim close behind me. Henry pointed out two plain-clothes cops seated at the bar near the door. I went up to them immediately, furious. "Are you guys cops?" I said.

"Yes," one of them said. He seemed a little sheepish, and I could feel immediately that something was amiss.

"Let me see your credentials," I said, and they both pulled out badges.

"And you say I'm drunk?"

"Yes, sir," the cop said.

"Well, I've got witnesses here to testify that I'm not. And you, at this very moment, know goddamn well that I'm not. Now here are *my* credentials," and I showed him the contents of my wallet. "I'm a journalist," I said, "and I make one hell of a credible witness. You picked the wrong guy. If you are trying to shake this place down, you better have your shit together when we get to court, fella, because I'm gonna take you apart."

I assured Henry that I would testify for him and urged him to get the names of the other people in the place to serve as witnesses, if need be. I left Jobim and Gerry and went immediately home and sat down at the typewriter and wrote out precisely what had happened, including the dialogue. I lost those notes in the same fire that took the tape of Bill Evans and Jobim and me, but the fact of writing them fixed the details in memory.

I went back to see Henry the next day. He told me that I had guessed right about the shakedown. Restaurant, bar, and nightclub owners were constantly subject to shakedown by a corrupt police department. He said he'd got fed up with it. Recently some of the precinct boys had been around with their hands out, and he had refused them. That's what this was all about.

In Jim and Andy's I talked to Jim Koulouvaris about it. "The damn fool," Jimmy said. "He should have paid them."

"Do you?" I said.

"Sure," he said matter-of-factly. "They've got you coming and going. There are so many regulations that they can walk into your john and scatter some cigarette butts on the floor and charge you with running an unclean establishment and close you down. The cops are part of your operating expenses."

Henry Solomon was charged with permitting a drunk to be served a drink, a misdemeanor. Jobim and Gerry were by now not in New York. I went to court with Henry and his lawyer. Only one of the two detectives testified.

He said that two of the men were embracing and kissing, implying that they were homosexual. He said he heard one of them— he pointed to me—say that if he had another drink he'd have a heart attack. And, the ultimate proof of drunkenness, the men were singing!

I asked Henry Solomon's lawyer to ask the judge's permission to let me question the detective. The judge gave it.

I stood up, walked to the witness stand, and said, "Officer, can you tell me the nationality of the man who was embracing me and kissing me on the cheek?"

"No, sir," he said.

"Your honor," I said, "the man is Brazilian. Embracing and

kissing on the cheek are common Brazilian custom. Now, officer, do you know who the two men were who were with me?"

"No sir," he said.

"One of them was Gerry Mulligan," I said, and I think I caught a flicker of recognition of the name in the judge's face, "one of America's great musicians. The other was Antonio Carlos Jobim, the great Brazilian composer. And the songs we were singing are quite famous, and Jobim and I wrote them, and we were showing them to our friend Mr. Mulligan. Your honor, that's a musician's bar, and music in there is commonplace. Everybody who goes in there is a musician."

The judge threw the case out.

But Henry Solomon's troubles were not over. Despite the proscription against double jeopardy in Anglo-American jurisprudence, a bar owner in New York does not enjoy its protection. Henry now had to face a second hearing before the state liquor licensing board to retain his license. The cops know perfectly well what it costs to defend oneself against even as false an accusation as the one that detective had laid, which is why their extortion tactics are so effective. Henry told me that he couldn't afford to fight on to retain his license, and he closed Junior's down. That's what killed Junior's: some faceless precinct captain and a couple of plainclothesmen on the take.

After that Jim Koulouvaris died, and Joe Harbor. Charlie was dead. And all four of those unforgettable jazz musicians' hangouts were gone. Even if they hadn't been, there was no Ed Sherman to chronicle their humor. He died of a stomach ailment. He was thirty-seven.

As the 1960s ended, I left New York, spending the next four years in Toronto, where for the most part I was writing and performing in television. Once Gerry and Sandy came up to be guests on one of my shows. The band was led by Rob McConnell, so I had the pleasure of hearing Gerry and Rob play together.

Then my wife and I moved to California, and I would see Jobim when occasionally he came to Los Angeles. Jobim and I wrote a few of our songs in California. By now he was an international celebrity, touring the world in concert, living still in Rio, though no longer in that little house at Ipanema.

It is interesting to ruminate on what Brazilian music would be like today if Skinnay Ennis hadn't hired Claude Thornhill and Gil Evans at the same time to work in his band on the Bob Hope radio show. The flow of inspiration from Evans to Mulligan to Jobim would never have occurred. Tinker to Evers to Chance.

Gerry and Sandy parted. I don't know why, and would not ask. Gerry married a tall and aristocratic Italian photojournalist named Franca Rota. He met her at a recording session in Milan. At the time she was working on a story for *Harper's Bazaar*. Now they divide their time between a house in Connecticut and a refined large apartment in Milan in whose living room Gerry's piano overlooks a charming treed square. I visited them there once.

I would see him and Franca when they came west, usually for a concert. One of these was in Hollywood Bowl with the Los Angeles Philharmonic playing Gerry's pieces, including an extended work called *Entente for Baritone Saxophone and Orchestra*. I inadvertently insulted Gerry after that concert, but in my own defense I must cite one of our conversations over dinner in a restaurant on West 80th Street, just in behind the Museum of Natural History, to which we were particularly partial. I asked him why he had never written for symphony orchestra, and he said with utter candor: "Because I'm afraid of the larger forms."

I remembered it as I listened to this lovely symphonic writing in Hollywood Bowl. I also remembered something André Previn once said: a symphony string section was not to be treated as if it were simply the world's largest sax section. This writing did not treat it that way.

And thus after the concert that night I said to Gerry, "Who orchestrated?"

He drew himself up, I cannot say whether with pride or indignation. Possibly both. He said, "*I* did."

And so Gerry is writing, richly and well.

Gerald Joseph Mulligan, native New Yorker, though he went to high school in Reading, Pennsylvania, turned sixty on April 6, 1987. Once the young Turk, he has become an elder statesman. The strawberry blond eyelashes and eyebrows have turned white, as has the handsome mass of straight hair. For several years now he has had a white beard, and since the map of Ireland is all over his face, this has the effect of making him look like a very tall leprechaun. He has never been a heavy eater, and he remains as slim as a boy, and watching him on a stage, slinging that sixteen-pound saxophone around, he still looks like one.

I asked him, during a recent phone conversation, some detail or another about our days in Jim and Andy's and Junior's and Charlie's and Joe Harbor's. He chuckled and said, "The only way I could remember some of that is to get juiced, and I don't do that any more."

We talked about Gene Williams, and wondered what had happened to him. Gerry had a couple of leads, which I followed up. We found Gene in Fort Lauderdale, Florida, alive and well and happy and still tending bar.

I think of those days sometimes, the 1960s in New York, and the friends Gerry and I had there who are gone now. Judy, Gary McFarland, Bill Evans, Nick Travis, Ben Webster, Coleman Hawkins, Sonny Stitt, Buddy Rich, Hank d'Amico, Willie Dennis, Willie Rodriguez, Philly Joe Jones, Jo Jones (the two Joes died the same week), Oliver Nelson, so many more, including Jim Koulouvaris himself. Even Sidney Frey is dead.

Generations are always passing.

In 1980, Gerry mixed and released on the DRG label the album he made with Judy in 1960. He sent me a copy. Hearing that sweet naive voice again, with its half-missing r's, and a sadness hidden in a smile, gave me the same strange amalgam of gentle affection and pain that her movies do when they turn up on television. Sometimes you get the feeling that you're running between the raindrops.

13

THE BACHELOR:
PAUL DESMOND

TWO PLATTERS of melon and cold cuts rested, along with a large deep bowl filled with ice and small bottles of wine, on a coffee table in a dressing room backstage at the Hollywood Bowl. On the open door were two names, Gerry Mulligan and Dave Brubeck. Gerry had just finished performing. Distantly, from the stage, we could hear Stan Getz. A girl appeared in the door and told Gerry that Dave was outside and wanted to say hello but didn't want to enter a roomful of cigarette smoke. There was in fact little smoke in the room. It seemed that almost all Gerry's guests had quit smoking, and Gerry, who has in recent years shown serious symptoms of moderation, smoked only occasionally.

I went outdoors with him. It was a warm smoggy night. Dave was wearing a white tuxedo jacket and ruffled shirt open at the throat. Gerry wore slim-legged black slacks and a white pullover shirt with loose sleeves that vaguely evoked the Middle Ages. I sometimes think Mulligan wishes he had lived then.

It was inevitable that we would talk about Paul. Desperate Desmond, as Gerry now and then had called him. "And what was that name he had for you?" Dave said. "G. Emily Guncloset," Gerry answered, and explained that this was what Paul had insisted the French emcee is saying on that Paris album wherein he announces. "Et maintenant—Zhe-hree Moo-leh-gahn!"

243

The last time I had seen Dave was at his home in Wilton, Connecticut—not all that far from Mulligan's present residence in Darien—and that had been at least fifteen years before.

Dave was slim and youthful at sixty-four. Paul had insisted, when they were young, that Dave must be part Indian. Dave doesn't seem to be all that sure about it himself; where his father grew up, a mixed white and Indian blood was fairly common, as it is in much of the American West. Anyway, whatever his roots, Dave does indeed look more and more like some distinguished Cherokee chieftain as he grows older.

Dave grinned—he has a wonderful embracing smile that makes his eyes crinkle—and he pointed at me and said, "I was thinking about you just the other day. I was remembering when you and Paul almost got us all shot in Indiana!"

"Oh God, yes," I said, laughing. "I've thought about it often. I think of you and me and Paul, lost at that crossroads amid all that corn in the middle of the night. We couldn't see over the cornfields to get our bearings."

"Would you say," Mulligan offered, "that this makes those people insular?"

And we told a few Desmond stories.

Paul was chronically tardy. In the early days, he would arrive in his car at the last minute to pick Dave up for their gig at the Band Box in San Francisco. The traffic lights near Stanford were set for forty-five miles per hour. Paul reasoned that they should also work at double that speed, and so he would go tearing to the job at ninety. "And on top of that," Dave said, "he'd be reading all the signs along the road backwards. And I just wanted him to watch the road."

Paul's early life is almost a blank. He never spoke of it to me, and perhaps to no one but Dave. Dave says Paul adored his father but not his mother. "If you knew the story," he said, "you could forgive him anything."

"I have nothing to forgive him for, Dave," I said.

Dave did. Paul's tardiness in the early days bordered on the truly irresponsible. Dave at one point told his wife, Iola, "I never want to see Paul Desmond again," and went a year without speaking to him.

Paul had an ability to maintain direct friendships with the wives of friends. Indeed he carried on suspended loves with some of them, curiously pure and innocent. One of them was my wife, to whom he said wistfully, "It seems to be my destiny to be in love with the wife of one of my best friends." Another was Iola, to whom he was very close. He was not of course the first man to resolve a fear of marriage by investing his deeper feelings in women who were safely out of reach.

After the months of estrangement, Paul turned up at Dave's house, doubtless looking woebegone. Iola went to the back porch, where Dave was hanging up diapers, and told him he would simply have to see Paul.

After that reconciliation, they never looked back.

Interestingly, though Dave repeatedly signed contracts with Paul, Paul never signed and never returned them—another symptom of his fear of commitment. Yet he never questioned the bookings and deals Dave signed on their behalf. And he became Uncle Paul to all Dave's children.

Stan Getz ended his segment of the concert. It was time for Dave's group to go on.

"I still miss him, Dave," I said.

And for a moment Dave looked bereft, truly lost. He said, "Oh boy, so do I."

Paul and Mulligan and I used to hang out together in New York in the 1960s. Desmond loved puns, the worse the better, and said he wanted to record an album called *Jazz Goes to Ireland*, containing such songs as *Fitzhugh or No One*, *The Tralee Song*, *Mahoney a Girl in a Gilded Cage*, and *Lovely Hoolihan*. He was the co-inventor of the most complicated pun I ever heard; I cannot recall who was his collaborator in this silliness. Dave says the joke dates back at least to 1954. It concerns a boy of Italian parentage named Carbaggio, born in Germany. Feeling himself a misfit, with his dark curly hair, among all those Teutonic blonds, he tries to be even more German than the Germans. In late adolescence he flees to Paris, where he steals one of those brass miniatures of the Eiffel Tower. Arrested by the police, he is given a choice of going to jail or leaving the country. He boards the first outbound ship and arrives in New York. Thinking he would like a career in communications, he goes to the RCA building in Rockefeller Plaza, takes an elevator, and walks into the office of General Sarnoff. Sarnoff tells him the only possible job is as a strikebreaker. The boy takes it. When the strike ends, he finds himself on a union blacklist. He goes to work making sonar equipment for a company owned by a man named Harris. After several years, his English is improved to the point where he gets a job on a radio station as a disk jockey. His show is called Rock Time. And he has fulfilled his destiny: he's a routine Teuton Eiffel-lootin' Sarnoff goon from Harris Sonar, Rock-Time Carbaggio.

I used to wonder what kind of mind would expend the effort of working out something like that.

Paul's kind. He numbered many writers among his friends, as Judy Holliday did, and he was an habitué of Elaine's, a bar on the upper East Side of New York City frequented by novelists and other scriveners. Sometimes you'd find him in one of his favorite restaurants, the French Shack, a few doors from his apartment building. One of Paul's writer friends was Doug Ramsey, a prominent television newsman, sometime jazz critic, and amateur trumpeter who combined in his personality two of the qualities Desmond prized most in people: musicality and literacy.

Ramsey describes Desmond's humor as "quiet, quick, and subtle," and tells of the time Paul first saw, in the Ramsey living room, a large oil painting of four cats stalking a mouse. "Ah," Desmond said, "the perfect album cover for when I record with the Modern Jazz Quartet."

Paul also had a taste for high-fashion models of which, in his travels, he had accumulated a considerable collection. Only recently a Toronto newspaper reporter friend of mine mentioned a famous Canadian model who had lived in his apartment building. Soliciting a Bloody Mary from him one hungover Sunday morning, she said, "I haven't been this tired since the last time Paul Desmond was in town."

Pianist Marian McPartland once wrote an article about Paul for me at *Down Beat*. It must have been about that time that I first met him. She asked Paul about his penchant for models. "Well," he said to her, "they'll go out for a while with a cat who's scuffling but they always seem to end up marrying some manufacturer from the Bronx. This is the way the world ends, not with a whim but a banker."

Paul was Dave's diametrical opposite. Once, in South America, a jazz fan possessed by that almost religious fervor for the music that you encounter in other countries asked me whether it was true that Paul and Dave had a homosexual relationship. I didn't even laugh. I was boggled by the question. Aside from the extraordinary rarity of homosexuality in jazz—the incidence is far below not only the other arts but the population norm, a statistical anomaly that is deeply puzzling—one could not easily imagine two men less likely to be so involved. Paul was a womanizer who doted on beautiful girls, and Dave is famous for an unshaken lifetime devotion to his wife, Iola.

Eight years after Paul died, I was at a party at Doug Ramsey's house. The rumor rose again: someone asked if it was true that Paul was homosexual. I doubt if many people knew Paul better than, or even as well as, Ramsey and I did, and the two of us said, in perfect unison, "Are you kidding?"

"I spent twenty years trying to get Dave Brubeck laid," Paul said with that idiosyncratic wicked laugh of his.

"He was always trying to get me drunk or get me to do something," Dave says with a smile.

"Sometimes," Paul said on another occasion, "I get the feeling that there are orgies going on all over New York City, and somebody says 'Let's call Desmond,' and somebody else says, 'Why bother? He's probably home reading the *Encyclopedia Britannica*.'"

"Yeah, but Paul," I said, "you probably are."

Home in those last years was a penthouse apartment at 55th Street and Sixth Avenue. Like Mitch Miller, Paul had a listed telephone number. Nobody ever thought to look it up, and fans rarely if ever called.

The living room of that apartment was a chaos, rivaled only by that of Glenn Gould in Toronto, of books, newspapers, records, tapes, tape recorders, crushed Pall Mall packs, and a black Steinway grand with a high gloss on which Paul played me tunes he wanted me to write lyrics for and for which, alas, I never did. In his will Paul left that piano to Bradley's as a wry act of kindness to musicians who suffer long with bad nightclub pianos. Paul and I went once to Bradley's to hear Jimmy Rowles. And now Jimmy plays Paul's piano there.

On that piano was the photo of a girl, taken long before, the wife of his best friend in the early years. Paul and she had fallen in love, which destroyed her marriage and of course the friendship. I suspect that Paul always carried a certain amount of guilt over it. It was that man, famous now himself, who broke the news to me at some social gathering in Los Angeles that Paul had lung cancer. And I could hear in his voice the trace of an old affection for Paul.

Paul was in fact an easy man to love. Everyone knew that but Paul. I once said that about him in print, and later he confessed that he had choked up on reading it.

Paul was quite capable, in his last years, of doing two quarts of whiskey a day, although I did not then and do not now consider him an addicted alcoholic. He obtained a syringe from his doctor and used to give himself vitamin shots in the thigh in the mornings, to diminish the hangovers. I used to imagine him, whiskey glass in one hand and a cigarette in the other, falling asleep on the sofa in front of a television set hissing with snow after the National Anthem, and maybe burning a hole in his trousers. He reminded me of Mitya, the Karamazov brother who wants to leap heels up into the muck to make himself as bad as he thinks he is and escape the burden of virtue in an ongoing corruption. In the end, Paul failed, because he was a very gentle man, and a very, very good one, haunted by his own romanticism, which he mocked in words and a wry choice of notes, and never finding that perfect love-for-a-lifetime he always, really, wanted. He was the loneliest man I ever knew.

Paul and Dave were native Californians. David Warren Brubeck was born in Concord on December 6, 1920. Paul Emil Breitenfeld (he said he got Desmond out of a telephone book) was born November 25, 1924, in San Francisco. His mother was Irish, his father German. Paul thought his father was Jewish until, near the end of his life, a relative told him he wasn't. His father was a theatre organist who became friends with a young cellist, also of German ancestry and native of San Francisco, named Hugo Friedhofer. Hugo and Paul never met. Hugo loved Paul's playing, which reflected that of Benny Carter and, among others, Pete Brown. I hear an echo of Johnny Hodges's upper register in Paul's playing, and of course a good deal of Lester Young. Doug Ramsey recalls that during a 1969 celebration of Duke Ellington's seventieth birthday at the White House, Paul played an impression of Johnny Hodges, so accurate that Ellington sat bolt upright in his chair in astonishment. Whatever his sources, Paul's assimilation of his influences was total, and he was a unique player. You could hear him for one bar and know it was he.

His playing was lyrical, romantic, soaring, and, in the very best sense of the word, pretty. If the saxophonists inspired by Lester Young played tenor as if it were alto, Paul played alto as if it were clarinet. Paul had at one time been able to play an octave even higher on the horn, but then an admirer asked him how he did it, and Paul tried to show him and lost that other octave forever. Dave confirms the story. Ralph J. Gleason told me years ago that Paul disliked fast tempos (he also disliked fancy changes and busy drummers) and that Dave, knowing this, and also knowing that Paul played his best when angry, would kick very fast tempos on purpose. Dave confirmed that story, too. Left to his own devices, Paul would have played ballads and medium-up tunes all evening. Notice on the albums he did without Dave how few (if any) really fast tunes there are. When I asked him how he had developed his sound, Paul said, "Welll—" in the way he had of drawing that word out "—I had it in the back of my mind that I wanted to sound like a dry martini." I quoted that in print, and it went around the world, quoted again so often that Paul said he wished he'd never said it. But in fact his sound did resemble the flavor of a dry martini; it had a sort of oval-shaped bitterness. On another occasion, I said to him, "Paul, what accounts for the melancholy in your playing?" And he said, "Wellllll, the fact that I'm not playing better." It happens that I asked the question while doing a formal interview with him, of which I have a tape. You can hear us both cracking up at that retort, but Paul's laughter crumbles into a dry raspy cough, the gift of his tobacco company and the presage of his carcinoma.

It was this sardonic quality that made Paul's romanticism work. It is impossible to write tragedy without a sense of humor. Humor lights up dark literature, like Rembrandt's underpainting. Without it the work is merely heavy, turgid. Make 'em laugh before you make 'em cry. Shakespeare does this deftly: the gatekeeper's scene in *Macbeth*, the gravediggers' scene in Hamlet. How smoothly Stravinsky does it in the *Firebird Suite*. Sibelius lifts your spirits before laying that tragic trombone melody on you in the *Seventh Symphony*. It is irony, mockery even, that makes Lorenz Hart the greater lyricist than Oscar Hammerstein. *My Funny Valentine*, for example—Hammerstein could never have conceived such a thought. Without an inner humor, tragic art becomes like the pathetic you-gotta-hear-my-story lapel-grabbing of a bar-room drunk. Here is one of the distinguishing differences between Tchaikovsky and Mozart. Mozart's restraint in sorrow makes his music only the more poignant. And Paul had that kind of elegance.

It was the fashion of some critics, who paid attention not to what he was doing but to what he had no intention of doing, to patronize his playing as "weak." There was of course nothing "weak" about it. Like someone sufficiently secure in his manhood that he is unhesitatingly gentle (a quality you encounter in some athletes), Paul never, as it were, had to raise his voice. He was too busy being funny, and in being funny was often heartbreaking.

Quotes in jazz are dangerous, and they can be corny, but Paul's were sly, humorous, and ingenious. When the quartet would play

Montreal, Dave says, Paul would quote *I'm a Dreamer, Aren't We All?* It was a play on words and music, in keeping with the principle of Cockney rhyming slang, which Dave knew to mean: I'm a Dreamer, Montreal. His mind worked the same way in words. Annoyed by an aggressive woman reporter who kept asking him banal questions, he said, "You're beginning to sound like a cross between David Frost and David Susskind, and that is a cross I cannot bear."

Both he and Dave would play telephone numbers in their solos. (The notes of a scale are numbered; any sequence of numbers can therefore be rendered as a melodic phrase.) When one of his girlfriends would arrive at a club, Paul would play her phone number into a solo. Dave came to recognize some of these numbers, and if two or more of Paul's ladies turned up at the same time and Dave was the first to see them, he would alert Paul by playing their numbers on the piano.

Dave and Paul achieved a close rapport in those years. Paul told me once, "When you do something good simultaneously, that's very interesting, but when you make the same mistake at the same time, that gets scarey." Dave Brubeck's career has been a mixture of acclaim and derogation. But one person you did not run Dave Brubeck down to was Paul Desmond. And he thought Dave comped for a horn player better than just about anybody.

He also loved the Modern Jazz Quartet. Connie Kay was probably his favorite drummer. On Christmas day, 1971, Paul joined the MJQ for their annual Town Hall concert in New York. The performance was recorded, though poorly. John Lewis worked closely with engineer Don Puluse to achieve a miracle of enhancement and issued the album on the Finesse label. "For Paul's friends," John said. "I think they'll like it." He was quite right: it is one of Paul's best albums. One hears immediately why Paul felt such an affinity for the MJQ. (It extended even to the conservative style of their dress.)

Paul recorded five albums for RCA Victor, a number for CTI, one in Toronto for Horizon; and the last thing he ever did was with Chet Baker. But of course the bulk of his recorded work was with the Brubeck group.

Once I ran into Paul on 55th Street, not long before the quartet disbanded. "Are you guys working?" I said.

"Are we working?" he said. "We're working as if it were going out of style—which of course it is." That's a typical Desmondism. You hear similar unexpected addenda to his musical phrases.

"The official disbandment of the quartet was at the end of 1967," Paul said. "It really should have been in Paris. It was the end of the European tour, it was the end of twenty years of playing together, seventeen of which we got paid for. The Paris concert was recorded. It was a logical time to end the whole thing, but we had two or three anti-climactic concerts left in the schedule."

Was it true that Paul actually founded what became the Dave Brubeck Quartet?

"Well," Paul said, "to the extent that it was a trio with a girl singer, and Dave and I did vocals, if you'd like to believe that."

"No kidding," I said. "I do find it hard to believe."

"I find it hard to believe myself."

"You I can sort of handle, but not Dave."

"How it all began was that Dave was working in a place called Geary Cellar in San Francisco with Norman Bates and a singer named Francis Lynn and a tenor player. And I used to go by and bribe the tenor player variously, so I could sit in with Dave. And, in one of the most courageous acts I ever performed, I stole his entire band and took them away, down to a place outside Stanford. I expected to be wrapped in cement and sunk in San Francisco Bay for several months thereafter."

Paul lacked the attributes of a bandleader. "When it comes to money," he said once, "I shouldn't be allowed loose in the street." Dave, on the other hand, is an organized individual, and gradually he became the leader. Though they were attracting a following, no record company was interested, and finally Dave recorded them with his own money, little though he had of it. The first albums were on Fantasy, but before long the group moved to Columbia Records and become the most popular jazz group in the world.

Paul was married briefly and once. Even Dave knows very little about the marriage, which occurred during or shortly after Paul's last year at San Francisco State University, where he was preparing himself to be a writer. The only reason I know about the marriage is that I met the girl, not long after their divorce and before I knew Paul. Paul never mentioned her to me, and I mentioned her only once, when we had both had a few too many drinks. Paul got tears in his eyes, and I never spoke of her again.

Paul in fact never talked about the women in his life. Contrary to what most women seem to think, few men boast of their conquests, and those who do are usually held in contempt by other men. It is considered unmanly. Paul was unusually reticent on the subject. I met a few of his ladies, however, and they were all great beauties.

Dave did something intelligent and generous: he made Paul in effect a partner in the group, receiving not only a salary but a percentage. They made a lot of money in those years, some of which Paul and Dave jointly invested. "Dave managed," Paul cracked once, "to find one of the few pieces of land on the California coast with no water on it."

But they lived very separate lives, which was inevitable, in view of their personalities, philosophies, and ways of living. Nonetheless, when Dave became gravely ill with mumps orchitis, it was Paul whom Iola called to help her take him to the hospital. Paul hated the uncivilized outdoors and all his life had a nightclub pallor to go with his lean and slightly stooped frame. With Paul and Iola holding his arms, Dave entered the hospital lobby. The staff was expecting them, and a nurse took one look at Paul and said, "Oh, Mr. Brubeck, let me get you a wheelchair."

Paul was perfectly happy to let Dave have the publicity and, when the hour came, simply walk onstage, play, and at concert's end leave with some girl.

One afternoon during that Indiana weekend when Paul and I almost got us all shot, he and I were invited to a party being held in some park by members of the Junior Chamber of Commerce. This was not exactly Paul's natural habitat. In the car, the thirtyish couple who had invited us took up the praises of some local singer, suggesting that Paul and I might be able to advance her career for which she would no doubt express her gratitude in an interesting (though not particularly original) way. The wife in the team made much of her friend's prodigious physical endowments. Somewhat amazed that I was actually hearing this, I said, "Does she have a husband?"

"Oh, yes," our hostess said brightly, as if nothing could be more irrelevant.

"What does he do?" I said.

"Bites his nails," Paul muttered darkly.

At the party, held in that great outdoors for which Paul had no taste, only beer was being served. And Paul had no taste for that either. "Split city," he said, and we did. It was that night that we almost got blown away.

My wife and I spent the first half of the 1970s in Toronto. Another thing Paul had in common with Glenn Gould was an addiction to the telephone. He would call, often very late, and begin the conversation with a cheery, "Hello there, this is your friend Paul Breitenfeld." If he didn't reach me, he would talk to my wife by the hour. He had in fact known her before I did, back in a time when he was dating a friend of hers in Detroit, inevitably a model. Paul was one of those men who genuinely like women, which no doubt was one reason he was so attractive to them.

One day I got a call from Paul Grosney, a well-known Toronto trumpet player who booked the performers for several jazz clubs, including Bourbon Street. Desmond had appeared in public very little in the last few years, and never in his life as a leader, except for that brief early experience in San Francisco. Grosney asked if I thought Paul would play Bourbon Street. I said that I doubted it, but it wouldn't hurt to ask him.

"Would you let me have his phone number?" Grosney said.

"Sure, but it's in the New York phone book."

Not long after that I got a call from Desmond, reporting on his conversation with Groz. "Do you think I should do it?" he said.

"Sure. You've done enough of being Achilles in the tent. It's a nice room, so come on up and hang out."

"I don't know," Paul said. "I'd have to practice. . ."

"So practice," I said.

"What about a rhythm section?"

"Ask for Don Thompson on bass, Terry Clark or Jerry Fuller on drums, and Ed Bickert on guitar."

"I've heard about Ed Bickert," Paul said. "Jim Hall told me about him. Jim says he's one of the few guitar players who scare him when he sees him come into a room."

Paul accepted the engagement. He called several more times. He said he was practicing, and he didn't intend to do any drinking until the gig was over. (He may have been referring to that period when he told Doug Ramsey, "I tried practicing for a few weeks and ended up playing too fast." He used to call himself "the world's slowest alto player" and "the John P. Marquand of the saxophone.")

He arrived in Toronto, held a rehearsal with the rhythm section, felt better about things, and came up to our apartment. He was surprisingly nervous about the gig but firm in his decision not to drink. I tried to keep him talking. "Have you started work on the book?" He was supposed to be writing a book on the years of the Dave Brubeck Quartet, the title for which was alone worth the price of admission.

"Only to the extent that I sold that one chapter to Punch and on the basis of that sold the book, so they gave me money, and now I have to do something about it."

"What's the exact story of that title?"

"At least once, and usually more often, a month, we'd get on a plane and. . . First would come Gene Wright with his bass. Then came Joe Morello—Dr. Cyclops, although he was always good-natured about his thick glasses. This procession would alert the flight attendants and passengers that something was happening.

"First the salesman in the second row behind Gene with the bass would say, 'Hey, are you going to tuck it under your chin and play some music for us?' That was inevitable. Then the stewardess would say, 'What band are you with?' And we'd say, 'Well, actually, it's the Dave Brubeck Quartet.' In the earlier days they would then say. 'Who?' And later on, they would say, 'Oh?' meaning much the same thing. Then, when the flight got comfortably under way, and they had some leisure, the stewardess would come back and sit down and say, 'How many of you are there in the quartet?'"

That of course was to be the title of Paul's book.

"How is it," I said, "that you never got into the Charlie Parker trap? You managed to go pretty much your own way."

"Well, that! I specifically tried to avoid it. I was starting out, and every saxophone player and alto players especially, and every musician, for that matter, was suddenly turned around and stunned by Charlie Parker. And many of them tried to adapt what he was doing, which meant they could only become copies, with varying degrees of effectiveness. And no matter how good the very best of them were, they were obvious, except for some who played different instruments. That's one cardinal rule for young musicians, in case you want any cardinal rules for young musicians. If you're going to imitate somebody, just imitate someone who plays a different horn, and you've got it made.

"I practically put ear muffs and blinders on to avoid falling into that quicksand, because I knew it would be the finish for me. Only after I felt reasonably secure, which was several years later, did I allow myself the luxury of sitting down and listening to a lot of Charlie Parker. Now, of course, it's a sheer delight.

"Jimmy Rowles was on a tour we did very early on—it must have been '52—with Charlie Parker and Chet Baker and Shelly Manne. And Jimmy noticed that effect, even as it was happening. The Charlie Parker effect. It was a weird time. It was . . . it's a ridiculous parallel, but it was almost a form of McCarthyism in music. It was equally analogous to a totalitarian state, in some ways. You either played the Holy Writ, or the party line, or you were outlawed. If you're a kid, starting out as a musician, Lord knows it's a rough enough situation anyway. You won't get gigs and you'll be starving to death and the only thing you'll have to value is the judgment of your peer group. And if you play one chorus, and they say, 'Good-bye,' that's it, you've been excommunicated. So whatever's going on, you've got to go along with it—or come up with something better. And come up with something better than Charlie Parker? Lot's o' luck.

"And what is that?"

Singing had broken out in the apartment above us. The lady who lived there, whom I had taken to calling Crazy Sheila, belonged to some fundamentalist religious group, and she and her friends would hold orgies of hymn-singing. They were always very out of tune.

"Amazing," Paul said, sitting in an armchair and staring at the ceiling.

But our conversation resumed, in spite of the accompaniment. I said, "I remember once asking you why you didn't write more, and you said, 'Because I keep getting constantly tinier screwdrivers and trying to fix up the first eight bars of the tune.'"

"Yeah," he said. "There's a way around that, which I haven't been able to get into yet. I should have done it ten years ago. Anybody who plays jazz of course is always composing. If you listen to your out-takes or concert records—somebody taking the last eight bars of somebody's chorus, and developing an entire chorus out of it—you can develop, as you know, certainly a song out of any four or eight-bar jazz phrase."

"Duke did."

"Right. And I hear fragments from all kinds of things that really should have been songs. Could have been. And that's the only way to do it. When you're playing jazz, obviously you have to keep going. You don't get to use your tiny screwdrivers and go back and rewrite."

"At least you got around to finishing *Take Five*," I said. Though it is widely assumed to be Dave's tune, *Take Five* was composed by Paul. Johnny Mandel collects antique mechanical musical devices. He owns one that plays brass discs with punch-out tines. The device is old, but, incredibly, some company somewhere still makes the discs, or did until recent years. And one of these discs is *Take Five*—with wrong changes. When Johnny played it for me, I tried to reach Paul by telephone in New York so that he could hear this terrible version of his tune, but he wasn't home and he never did hear it.

"*Take Five* was one of the exceptions to the rule," Paul said. "It was just going to be the original phrase. I had the middle part kind of vaguely in mind. I thought, 'We could do this, but then we'd have to modulate again, and we're already playing in five-four and six flats, and that's enough for one day's work.' Fortunately, we tried it, and that's where you get the main part of the song."

"That album, *Time Out*," I said, "was really the launch of all the new time figures in jazz. I don't think that Dave's ever been given credit for that album, really. I can remember one critic who panned Dave for affectation because of the so-called 'odd' time figures. Yet Dave pointed the way, and now those figures are comparatively common."

At this point, Crazy Sheila's Holy Rollers swelled into a rousing chorus. Then they subsided again. "I never did get that story straight about you and George Avakian and the phone call," I said.

"I did four albums on RCA with Jim Hall. Not counting the one with strings. When I began with RCA, George Avakian was very high up in the company. He was sort of second in command. Sometime between the album with strings and *Take Ten* there was a change in the management, and George Avakian was selling pencils in a tin cup outside RCA. He was really very much at loose ends. He had no office, so if you wanted to reach him, he still had a few freelance projects to complete. Like, he was assigned to completing what RCA regarded as my disastrous series of albums with Jim Hall. He was a freelance producer, and he would come in like a freelance drummer, and he would say to people, 'If you want to reach me, I'll be in Studio B at RCA between two and five p.m.' And so of course you would turn up for the date, and George would be there, and the phone would constantly ring, because those were his three office hours for the week. Ordinarily, that wouldn't make that much difference, because it was a very do-it-yourself operation anyway. We'd play until we thought we had something that sounded good and then go and listen to it back.

"There was one tune . . . we were really scuffling with it. And along about take twenty-seven, by then you should really face facts, if you're a jazz group. You should say, 'We're not going to do this tune now or ever, let's do something else.' We finally did a take, one where I thought the intro made it, and we solved the hassle in the chorus, and the rhythm worked out, and the solos sounded good, and nobody played any wrong changes, and the modulation worked out and the ending worked out, and I was getting a little punchy by then.

"So we stopped, and after the end of the take I looked at the control room, to see some sign of humanity, a nod, a wink, anything. And there's George on the phone. And that did it.

"I ran out into the hall. They had a pay phone there. I called RCA. I said, 'Can I have Studio B?' 'Certainly, sir,' then, 'That line is busy. Can you hold?' I said, 'Yyyyyesss, Ma'am.' She said, 'I can ring now.' Rrrrring. 'Hello, is this George Avakian?' 'Yes it is, who's this?' 'It's Paul Desmond. How was that last take?'"

Crazy Sheila's group was now into *Rock of Ages* or some such. "Good Lord!" Paul said. I steered him back to the subject of the book; I really wanted him to write it.

"Well, the whole book thing," he said, "it's kind of silly, really, in a way. I realized that when I began to hang out at Elaine's in New York. Mailer goes in there, and George Plimpton, and various lesser luminaries and occasional visitors, and I discovered that almost without exception—I'm not sure about Mailer, if he ever gets through with the bullfighting—but a lot of the other writers would much prefer being jazz players. Frank Conroy is a glowing example. He's an excellent writer, but he's also a very good piano player. He's worked obscure little places on the Cape, where he lives now, and in New York."

"Do you know why they all want to be musicians?"

"Possibly because being a jazz musician is one of the best things in the world to be."

"Why?"

"Uhhh . . . Well, if you can solve a few of the problems—a few? Ha-ha! Finding the right guys to play with. Finding people to pay you money to play. Traveling, because you can't stay in one place all the time and play really what you want to. Just the process of playing jazz is immensely rewarding. It's more transitory then other things, which is good in some ways, bad in others. Obviously, because if you play a lousy chorus, it's gone forever. Of course, if you write a lousy page you rip it out of the typewriter. That follows too. But there's no such thing as sitting staring at a blank piece of paper. The time comes to play, and you make noise, of some sort or another. I don't know whether you can do that in writing."

"All true," I said. "But there's something else. Walter Pater said it, and Conrad quotes it someplace: 'All art constantly aspires towards the condition of music.' And I think I know what he means. Music is direct emotion, and it is abstract. It requires no subject matter. All the other arts must work on the emotions indirectly. And painting, certainly since the invention of photography, is attempting to dispense with subject matter, resulting in some of the fraudulent nonsense of modern art. James Joyce and Gunther Grass have struggled to achieve something beyond narrative in the novel and as far as I'm concerned have attained only triumphs of technique. You see this attempt at abstraction in some of the crap that passes for modern poetry, and certainly in the more pretentious rock lyrics. Each art is at its best when it does what only it can do. It is not at its best when it is trying to do what another art does better. And music does abstraction better than any of the other arts. I think that's what Pater meant, and why those guys would rather be musicians than writers."

"Yes," Paul said. "I must engrave that line someplace. I like that a lot. There's another line that came from Milton, of all people. The most perfect definition of the state of mind required to play jazz—'with wanton heed and giddy cunning.' If you want to carve that any place, that's how you play jazz."

The afternoon waned. There was another outburst of hymnody from Crazy Sheila and her friends. Paul looked at the ceiling and said, "Does this group take requests?"

We drove him to the job. "I'm not like Zoot," he said. "Zoot can always go straight ahead, but I'm always very affected by what's going on around me."

The opening went beautifully. Paul was so in love with the new-found rhythm section that he was on the phone within days to record companies in New York. Eventually Creed Taylor recorded him and Ed Bickert (and Ron Carter and Connie Kay), and Horizon issued an album recorded at Bourbon Street with Thompson, Bickert, and Fuller.

We had wonderful times with Paul during that engagement. He played brilliantly. Not until the last set of the last night did he allow himself so much as one drink.

I had no way of knowing, of course, that I would only ever see him once more.

To be sure, he stayed in touch with us by telephone after we moved to California.

"Hello there," said the voice on the telephone one day, and I knew before he had completed the greeting that it was Paul Breitenfeld. The telephone line sounded exceptionally clear. "Where are you?" I said.

"Well actually, I'm in town. At the Century Plaza." A movie producer wanted him to do a score for a picture, and he was here for a day or so to discuss it. And he wanted my wife and me to have dinner with him that evening. There was an odd urgency to his tone. He hardly needed to press us to see him. I said we'd pick him up, and we set a time.

I suggested that we go to the Cock and Bull on Sunset Boulevard, a few paces from the border of Beverly Hills. It was a replica of an English pub so faithful that it surprised British visitors. I thought Paul would like it, and he did. It's no longer there.

We laughed a lot and retold old stories, including the one about the night we nearly got shot. The 1960 Indiana Jazz Festival was produced by a man named Hal Lobree, in Evansville. I was the master of ceremonies. On the evening of that Junior Chamber of Commerce party, the Brubeck Quartet played. Lobree was having a post-concert party at his house. Paul and I induced Dave—for once—to come along. Lobree told some young man connected with the festival to drive us to his place, and gave him directions.

He told us that if we got there before he arrived, we should simply open a window and let ourselves in.

The driver got lost. At some point we pulled up at the crossing of two unpaved country roads amid corn that seemed eight or ten feet high. There was a darkened grocery store beside which there was a telephone booth. Lighting matches to see, our driver tried to call someone or other to find out if they could tell him where we were from a description of this nameless intersection. Paul and I were standing in the middle of the road. He was recalling a Warner Brothers animated cartoon in which the coyote tries to drop an anvil from a great cliff onto the roadrunner. His sound effects were vivid, and we were laughing madly and sophomorically.

The driver returned none the wiser and we got back into the car and resumed our feckless wandering through the Indiana night. And suddenly the terrain began to fit Lobree's description. Then we came to a house that just had to be his. It was all in darkness. While Dave and the driver waited in the car, Paul and I walked up the driveway and opened a window. I put one leg over the sill and was halfway into the living room when a light went on at the top of a flight of stairs and a man descended them. He was wearing an old-fashioned nightshirt and, more significantly, he was carrying a shotgun. For what seemed an eternity I tried to process this information, and then understood and said, "Run like hell, Paul, we're in the wrong house!" And we pounded down the driveway and leaped into the car, landing on top of Dave. "Go go go!" we shouted to the driver, who took off. We disentangled the arms and legs, and Paul and I gasped with laughter. "Can you imagine the headline?" I said. "Jazz Musicians and Writer Killed in Burglary Try." And that sent Paul into another strangled fit of laughter.

We never did find Hal Lobree's party.

We laughed about it again in the Cock and Bull. And then Paul began to talk. He seemed to have a great need to do so that night. He told us about a girl he had been seeing, which was unusual enough in itself. He talked about his life at length and in detail. Never before had he been so self-revealing. Deliberately so. He seemed curiously happy. Finally he said, "Don't you think this'd make a good book?"

"Yes," I said. "Why don't you write it."

"No," he said softly but firmly. "You write it."

I was puzzled. Later I realized that he was in possession of a bit of information that I was not. He knew he was dying.

It was in May 1977 that Paul told Doug Ramsey that his doctors had decided to discontinue both radiation and chemotherapy. About a year before, they had turned up a spot on his lung. His liver, however, had been given a clean bill of health. "Pristine," Paul told Doug. "One of the great livers of our time. Awash in Dewars and full of health."

In the months after that, Mulligan kept me posted on the telephone. Even as Paul wasted away, he made us laugh. When Gerry asked him how he felt, he said, "As if I had just driven non-stop from Vancouver for a one-nighter."

He spent his last weeks at home. In time he became too weak to go to the door to admit friends, so he left it unlocked. The doorman downstairs knew who was to be admitted. Among them was Charles Mingus.

Mingus walked into the bedroom, where Paul lay sleeping. Mingus stood there for a long time in vigil. Then Paul awoke. Mingus was dressed all in black, including a cape and a leather hat. "I thought The Man had come for me!" Paul told Dave later.

Mingus also told the story, and said, "Will you come to my bedside when I'm dying, Dave?" But Mingus went to Mexico in a vain search for effective treatment and died there. "So I wasn't able to go to him," Dave said. "It really bothered me."

Paul specified in his will (which left his money to the Red Cross) that he be cremated "because I don't want to be a monument on the way to the airport." All the highways to New York airports seem to pass cemeteries.

His wishes were followed. Another old friend, Jimmy Lyons, the one-time San Francisco disk jockey and founder of the Monterey Jazz Festival, who had known him since the early days, took the

urn containing Paul's ashes and a pitcher of martinis up in an air-
plane over the sea off the rugged coastal stretch known as Big Sur,
which Paul loved. He opened the plane's window to scatter the
ashes and drink a last martini to Paul, and the wind blew both in
his face.

"Thanks a lot, Paul," Jimmy said, and laughed.

A day or two after the Hollywood Bowl concert, Gerry and his wife
Franca drove the seventy miles from Los Angeles to spend the day
with us in Ojai. We went to lunch at the Ojai Valley Country Club,
because the food there is adequate and the scenery beautiful. And
again, we talked of Paul and his way with a phrase and his talent
for laughter. Paul said that listening to Ornette Coleman was like
being locked in a red room with your eyelids pinned open. He said
that Miles Davis solos reminded him of a man constructing a
mobile while riding a unicycle.

Gerry said, "When Eubie Blake made that remark that if he'd
known he was going to live this long, he'd have taken better care
of himself, I laughed. And then I thought, 'Hey, wait a minute.
That's not so funny. He's got a point.'"

"Paul must have operated on Joe E. Lewis's maxim," I said.
"'You only live once, but if you do it right, once is enough.'"

Somewhere I read an obituary, published in 1860, which said of
a man that, having lived all his life in good health, "he succumbed
to old age and died at fifty-one." Now some of our sexual and
romantic ikons, such as Linda Evans and Raquel Welch, are in
their forties, a top model is in her fifties, and Ricardo Montalban
is in his sixties. In the old film *Strike Up the Band,* the woman who
plays the mother of the sixteen-year-old high school bandleader
played by Mickey Rooney is elderly, plump, dowdy, and wears her
hair in a bun.

"That's right," Gerry said. "In those days the mother was played
by Jane Darwell. The attitude has changed. That's what makes the
difference."

Paul was fifty-three when he died.

Mulligan does not easily admit to sentiment. And like Paul, he expresses his romanticism in his playing, tempering it with a smile. But he has confessed on occasion that he too misses our friend quite badly.

Gerry said, just before we left the restaurant, that he had no idea what an avocado tree looked like. As we emerged into the bright sunlight, I pointed up to the mountains and said, "There, these rows of trees on the slopes, they're avocados."